The Church of England - Charity Law and Human Rights

IUS GENTIUM

COMPARATIVE PERSPECTIVES ON LAW AND JUSTICE

VOLUME 36

For further volumes:
http://www.springer.com/series/7888

Kerry O'Halloran

The Church of England - Charity Law and Human Rights

Springer

Kerry O'Halloran
The Australian Centre for Philanthropy
and Nonprofit Studies
Queensland University of Technology
Brisbane, Australia

ISSN 1534-6781 ISSN 2214-9902 (electronic)
ISBN 978-3-319-04318-0 ISBN 978-3-319-04319-7 (eBook)
DOI 10.1007/978-3-319-04319-7
Springer Cham Heidelberg New York Dordrecht London

Library of Congress Control Number: 2013958451

Printed on acid-free paper

Springer is part of Springer Science+Business Media (www.springer.com)

Contents

Introduction

This book concerns a conflict of laws: canon law, charity law and human rights law. It regards the Church of England in its present circumstances as providing a particularly fruitful case study – transparent and visibly sensitive (if not always responsive) to both internal dissension and external challenge – for examining the causes and effects of that conflict. While such a study of the Church and the wider Anglican Communion would be sufficient and justifiable in itself, it is also intended to use that focus to shed some light on the broader conflict implications for contemporary western society. Hopefully, by adopting an enquiring rather than a pedagogical approach, *The Church of England: Charity Law and Human Rights* may add more to an awareness of the complexity than to the polemic that now surrounds any discussion of the role of religion and the meaning of the 'culture wars' in contemporary society.

The Church of England is undoubtedly in a difficult position. Having had its body of religious doctrine embedded and protected for almost five centuries in canon law, the Church in the twenty-first century now finds itself exposed to the effects of law reform relating to both charity and human rights, some of which interlock and have a direct bearing on its core religious beliefs. Running alongside, and interacting with the prevailing legal framework, there are also significant cultural changes to long-established social mores in some developed western nations. The resulting convergence of powerful contemporary pressures from cultural change, charity law reform and developments in human rights law has compromised the 'established' status of the Church, its traditional role in society and, most importantly, some of its beliefs. These difficulties are clearly representative of themes that now face many western societies.

The cultural hegemony of a cohesive and structured English society, transplanted via the British Empire to many of the countries comprising the Anglican Communion, would seem to have given way under the many pressures of modern life: not the least of which has been economic migration and the accompanying cultural dislocation, the effect of ever changing global trends, and the frequent substitution of lifestyle choices for religious beliefs. In addition, within the progenitor Anglican nation and elsewhere, there is now much evidence of what could be seen as a tussle between the levelling effect of social justice principles – such as equity, equality and non-discrimination – and the effects of a somewhat rampant egalitarianism. It is clear that the nature and scale of social change cannot be attributed solely to the politics of pluralism: advances in science and medicine, the loosening of family and community ties, the internet as a communications medium and other contemporary developments are all in the mix. The outcome, however, presents a stark challenge to some of the Church's traditional and most fundamental beliefs. Secularism, nontheistic beliefs, gay marriages, same gender parents, together with female and gay clergy, and many other indicators of a break with tradition, are relentlessly requiring Christianity to make further adjustments and compromises.

A response to these and other social changes in recent years has come from the fields of both charity law and human rights law. National charity law reform, combined with equality legislation and significant case law developments in the European Court of Human Rights (ECtHR), have directly impacted upon the Church of England. This has been matched by comparable initiatives in many other leading common law nations.

Some charity law reform processes have recently concluded with legal definitions of 'religion' and with new legal requirements for religious organisations to be registered as charities (among other matters). It is not impossible that other common law countries will in due course, either explicitly by statute or by following case precedents, accept the lead given by England & Wales and similarly adopt a statutory definition of religion that removes the necessity for a belief in God or Gods. In addition, an important aspect of the reform processes has been the attention given to the 'public benefit test' as a condition for attaining or retaining charitable status. Again, the initiative taken in England & Wales (since followed by Scotland and Northern Ireland) to reverse the centuries old legal presumption – that religious purposes, the activities of religious organisations and gifts for their use are assumed to satisfy this test – presents a serious challenge to established law and practice. There is now the prospect of this presumption being replaced in other common law jurisdictions, as it has been throughout the UK, by a legal requirement that all religious organisations wishing to become or remain charities must demonstrate how they will promote the public benefit. This initiative, alone, has the potential to fundamentally alter the future relationship between charity and religion. If other such jurisdictions choose not to follow suit this will be extremely divisive. Either way, the changes introduced will have huge implications for the type and number of organisations already registered, or which may in future be registered, as charities.

Developments in human rights case law and equality legislation, occurring in conjunction with charity law reform, have also played their part. These have changed the operational context for the Church of England and its counterparts elsewhere and, more generally, have moderated the checks and balances that regulate the interests of those with and without religious belief in contemporary western societies. The consequences can be seen in the contention generated by issues such as: proselytism, the compatibility of philosophical and religious beliefs, the rights of secularists, same sex marriages, government funding for religious charities, the charitable status of faith based schools and other facilities, religious charities and their discriminatory employment and service provision practices, and the right of religion based adoption agencies to choose not to accept same sex applicants. These and an ever-growing range of such issues certainly present a fundamental and pressing challenge for the Church of England but they also carry serious implications for society as a whole.

In fact, the role of religion in modern society is generating considerable controversy. Often this is centred on doubts regarding its capacity to promote equity, equality and pluralism and to further social cohesion instead of fostering social division. Disenchantment may be giving rise to what Baroness Warsi, Britain's first Muslim cabinet minister, has termed 'a militant secularism'. Human rights litigation, bringing with it a heightened awareness of discrimination in any form, is rapidly adding extra complexity to an already entangled area where law, morality and social policy converge. The dissonance within the Church caused by the incremental abandonment of what were traditionally held to be red line issues for its religious beliefs, and the resulting disruption to the fabric of the Anglican Communion, are raising profound questions regarding what now needs to be done to realign the legal framework and core religious beliefs and restore coherence.

For such reasons this is an opportune time to examine the problems now facing the Church of England. While its difficulties call for analysis in their own right, they also make an ideal case study to explore issues of equality that have a much wider application.

This book, therefore:

- provides an objective and informative study of the Church of England, its distinctive doctrines, developmental history, organisational structure etc.;
- in particular, it focuses on the difference made by its locus standi as the 'Established Church';
- identifies and assesses the impact of charity law reform and human rights requirements upon the Church of England, and examines their wider implications;
- considers that which now constitutes 'religious belief' and compares and contrast this with other theistic and non-theistic beliefs;
- reflects on the arguments for and progress made by secularism;
- assesses the practice and significance of government funding for the Church and for other religious bodies;
- identifies and analyses what might be termed the core 'moral imperatives' the bright lines for religious bodies as they interface with human rights; and it
- suggests some possible ways forward as indicated by current case law.

Its main themes are:

- private piety as a public good;
- human rights and discriminatory practice by, or in favour of, religious bodies;
- the extent to which religion and the activities of religious organisations do or should satisfy a public benefit requirement;
- the roles of law and charity in moderating the balance between religion's capacity to generate social cohesion (instilling values of compassion and altruism, providing

health and educational facilities etc.) and its tendency to promote social divisions (polarising communities, accentuating differences etc.); and
- religious belief and 'moral imperatives'.

The Church of England: Charity Law and Human Rights begins with a background section of two chapters: 'Boundaries and Interfaces' and 'Religion, Charity and the Law'; the first outlining and assessing some of the parameters that currently constrain religion; and the second identifying and explaining the core concepts, principles, precepts and legal definitions relevant to religion and charity. The second section focuses on the Church itself and does so in three chapters: 'Establishing the Church of England', 'The Established Church: Governance, Organisational Structure & Theology', and 'Anglicanism at Home & Abroad'; the first gives an historical account of the origins and development of the Church; the second explains its status as the 'established' Church, describes its organisational structure and modes of governance, and deals with its distinctive theological underpinnings; while the third provides a contemporary profile of the Church, considers its role within the Anglican Communion, and identifies the management structures employed by both Church and Communion. The final section is again in three chapters: 'The Impact of Charity Law Reform'; 'The Impact of Human Rights' and 'Moral Jeopardy: the Challenges For the Church and For Religion Internationally'; the first identifies the drivers for reform relating to religion, explains the outcomes and assesses their effect on religion and the Church, giving particular attention to implications arising from changes to the public benefit test; the second considers the impact of human rights on religious beliefs, discrimination and the Church, drawing on case law arising from the Equality Act 2010 and Articles 9 and 14 of the European Convention; while the last chapter examines the capacity of religion to accommodate pluralism, taking stock of such guidance as has emerged from case law relating to clashes between religious beliefs and human rights, and identifying those areas where judicial clarification has at least been helpful and those where some resolution has been reached on 'moral imperative' issues. The book ends with a 'Conclusion' which reflects on the significance of the various challenges that now threaten the Church of England and the Anglican Communion and considers some of their wider implications.

Chapter 1
Boundaries and Interfaces

1.1 Introduction

> We have granted to God, and by this our Charter have confirmed, for Us and for our Heirs for ever, that the Church of England shall be free, and shall have all her whole Rights and Liberties inviolable.[1] We have granted also, and given to all the Freemen of our Realm, for Us and our Heirs for ever, these Liberties under-written, to have and to hold them and their Heirs, for us and our Heirs for ever.[2]

With these opening words the Magna Carta[3] established the overarching authority of Church and State: thereafter, English citizenship would include respect for the Church of England as the nation's governing religious institution; albeit subject to the denominational adjustment achieved by the Reformation. It then proceeded to address, as a subsidiary matter, the relationship between the monarch and his barons; the latter championing interests that, in due course, would come to be represented by Parliament. This, the single most important document in English history, stands as a constitutional landmark giving separate recognition to sources of authority which, despite subsequent changes within each and in the balance struck between them, has ever since governed the lives of its citizens. However, while the dual interests of Church and State as then defined proved to be the most enduring and relevant frame of reference for the purposes of this book, other boundaries and interfaces have also been significant and their variable bearing, over time on the role of the Church, must be borne in mind.

This chapter begins with a brief historical overview of the evolving relationship between Church and State in the centuries leading up to the Reformation, identifying themes that carried on through it, and which continue to influence the contemporary social role of the Church of England. It then turns to consider other frameworks that have come to condition the part played by religious belief. As firmer boundaries

[1] *Quod ecelesia Anglicana libera sit et habeat jura sua integra et libertates suas illæsas.*

[2] Magna Carta, Clause 1.

[3] Also known as the 'Articles of the Barons'.

K. O'Halloran, *The Church of England - Charity Law and Human Rights*, Ius Gentium: Comparative Perspectives on Law and Justice 36, DOI 10.1007/978-3-319-04319-7_1,

gradually separated the interests of Church and State, the space created allowed other entities to flourish, mutate and in so doing to alter the established pattern of subservience to both. The chapter therefore focuses in turn on: the family unit and the effect of changes in its definition; the evolution of new mediating forums between citizen and State such as collectivism, political ideology, legal rights, the professions and trade unions. It considers the consequences of advances in science and medicine that have probed the frontiers of knowledge, causing sacred verities to give way to secular, and concludes by reflecting on the ever more worldly role of some religious charities. In essence, this chapter identifies the factors that have intervened to constrain the traditional role of religious belief and put in play the different strands that now converge to compromise the Church of England.

1.2 Church and State in the Pre-reformation Era: A Brief Overview

When King John fixed his Great Seal to the Magna Carta in the meadow at Runnymede on 15 June 1215, he sought closure on a long history of fractious monarchical dealings with secular and religious powers. This turning point in English history, of lasting significance in the evolution of Church/State relationships, proved to be also important because it introduced the beginnings of parliamentary democracy which ultimately prised apart the parties that for centuries constituted a theocratic form of governance. As the shared ground for mutual support, formerly based on religious doctrine, was gradually eroded, the jurisdiction of the Church shrank and the State steadily took more responsibility for matters affecting the lives and property of its citizens in a process that also triggered some readjustment to the latter's traditional fealties.

1.2.1 Monarch and Pope

Among the monarchical concessions included in Magna Carta was the requirement that King John surrender his crown and kingdom into the hands of the Papal legate to be received back from him as a fief which he and his successors were to hold of the Pope for an annual rent of 1,000 marks. King John in effect made England a Papal fiefdom. In ceding so much, the monarch achieved a strategic success that at the time was significant and welcomed by all parties but would later come to be viewed as having sorely compromised the monarchy.

1.2.2 Rome in England: Catholicism and Papal Power

In the thirteenth century, Catholicism experienced a growth spurt as the mendicant orders of Franciscan and Dominican friars developed, spread throughout Europe, and became widely established in England. Indeed, thereafter "for more than

300 years the mendicant Friars in England were on the whole a power for good up and down the land, the friends of the poor and the evangelisers of the masses".[4] They, together with the many Catholic religious orders that built and operated a network of abbeys monasteries and Cathedrals across England, contributed much to social care provision and to generating a sense of national solidarity. This period also saw the conclusion of the crusades (1095–1291) which had seen Church and State co-operating to retrieve the Christian Holy Lands from 'unbelievers': a time when Archbishops and Kings had marched into war together.[5] During this and the succeeding century a working relationship was forged between the Church and monarchy in England and between them both and the Papacy in Rome.

1.2.3 The Ecclesia Anglicana

This term would seem to have first come into use during the reigns of Edward I and III when the Catholic Church in England cultivated a direct and wholly subservient relationship with the Papacy. In this it was not alone: Catholicism (like Judaism) was trans-national and trans-racial, its adherents owed loyalty equally to their national rulers and to the Pope; but on issues where faith and secular fealty were in conflict, the Catholic citizen looked first to Rome. As Maitland expressed it: "the Pope is above the law … to dispute the authority of a papal decretal is to be guilty of heresy, at a time when deliberate heresy was a capital crime"; this being "a principle to which archbishops, bishops and clergy of the province of Canterbury have adhered by solemn words".[6] The earlier State sanctioned murder of an Archbishop[7] had had a chastening effect on both Church/State relationships within England and between the latter and Rome: all parties wished to step back from what had been deemed to be a heinous affront to God and his Church. Although in general this was a period of building close and mutually respectful relations between England and Rome, there were rumblings of discontent within the *Ecclesia Anglicana*. One such emanated from Wycliffe[8] who, in leading a movement that opposed the medieval Church and some of its dogmas and institutions, prepared the doctrinal ground for

[4] Jessopp, A. 1885. *The coming of the Friars and other historical essays*. Whitefish, Montana, USA: Kessinger Publishing.

[5] For example, Baldwin the Archbishop of Canterbury accompanied Richard Coeur de Lion on the Third Crusade in 1190.

[6] Maitland, F.W. 1898. *Roman canon law in the Church of England*. London, UK: Methuen, at 17 citing the "Provinciale" of Bishop Lyndwood (1435).

[7] The lengthy dispute between Henry II and Archbishop Thomas Becket crystallised with the issue of the Constitutions of Clarendon in 1164 which redefined Church/State relations, restricted ecclesiastical privileges and curbed the power of the ecclesiastical courts. The dispute culminated on the afternoon of 29 December 1170, in Becket's murder following the King's provocative suggestions. The death was treated as martyrdom and became a pivotal landmark in relations between the Church in England, the monarchy and the Papacy.

[8] John Wycliffe (1330–84) was a philosopher, theologian, lay preacher and translator who taught at Oxford University.

the Reformation. In particular his 1378 treatise *De Veritate Sacræ Scripturæ* advanced the proposition that the Holy Scripture was the central and perhaps the sole necessary Christian belief. His further suggestion that this could be open to individual interpretation flew in the face of centuries of Church accumulated dogma, doctrine and canons but is very much in accord with the views of some English judiciary in the twenty-first century. Dissent within Protestantism and a small but often powerfully connected residual rump of Catholicism, were constant factors accompanying the growth of Anglicanism.

1.2.4 Christianity and Charity

In the centuries preceding the Reformation, Christianity and charity were inextricably linked. The Church provided shelter and succour for the poor and needy and engaged in other such charitable activity. The State supported the Church and enforced its doctrinal edicts. However the feudal system, with its basis in land tenure – underpinning the authority of the monarch and providing stability for the State – was gravely threatened by aspects of the Church's charitable role and this gave rise to tensions in the Church/State relationship that were not resolved until the Reformation.

1.2.5 Church, State and Charity

Records show that the role of the mediaeval Church, with its blend of saintly and secular concerns, received powerful support from the State which, through laws proclaiming that "God's churches are entitled to their rights",[9] required taxes to be paid to the Church and imposed severe penalties for non-payment.[10] The instilling of Christian beliefs, accompanied by charitable provision for the disadvantaged, was an area of shared common interest between Church and State. Indeed[11]:

> The enormous status and prestige of the early and mediaeval Church enabled her to assume jurisdiction over whole areas of social life which today would rightly be considered the concern of secular government. Indeed not until the mid-nineteenth century did the ecclesiastical courts in England lose their jurisdiction over marriage and matters relating to the probate of wills.

[9] See, King Edward's code promulgated at Andover (c. 963). Also, see, the laws of the West Saxon King Ine (688–694) which directed that "Church-scot is to be given by Martinmass; if anyone does not discharge it, he is liable to 60 shillings and to render the church-scott twelve-fold", as cited in Brady, J. 1975. *Religion and the law of charities in Ireland*, 6. Belfast: Northern Ireland Legal Quarterly.

[10] See, Whitelock (ed.), *English Historical Documents 500–1042*, at p.365; as cited in Brady, ibid.

[11] See, Brady, J., *Religion and the Law of Charities in Ireland, op cit*, at p.6.

To some extent the rise of the monastic orders in the thirteenth and fourteenth centuries largely displaced the previous parish based charitable activities of the Church as religion focused more on the salvation of souls than on temporal welfare.

1.2.6 Mortmain, Frankalmoigne and the Pious Use

While the donor role of the Church received State support and reinforcement, its capacity to attract enormous wealth, in perpetuity, from benefactors who believed the salvation of their souls could be ensured by offerings of property for religious purposes, was a source of increasing tension.

Feudalism, a centralised system based on land ownership, had become the basis for determining the loyalty, services and tithes due to rulers; included in the duties owed by a landowner was the obligation to provide knights, the number being determined relative to the size of the owner's property, for service in defence of the realm. For centuries, this system of land tenure underpinned feudalism and provided the basis for ordering society. From the perspective of the rulers, a significant threat to the system arose from the growing practice of mortmain. This Norman French term *morte meyn* or 'dead hand' referred to the practice whereby a donor would tie-up his lands in perpetuity by gifting them to the Church. It was customary for a penitent donor to make a gift to the Church for a pious use coupled with a request that prayers or masses be offered for the salvation of the donor's soul. Such gifts for pious uses were recognised as charitable gifts in the years prior to the Reformation. As Coke has explained[12]:

> The lands were said to come to dead hands … for … by alienation in mortmaine they lost wholly their escheats and in effect their knights services for the defence of the realme; wards, marriages, reliefes and the like; and therefore was called a dead hand, for that a dead hand yeeldeth no service.

Once property passed into the 'dead hand of the Church' it remained there as the latter prohibited any alienation of its property.[13]

Much land came to be owned by the Church on the basis of 'tenure by frankalmoign'; the gift of property having been made subject to a condition that it be held for the use of specified persons, usually the donor and/or his family. As has been said[14]:

> Tenant in frankalmoigne is where an abbot, or prior, or another man of religion or of Holy Church, holdeth of his lord in frankalmoigne that is to say in Latin, *in liberam eleemosinam*, that is, in free almes, and such tenure beganne first in old time.

---

[12] See, Coke, Co.Litt., 2B.

[13] Such was the enduring secular hold of mortmain on the adherents of Christianity in this jurisdiction that it was not abolished until the mid-twentieth century by the Mortmain (Repeal of Enactments) Act, 1954.

[14] See, Littleton, S., 133; Co.Lit., 93(b).

The statute *Quia Emptores* 1290[15] defined the services owed by a tenant in frankalmoigne to their feudal lord as follows:

> S.135(b). And they which hold in frankalmoigne are bound of rights before God to make orisons, prayers, masses and other divine services for the soules of their grantor or feofforn and for the soules of their heires which are dead, and for the prosperity and good life and good health of their heires which are alive. And therefore they shall do no fealty to their lord, because that this divine service is better before God than any doing of fealty: and also because that these words (frankalmoigne) exclude the lord to have any earthly or temporal service, but to have only divine and spiritual service to be done for him.

As time passed and the Church accumulated vast estates, thereby depleting State revenues and the availability of knight services, so feudal rulers came to regard mortmain and frankalmoigne as undermining the security of the State.

1.2.7 The Boundary Between Ecclesiastical and Secular Jurisdictions

In Europe, throughout the Middle Ages, the authority wielded by the courts of the Catholic Church operated in tandem with and often rivalled those of national monarchies. While the jurisdiction of the latter was largely criminal with a growing civil and constitutional remit, the jurisdiction of the religious courts was primarily concerned with sacramental matters particularly marriage and baptism. They had exclusive jurisdiction over all internal disputes concerning the Church such as the administration of property, tithes and benefices, and in relation to oaths and vows, and heresy. In addition, this jurisdiction was partially secular as all matters regarding the conduct of clergy, including criminal activity, were justiciable by the ecclesiastical courts. They also had exclusive jurisdiction over cases involving defamation and wills which, in England,[16] for many centuries, extended to matters of succession to personal property.[17] Although the ecclesiastical and secular courts had separate jurisdictions, in the virtual absence of any civil legislation, the former followed the common law principles established by the latter. Moreover, as a representative of the 'established' Church, the ecclesiastical court functioned as part of the State and was therefore required to ensure that, where there was a jurisdictional overlap, its decisions conformed with those of its secular counterpart.

Wherever heretics were so strongly entrenched that it was thought necessary to repress them, the special ecclesiastical court of the Inquisition was employed. In that context, Church and State functioned in unison as the latter were obliged under

[15] 18 Edw. I. c. 1. A statute passed by Edward I which forbade the practice of giving estates 'for the use of others' as a device for owners to retain the fee simple. It thereby facilitated the full and permanent transfer of property.

[16] See, further, Outhwaite, R.B. 2007. *The rise and fall of the English Ecclesiastical Courts, 1500–1860*. Cambridge: Cambridge University Press.

[17] See, further, Denning, Lord. 1944. The meaning of Ecclesiastical Law. *Law Quarterly Review* 60: 235.

pain of excommunication to pass the most severe sentences. This complementarity was illustrated by the statute *De hæretico com burendo* of 1401 which provided that heretics convicted before a spiritual court, and refusing to recant, were to be handed over to the secular authorities and burned to death.

Salus animarum suprema lex

Ecclesiastical law, as administered by the Church through its own network of courts, has always been governed by the one overriding principle – salvation of souls is the supreme law.[18] Unlike their secular counterparts, the outcome of proceedings in the ecclesiastical courts were intended to reform the offender *pro salute animae*, so as to secure the salvation of their soul rather than to compensate any victim; both nonetheless involved punishing an offender.

1.2.8 Confining the Jurisdiction of the Ecclesiastical Courts

By the fourteenth century, as the administration of royal justice increased, so did tensions between the secular and ecclesiastical powers. The former found ways to diminish the powers of the ecclesiastical courts. One was through appeal by writ of error in the secular courts. Then, in more subtle ways, the ecclesiastical jurisdiction was restricted to spiritual matters. The civil contract of marriage, for example, was separated from the sacrament. Other contracts and wills were similarly brought into the secular sphere. By the sixteenth century on the continent, the ecclesiastical courts had largely ceased to have any secular functions.

The gifting of property to the Church for pious uses was also a source of contention and one which became increasingly problematic for feudal rulers. Unsurprisingly, they regarded a grant of land to the Church by a subject as incompatible with the latter's feudal duties and, from the time of Magna Carta,[19] they sought to curtail this practice through successive statutes.[20] However, the systematic avoidance of statutory

---

[18] See, for example, the ruling of the Court of the Arches in *Breeks v. Woolfrey* (1838) 163 English Reports 304 where it was noted that "touching and concerning [the] soul's health … is the usual style and language of the proceedings of the [ecclesiastical] court". See, further, Chadwick, O. 1990. *The secularisation of the European mind in the 19th century*, Canto original series. Cambridge: Cambridge University Press.

[19] See Clause 43 which provided:

> It shall not be lawful from henceforth to any to give his lands to any religious house and to take the same land again to hold of the same house: nor shall it be lawful to any house of religion to take the lands of any and to have the same of him of whom he received it. If any from henceforth give his lands to any religious house, and thereupon be convict, the gift shall be utterly void, and the land shall accrue to the lord of the fee.

[20] See, statutes of Henry 111, 1217, of Marlborough 1267, of Edward 1 in 1279 and 1285, Richard 11 in 1391 leading eventually to Poynings Law in 1495.

constraints allowed the Church, and particularly the religious orders, to continue acquiring more power, land and political influence until Henry VIII's fateful intervention in the Church/State crisis that became the Reformation.

1.3 Family, Religious Belief and the State

The Christian family model, based on the original Nazarene unit of married parents and the child 'of their marriage', has always been a fundamental benchmark of personal and societal relationships for the Church of England as for other Christian religions. For centuries, culminating in the moral code of the Victorian era, the legal status of marriage was upheld by Church and State as an inviolable building block for constructing a sound Christian society. Only in fairly recent times, perhaps since the mid-twentieth century, has the monogamous, lifelong union of a heterosexual couple, parenting the children of their marriage, ceased to be the ubiquitous norm it once was.[21] Any appreciation of the impact of contemporary social norms upon traditional religious beliefs, such as those held by the Church of England, must take into account: the nature of the interpretation initially given to the legal status of 'marriage' and 'family' by the ecclesiastical courts; the depth and continuity of the Church's investment in defending its beliefs as manifested in the context of the marital family; and the extent of subsequent secular changes that have steadily eroded the Christian definition of that unit.

In considering these matters it is instructive to reflect on the rules devised – first in the ecclesiastical courts and subsequently in the common law courts – to distinguish, and discriminate, between marital and non-marital families, between the patriarchical powers of the husband and the servile duties of his wife, the respective property rights of the two spouses and the inheritance rights of 'legitimate' as opposed to 'illegitimate' children. Issues of equality and discrimination, even if not recognised as such, were then certainly very much in evidence. Arguably, then as now, it was not until statute law laid down new principles for redefining 'marriage' and 'family' and provided for a more equitable approach towards the parties concerned, that the Church reluctantly followed the lead taken by the State.

1.3.1 Marriage

For many centuries marriage law was canon law as administered by the ecclesiastical courts.[22] Its key legal characteristics evolved in that context. One such was the

[21] See, for example, Wohl, A.S. (ed.). 1978. *The Victorian family: Structure and stresses*. London: Croom Helm Ltd.

[22] It was the Clandestine Marriages Act 1753 that introduced formal requirements for the ceremony of marriage: publishing of banns; ceremony to be public and conducted in a Church; consent of a minor's parents to be obtained; and the marriage to be registered.

heterosexual basis for a legal marital relationship[23]: although this goes unmentioned in Christian teachings, it was clearly understood as a 'given'; as illustrated by the fact that it was interpreted in canonical terms as being primarily for the purposes of procreation; indeed impotence or wilful refusal to consummate were recognised at an early stage as grounds for annulling a marriage. Other traditional characteristics included: not being already married or within the prohibited degrees of consanguinity or affinity[24]; and being monogamous.

1.3.2 The Marital Bond

Christianity viewed the marital bond as of fundamental importance both in a religious and social sense. It bound: the spouses in an exclusive mutually supportive union for procreative purposes, granted legal rights to maintenance and property and provided the only context in which sexual relations and the children born thereof could be legitimate; the families and relatives of the spouses in a kinship network; and the marital family to the State as a unit that conformed the latter's laws, thereby fulfilling a deep civic contract between family and society. Especially in a hierarchical society – where lineage, class and the orderly devolution of family estates have always been important (unlike the more lateral and collective social structures of the clan system in Ireland and Scotland) – marriage was a key social institution.

It was primarily a public rather than a private bond. At a time when England was more socially and religiously homogenous, marriage was wholly accepted as the appropriate way to seal the above bonds: as a proportion of the total population, the number of those choosing to cohabit and/or to rear 'illegitimate' children, was tiny; they were seen as deviant.

1.3.3 Family: The Marital Unit

In law, the family was in effect defined by marriage, which in turn had been defined by the Church. The legal status of spouses and their children with all attendant rights and duties were only acquired as a consequence of marriage; those in non-marital relationships were not so legally bound.

[23] Not until the mid-nineteenth century was marriage so defined in English law when Lord Penzance, in *Hyde v. Hyde* (1860) LR. 1, P&D 130, declared that a Christian marriage was "the voluntary union for life of one man and one woman, to the exclusion of all others" at p.135 (see further, Chap. 7).

[24] Consanguinity being the proximity of relationship derived from blood-links. Affinity being the proximity of relationship derived from marriage.

1.3.4 Legal Obligations of Spouses

In legal terms, marriage was viewed as unifying the persona of husband and wife: in effect they assumed one legal identity, that of the husband. As has been explained[25]:

> [the] very being or legal existence of the woman is suspended during the marriage, or at least is incorporated and consolidated into that of the husband under whose wing, protection and cover she performs everything.

It provided the spouses with mutual legal rights and obligations unavailable to unmarried couples. These included: provision of home and adequate maintenance; mutual consortium[26]; and succession rights to family property. It was a status that also had the consequence of: transferring to the husband all property, other assets and entitlements previously vesting in his wife; and requiring the wife to assume the same domicile and citizenship as that of her husband. In keeping with its recognition of a husband's almost proprietary rights to the services of his wife,[27] the common law also provided him with the means for suing third parties when they were responsible for the loss of those services: an adulterous relationship, for example, would provide grounds for him to bring an action for 'criminal conversation'. For centuries this process gave a husband the right to sue a third party for the loss of 'conjugal rights' to which, as spouse, he was entitled; but to which, in reverse circumstances, provided a wife with no equivalent recourse.

1.3.5 Parenting

Only spouses were vested with specific parenting rights and duties for which they could be held accountable by the ecclesiastical courts, and later by their secular counterparts, in the event of a breach. In the patriarchical culture of that time, the duty to ensure adequate maintenance and the right to determine matters of upbringing (e.g. schooling and religious adherence) and to administer 'reasonable chastisement'[28] to their children, which could extend to serious beatings, were the exclusive responsibility of the marital father.[29] Also, the Church evolved certain practices for conferring status, available only to spouses in relation to their children, including christening and the appointment of godparents.

---

[25] See, Blackstone. 1824. *Commentaries on the Law of England,* vol 1, 8th ed, 449.

[26] A term which implies a breadth, duration and proximity of companionship in which sexual relations may, but need not, play a part. Like most legal aspects of the marital relationship, consortium was usually understood to vest rights in the husband and reciprocal duties in his wife: see, for example, *R v. Lister* (1721) 1 Stra 478; indeed a husband could not be charged with rape in respect of his wife.

[27] For example, the writ of trespass *vi et armis de uxore rapta et abducta* was available only to a husband.

[28] See, for example, *R v. Hopley* [1860] 2F and F 160.

[29] The first statutory acknowledgment of a paternal right to custody was in s.8 of the Tenures abolition Act 1660. Until 1839 the custody of a 'legitimate' child vested exclusively in the father. As Bowen LJ explained in *Agar-Ellis* (1878) 10 Ch D:

1.3.6 Breaking the Marital Bond

The importance attached to the legal status of 'marriage' and 'family' was reflected in the few and tightly controlled grounds for ending a marital relationship. Because it was viewed as a public institution, there could be no question of a marriage being terminated at the discretion of either or both of the parties: strict conditions had to be met, to the satisfaction of the court, if such a crucial bond was to be broken.

1.3.7 Nullity

While marriage was deemed to be a lifelong commitment, ecclesiastical law at an early stage developed certain legal means for ending it. The first such procedure was the decree of 'nullity' which allowed a marriage to be annulled when it was either void or voidable: void when certain pre-conditions had not been satisfied, due perhaps to one party already being in a valid and subsisting marriage, it was then viewed as invalid *ab initio*; or voidable, at the petition of either party, but only if one was unable to consummate the marriage or was unable to enter into and sustain a normal marital relationship, perhaps due to a lack of informed consent, being underage[30] or within the prohibited degrees of relationship,[31] or the parties were not respectively male and female. In either case all children of such a relationship would be deemed 'illegitimate'.

The ability to rule that a marriage was void, with full discretion to interpret the relevant grounds as they saw fit, placed great power in the hands of the ecclesiastical courts. When exercised after the death of a spouse serious implications could arise for the devolution of family property. Not until the Reformation was this power removed from those courts.

1.3.8 Divorce

A form of divorce known as *a mensa et thoro* was available from the ecclesiastical courts on the limited grounds of adultery, cruelty or unnatural practices. This decree, relieving a petitioning spouse from the marital obligation to share 'bed and board', essentially provided a form of legal separation which allowed the spouses to cease

---

The strict common law gave to the father the guardianship of his children during the age of nurture and until the age of discretion. The limit was fixed at fourteen years in the case of a boy and sixteen years in the case of a girl …

[30] Until 1929 the minimum age limits for marriage in England were 14 for the male and 12 for the female.

[31] A marriage between persons who are within the prohibited degrees of consanguinity (relationships by blood) or affinity (relationships by marriage) is void.

cohabiting but, as it did not end their marriage, neither were free to remarry. Desertion was never sufficient grounds for such a decree, the only remedy then provided by the ecclesiastical courts was a decree for the restitution of conjugal rights. Having obtained a divorce *a mensa et thoro* from the ecclesiastical court, the only way in which a person could then acquire the freedom to remarry was by petitioning Parliament and obtaining a private act of Parliament. Such recourse being made available to prevent 'illegitimate' children being foisted on "the unhappy husband whose bed had been violated".[32]

Statutory divorce, introduced in England in 1857, provided for the dissolution of marriage, altered the legal status of the parties from spouses to unmarried persons, thereby allowing both to remarry. However divorce proceedings were very seldom utilised: the grounds were restricted; they were expensive as they involved lawyers; and they tended to attract social disapproval.

1.3.9 Family: The Non-marital Unit

Traditionally, none of the legal characteristics of a marital family applied to its non-marital counterpart. Whether 'non-marital' or 'extra-marital' it was seen as deviant and all parties involved were legally and socially stigmatised.

1.3.10 Parents

An unmarried father was denied any rights in respect of his children.[33] All parental responsibility vested exclusively in the mother.

1.3.11 Children

A child born of a non-marital relationship was in law an 'illegitimate' child. Under common law, being *filius nullius*, such a child had no legal relationship with anyone. He or she had no rights, for example, to maintenance or to inherit property; nor did anyone owe such a child any duty, for example to protect him or her from harm.

1.3.12 Penalising Non-marital Relations

The ecclesiastical and secular authorities were united in their approach to strengthening the legal significance of marriage by at least stigmatising, if not criminalising,

[32] *Mr Lewkenor's Case*, 13 State Trials 1308: as cited in Cretney, S.M. 2003. *Principles of family law*, 7th ed, 270. London: Thomson, Sweet & Maxwell.

[33] In particular he had no right to custody: see, for example, *R v. Moses Soper* (1793) 5 Term Rep 278.

non-marital relations. Unlawful carnal knowledge, for example, was designated and treated as both a sin and a crime.

1.3.13 Church, State and the Enforcement of Christian Morality

In late mediaeval England the ecclesiastical courts had a wide and punitive jurisdiction on matters of morality. The authority vested in them to decide matters such as disputes relating to marriage, divorce, wills, and defamation provided considerable scope for monitoring and regulating public morality, but it was in relation to the family that they had a particular and lasting effect and where their rulings significantly influenced the approach taken by State authorities. Christian principles guided the deliberations of ecclesiastical courts.

1.3.14 Sexual Relations

For some centuries the religious doctrine of the established Church was underpinned by statute and common law to prohibit any infringement of Church approved morality. In particular, sexual transgressions attracted the approbation of the ecclesiastical courts and the principles applied there, which in time became transmuted into legislative provisions, included: a rejection of non-marital sexual relations; and the prohibition of adultery, bigamy, unlawful carnal knowledge, incest, sodomy, etc. Christian principles established certain 'moral imperatives' that came to inform the law relating to the family and continue to provide the grounds for sustaining such traditional religious beliefs as that in monogamous, heterosexual marriage for life. Indeed, given the Scriptural endorsement of marriage, it is unsurprising that adultery was viewed with singular approbation and that divorce legislation was initially introduced to provide a remedy for a legal wrong, to publicly shame those who had violated that bond and to free the blameless spouse to make a fresh start.[34]

From this Christian perspective other consequences followed such as: the stigmatising of unmarried mothers, non-marital children, those who entered into partnership relationships or who divorced; upholding patriarchical authority; and a renunciation of all methods of birth control. The assidious vigour with which the authorities of both Church and State pursued their joint mission to police any laxity in the virtues of English citizens was evident in "the thousands of men and women cited and punished each year by secular and ecclesiastical courts for fornication

[34] See, Ingram, M. 1990. *Church courts, sex and marriage in England, 1570–1640*. Cambridge: Cambridge University Press.

and adultery".[35] In the light of that background, the comment recently offered by an ex-Archbishop that "it is at least worth asking why the most bitterly contested issues within some traditional religions at the moment, certainly in the Christian churches, are not doctrinal in the strict sense but matters on the dangerous frontiers of sexuality and power"[36] seems at best strangely disingenuous.

1.4 New Forms of Collective Action Mediating Between Citizen and State

By the twentieth century, simple submission to the combined authority of Church and State, characteristic of citizenship in the Middle Ages, had been broadened by a range of intermediary forums and membership opportunities that loosened and tended to dilute the ties between citizens and their spiritual and secular rulers. The perception that a vesting of personal trust, respect and sense of 'belonging' might be better served by diverting wholly or partially from traditional obligations towards routes selected on the basis of offering immediate answers to pressing problems, was likely to be accompanied by an attitude less accepting of prevailing circumstances or prone to automatic deference and more open to challenging previously unquestioned sources of authority. The three main such routes were: collectivism, politics and other forms of action for social policy purposes; professions or other special interest groups; and legal rights accompanied by trade union activity.

1.4.1 Collectivism and Politics

Prior to the late seventeenth and early eighteenth centuries, apart from the work of religious organisations, there had been little evidence of consensual and peaceful, constructive group action for social improvement purposes.

1.4.2 Collectivism

In England, towards the end of the nineteenth century, as the State poor law regime faded, collectivism as a basis for organised mutual support became evident in initiatives such as those that launched the Friendly Societies.[37] There was also greater

[35] See, Poos, L.R. 1995. Sex, lies, and the church courts of pre-reformation England. *The Journal of Interdisciplinary History* 25(4, Spring): 585–607.

[36] See, Williams, R. 2012. *Faith in the public square*, 20. London: Bloomsbury.

[37] The 1874 report of the Royal Commission on Friendly Societies offered support for the new forms of intervention into the circumstances of the poor.

awareness of the extent and effects of poverty as a result of a series of late-Victorian and early Edwardian social surveys, notably those conducted by the wealthy liberal businessmen Charles Booth[38] and Seebohm Rowntree.[39] In the aftermath of generalised unrest that threatened to spark social revolution in 1848, the growth and spread of socially concerned groups, actively involved in ameliorating poverty, did much to stabilise English society.

A new pattern of social activism emerged represented by the creation of associational charities.[40] Prominent liberal activists, including Mary Wollstonecraft,[41] Mary Carpenter,[42] and Octavia Hill[43] generated public awareness of contemporary issues of social inequity. The Evangelical clergy also played a pioneering role with Henry Thornton, Thomas Babington, Hannah More and William Wilberforce and other members of 'the Clapham Sect' challenging the orthodox institutional role of within the established church. Leadership for a new approach was provided by 'chocolate philanthropists' from the Quaker families of Fry, Cadbury and Rowntree.[44] Their construction of model villages enabling whole communities to be self-sufficient and mutually supportive offered a new challenging interpretation of philanthropy. This approach contrasted sharply with the previous centuries of provision by Church and State of alms and the workhouse, respectively, that led to consequent ignominious dependency.

1.4.3 Mutual Benefit and Other Organisational Structures

The new ethos saw the birth of organisations formed to provide sustained economic security for its members such as, guilds, mutual benefit associations and the Credit Union movement[45] which were organised around principles that required ownership, labour and profits to be shared among their members. The Industrial and

[38] Charles Booth (1840–1916), a social researcher noted for his studies into pauperism in London; see, *Life and Labour of the People of London* (1891–1903).

[39] Seebohm Rowntree (1871–1954), noted for studies measuring poverty and analysing its effects in York at the turn of the century; see, further his reports, for example *Poverty a Study of Town Life* (1901), *Poverty and Progress* (1936) and *Poverty and the Welfare State* (1951).

[40] See, Hitchcock, T. 1992. Paupers and Preachers: The SPCK and the parochial workhouse movement. In *Stilling the grumbling hive: The response to social and economic problems in England, 1689–1750*, ed. L. Davison et al., 145–66. Stroud, London: Allen Sutton.

[41] See, for example, Gordon, L. 2004. *Mary Wollstonecraft: a new genus*. London: Little Brown.

[42] See, Carpenter, M. *Reformatory Schools for the Perishing and Dangerous Classes and for the Prevention of Juvenile Delinquency*, published in 1851.

[43] Founder member of the Charity Organisation Society; see, Hill, O. 1875. *Homes of the London poor*. London: Macmillan.

[44] See, further, Cadbury, D. 2010. *Chocolate wars*. London: Harper Press.

[45] Organisations set up for the mutual benefit of members have, of course, consistently been refused charitable status: see, for example, *Nuffield (Lord) v. Inland Revenue Commissioners* (1946) 175 LT 465.

Provident Societies, the Friendly Societies, co-operatives and community benefit societies, all with a mission to conduct business for the benefit of their members or community, became established in the nineteenth century. Many mutual benefit organizations were also self-help in nature, often short-term with a single-issue focus and with governance arrangements heavily weighted in favour of user representation. These included housing associations, community development organizations, and training for employment associations. Together with other forms of associational activity dedicated to the pursuit of social improvement, such organisations shifted the concept of citizenship away from simple subservience to Church and State by laying the foundations for what was to become the nonprofit sector, thereby forming the basis of a new strategic socio-economic balance with the government and commercial sectors.

1.4.4 Politics

Politics has probably always played a role in guiding human affairs: planning with others to effect change in temporal circumstances is part of the human condition. In medieval times it would have been constrained by pre-ordained feudal loyalties, restricted mainly to leadership issues and focused largely on strategies for dealing with enemies. Politics as we now know it – collective movements, organised around an agreed agenda of policy and principles, intending to acquire the authority necessary to effect nationwide change and then organising to do so – is a relatively recent phenomenon and for many is one which has undoubtedly impacted upon their relationship with religion and charity. While it is usually perfectly compatible with religion, politics, or more accurately political ideology, can itself become the higher authority – transcending circumstantial everyday concerns – to which individuals can turn for a sense of belonging, fulfilment and a feeling of contributing to a greater good. Incompatibility is also clearly possible, particularly on the agenda of contemporary social issues involving medical intervention on matters relating to life and death (including but certainly not limited to, abortion, birth control and euthanasia) where religious belief and social policy can often be in conflict. Then again, strains of politics and religion can merge as in the conjoining of neo-conservatism and evangelical Christianity in the US at the end of the twentieth century.

Where politics and political debate invariably succeed is in their capacity to generate a greater awareness of the cause and effect of good and bad social phenomena, and a realistic grasp of the resources available to address current issues and plan future developments. For those accustomed to investing their trust in evidence based outcomes, where accountability can be readily established, the political route has proved attractive; though not necessarily to the exclusion of religious belief.

1.4.5 *Unified by religion*

Theocratic states have a long history. From the records of Mayan and Egyptian dynasties, with their worship of rulers who were held to be deities or the incarnation of deities, to the conduct of rulers in contemporary Islamic states, it is demonstrably clear that some cultures find it appropriate that their affairs be governed by an authorative fusion of Church and State. Currently Iran is perhaps the leading contender for recognition as a theocratic nation state. In such states, as religious belief is politically determined, the scope for individual manifestations of belief is negligible; citizenship carries a prescriptive requirement for the uniform expression and practice of a politically designated religious belief.

For most of the twentieth century, communism, and to a lesser extent socialism (and some forms of fascism), sought to create a society that would have need for neither religion nor charity. The attempts in eastern Europe to achieve this on a nation state basis have conspicuously failed and the countries concerned, having now emerged after many decades from under their totalitarian blanket, have returned to creating space for religious belief and welcoming modern philanthropic initiatives. The collapse of ideology (communism, fascism and Maoism among others) as a driving force and its replacement by centre left politics with its focus on socio-economic management would seem to have given permission for a break with *en bloc* loyalties. Instead of continuing the family tradition of adherence to an institutionalised religion, many in England and elsewhere elected to either forego religion or form or join one of a rapidly expanding range of new sects and philosophical groups.

1.4.6 *Modern Democracies, Pluralism and Faith Based Organisations*

In England, as in other modern democratic nations of the common law world, governments are currently in the business of managing a sustained influx of immigrants, mostly economic refugees, which requires initiatives to respect and reinforce their cultural background while simultaneously endeavouring to protect the established domestic culture. The policy of pluralism has been developed to cope with these tensions and balance the interests of all concerned. However, this is an imperfect science and many government grants and planning permits, issued to nurture cultural identity, have instead resulted in community discord. A pluralism policy, operationalised by government grants to religious organisations for the purpose of assisting them to support ethnic groups and affirm their cultural identity, all too often achieves little more than sanctioning the creation of cultural ghettoes. When the policy is rolled out by way of facilitating a cultural mix, it can end up accentuating differences and exacerbating community tensions (see, further, Chap. 7).

1.4.7 *Professions and Other Special Interest Groups*

The collapse of the customary buffers between family and State – the kith and kin support networks and good neighbor relationships of settled communities – increased the likelihood that individuals in difficulty would turn instead to either charity or the Church and, in all probability, this was often the case. However, the likelihood of that happening was reduced by one of the more significant twentieth century developments affecting the relationships between citizen, family, and the State – the rise of the professional as the mediator of issues occurring within that relationship context. By mediating in that space the professions have, perhaps, deskilled or demoted the family and further distanced the individual from traditional sources of support, but they also provided a tangible and accessible resource to which those with problems could turn and expect a response that would not require submissive deference. The anonymity, confidentiality and problem solving characteristics offered by a relationship with a chosen professional may often have influenced those who might otherwise have sought help from Church or charity.

This rise of the professions also led to the forming of profession specific bodies, set up to represent the interests of their members, which negotiated with government and other entities. To an extent these representative bodies were following in the footsteps of the guilds and confraternities that preceded them by several centuries. They differed from their predecessors by being powerful negotiating bodies assured of access to relevant government policy-making forums on which they exercised considerable leverage. Again, they offered a different model – one that featured assertive action on behalf of members to address problems and improve collective best interests – which contrasted sharply with the role of Church and charity.

1.4.8 *Legal Rights, Trade Union Activity etc.*

The common law was essentially grounded on the rights and duties of the individual. There was no sense of collective legal interests, no provision was made for class or community actions; the law consisted merely of categories of causes actionable by or against individuals. Similarly, employment was a matter settled in time-honoured fashion on terms set by the employer which an employee was free to accept or reject. The approach in both contexts was personal: goals were to be pursued on an individual basis, which was very much in keeping with that adopted in respect of religious belief; the system was as it had always been and it was left to the individual to apply and hope their needs would be acknowledged. The changes introduced by concepts of legal rights, social justice and collective bargaining shifted the dynamic from the personal to the public domain. It may also have encouraged a more utilitarian or even an entitlement approach that weakened the resolve of those accustomed to placing their trust in religious belief.

1.4.9 Legal Rights

The legal rights approach provides for assertive action in the courts by individuals for alleged breach of specific rights as established in national legislation and/or in international conventions. Legal rights and corresponding legal duties, usually underpinned by moral authority and enforced by legal powers, form the basis for national legal systems. This approach is characterized by: acknowledgment of specific rights held by individuals; a process for obtaining formal recognition of individual entitlement; objective adjudication on alleged breach and appropriate recompense; and a process for enforcement. As nation states became steadily less cohesive, uni-cultural, homogenous, and more independent entities, so legal rights acquired a trans-national remit.

Certain rights have gained international recognition as being of greater importance than others. In particular the rights embodied in the European Convention for the Protection of Human Rights and Fundamental Freedoms 1950 have been seminal (see, further, Chap. 7).

1.4.10 Social Justice

In contrast to an approach based on the rights of the individual, but complementary to it, social justice provides a blanket safety net of provisions. It requires universal standards of equity, equality and non-discrimination to be entrenched in legislation and applied uniformly across society. In particular the prohibiting of discrimination is now to be found in many laws applying that principle in relation specifically and separately to disability, race, religion or belief, sexual orientation, equal pay and fair employment etc., requiring more general social legislation to be proofed against those principles and providing for an independent overview by regulatory bodies, commissions or tribunals coupled with power of referral to the court.

The collective approach to justice is most apparent in national legislation dealing, for example, with civil liberties and freedom of information, but is also reinforced by international conventions. Both legal rights and social justice represent the development of a relatively recent rights sensitive culture and an awareness of the need to nurture, across all subscribing nations, the same basic conditions for the growth of civil society. Both also have provided forums for the redress of temporal injustice, the assuaging of need, and a procedural model for those seeking self-affirmation and a problem solving resource, which again may have diverted some from their traditional loyalties.

1.4.11 Trade Unions

It would be wrong to overlook the positive contribution made by trade unions, not only to improving conditions for workers, but also in providing debating forums and social facilities that offered a supportive environment within which members could build a sense of collective solidarity and learn self-help strategies. The concepts of group representation, of bargaining and contract that took hold over time have undoubtedly done much to erode certain attitudes – submissiveness, acceptance and compliance with authority – which contributed to sustaining the social functions of charity and religion. Throughout times when other nations were riven by totalitarian conflict and revolution, the trade unions in England seemed to stand on a middle ground demonstrating that collective bargaining could effect sufficient change in the lives of workers and their families to warrant rejecting alternative and more violent strategies.

1.5 From the Sacred to the Secular

For all religions, the steady inroads made by modern scientific discoveries into areas hitherto clothed in religious belief have presented a continuous, and increasingly serious, challenge. There are those who consider that science has come to offer an alternative frame of reference to the inherited ancestral beliefs that pictured a transcendental dimension to human life. Some contend that the transcendent is no longer necessarily embodied in religion: its belief systems and spiritual and moral values for leading a 'good life' have perhaps been gradually displaced by, or swapped for, the verities of scientifically established knowledge; the derived values from which have come to inform the way we now live; providing, for example, the transcending set of fundamental human rights.

The challenges have not always been external – religion has itself been undergoing change. Always prone to schisms, the major religions have lately experienced a greater number of subdivisions with, for example, more extreme Islamic organisations and more evangelical Christian groups gaining adherents and prominence. The consequent tensions between the traditional parent religion and its more recent and radical offshoots parallels the growing acrimony between those with and those without religious belief. All of which has led to the present sharp interfaces between science and religion, secularism and religion, between and within religions and between religious and philosophical beliefs (see, further, Chap. 7).

The secular also impinges upon religion in other more mundane ways. Increasingly, for example, all charities including religious organisations, and certainly including the Church of England, are having to look to the marketplace and initiate or maintain commercial ventures, and probably experiment with new entrepreneurial initiatives, in order to offset their fall in income from government grants and public fundraising. Again, and like other charities, the Church is having to cope with new government anti-terrorism provisions for monitoring cash flows.

1.5.1 The Interface Between Science and Religion

The boundaries of human knowledge, circumscribing the early years of the Church of England and providing the context in which it forged its beliefs, were tightly drawn but have since been steadily pushed back by the advances of scientific research.

While the range of scientific discoveries impinging upon established religious belief is considerable, the impact of developments in medical science relating to human life – its beginnings, alteration (e.g. gender change) and end – present the area of greatest difficulty for religion. But medical intervention in life more broadly is also problematic. The ongoing process of having to make room for alternative, evidenced based, explanations for matters handed down through the previous generations as inviolable religious truths, is inevitably weakening the authority of all religions.

1.5.2 Medical Intervention in Matters of Life and Death

Developments in medicine and law have greatly impacted upon parenting: increasing the extent to which maternity is now a chosen option as pregnancy may be achieved by artificial insemination, avoided through the use of improved contraceptives, or terminated by abortion. Surrogacy, while decreasing the relevance of paternity and rendering obsolete any residual traces of patriarchy, has also rendered the choice to parent a gender free option: its availability to single prospective parents[46] as well as to same-sex couples has done much to broaden the diversity of contemporary family forms. At the other end of the scale, medical advances are now such that people are living longer and assisted euthanasia can offer relief for the terminally ill, even if permission for such relief is not yet lawful.

The field of genetic science is perhaps where the interface between medicine and religion is becoming most fraught. Genetic counselling, for example, is available to prospective parents at risk of perpetuating a family chromosome disorder and for whom avoidance of pregnancy may be advised. Where tests confirm the presence of a damaged foetus, or one likely to carry the chromosome disorder, a termination that could then be legally sanctioned on medical grounds would be in breach of religious beliefs. The number of cases coming before the courts on such issues (e.g. the legal challenge to commercial patenting of DNA) testifies to the difficulties now presenting at this interface. Again, body tissue 'grown in test tubes' can be used to repair and sometimes replace damaged human organs. Indeed, recent discoveries in sequencing the human genome are believed likely to advance the diagnosis and treatment of diseases, offer new insights into many fields of biology and lead to an understanding of human evolution itself – leading also to even more acute interface problems.

1.5.3 Other Scientific Advances

The range and rapidity with which new scientific discoveries are extending the boundaries of human knowledge and, though this is hotly contested, shrinking those previously in the domain of religious belief, has become difficult to

[46] See, for example, Mucklejohn, I. 2005. *And then there were three: The exceptional story of a remarkable surrogacy family*. London, UK: Gibson Square Books Ltd.

assimilate and impossible to do justice in this context. For present purposes, however, it is worthwhile to reflect on the implications for religion of some of the more recent advances.

For example, breakthroughs in biogenetic engineering have seen crop modifications that increase yield and disease resistance and have made possible the cloning of animals. With the latter has come the realisation that the cloning of humans is now also technically possible. The discovery of a new galaxy has shown the universe to be much bigger than previously realised and increases the probability of other life forms being present in it. The Higgs Bosun discovery at CERN in 2012 provides evidence to confirm how all other particles, including human beings, acquire mass. These and many other scientific discoveries in nano-technology, physics, biology, and in other areas, have also increased our awareness of the interconnectedness of all life forms on this planet and how their current increasing exposure to global warming, within a degrading environment, could threaten the planet's future. This awareness may be counter-intuitive for those with religious beliefs.

1.5.4 Secularism and Religion

From at least the mid-nineteenth century secularism[47] has had a marginal if expanding social profile, but the interface between religious belief and what to some has since evolved into 'a militant secularism'[48] is one that, although already tense in the closing decades of the twentieth century, is set to become more so in the twenty-first.

1.5.5 The State and Religion

The question of whether all matters of government should be entirely separate and insulated from religion is one that has exercised policy makers in many countries: there is no equivalent in England to the constitutional separation of Church and State in the U.S. Indeed, following the Reformation, all State institutions were permeated by and aligned with Protestantism, as represented by the Church of England, and although this symbiotic Church/State relationship has faded somewhat over the past century it remains formally in place and still retains a good deal of potency.

The problem is often given a sharp focus in the context of eligibility for government funding. In this jurisdiction it has long ceased to be State policy to give

[47] The term 'secularism' was first coined by George Jacob Holyoake (1817–1906).

[48] A term used by Baronness Warsi, Britain's first Muslim cabinet minister and chair of the Conservative Party, in response to the ruling of Ouseley J in *NSS v. Bideford Council* [2012] EWHC 175 (Admin) when he declared it unconstitutional for Bideford Town Council to continue with its long-standing practice of holding prayers at commencement of their meetings.

preference the Church of England in any disbursement of financial grants; indeed, that policy is to taper off any such grant aid to all charities whether religious organisations or not. Instead, the issue is more likely to arise in relation to public benefit service provision contracts. As these go out to tender they become contentious because religious charities often have greater capacity and are better positioned than competing secular commercial and nonprofit organisations to deliver services such as schooling, health and social care. Not all government bodies are able to adopt the wholly non-partisan stance of Munby J in *X v. X*[49] when he declared that "although historically this country is part of the Christian west, and although it has an established church which is Christian, I sit as a secular judge serving a multi-cultural community". When, for example, approximately one quarter of the nation's primary schools educating one fifth of all schoolchildren are owned by the established Church, government subvention of education services will inevitably be skewed to some degree.

It may be argued that in circumstances where the cultural identity of a nation has become indivisible from its association with a particular religion (e.g. Italy, Ireland, Spain and the Catholic Church), then there is justification for the State to permit its public institutions to reflect that mutuality and for it to preference the interests of related religious organisations against all others. On the other hand, the equality principle as upheld by the ECtHR does seem to require the State to be neutral in its relationship with religion. In which case the public arena needs to be treated as either: an open market in which all religions are equally free to proclaim and manifest their beliefs, compete for adherents and be assured of equal respect and engagement with State authorities; or, alternatively, as one in which all religions are equally prohibited from exercising any presence, that space is reserved entirely for secular entities and their activities, and all religions can be equally assured that they will be ignored by the State authorities. The privileged position of the Church of England as the 'established' religion does, however, seem to complicate that neat dichotomy.

1.5.6 Those with and Those Without Religious Beliefs

The rift between these two groups has become steadily more contentious as secularists grow in number and both adopt opposing and intransigent positions on an increasing range of matters. The area of contention is partially to do with the propriety of any form of government support for or engagement with religion, particularly in relation to a specific religion, and of its links to bodies associated with a religion. Secularists would be very alert, for example, to the vulnerability of public institutions, such as schools, to penetration by covert proselytism either in the classroom (through use of teachers, teaching materials or fixtures that suggest particular, or

[49] [2002] 1 FLR 508, at para 112.

any, religious belief) or in pastoral care (through the role of chaplain etc.).[50] In recent decades contention has grown more acrimonious in respect of an ever extending agenda of social issues with a high moral content. Mostly, in England as elsewhere in the developed western nations, these are issues – such as abortion – that turn on a Christian principle (see, further, Chaps. 7 and 8).

While the interface between the religious and the secular is fraught so also are those that lie between and within religions and, to a lesser extent, those which lie between religion and philosophy or other belief systems. For the Church of England these boundaries and interfaces are acquiring greater salience as the twenty-first century gets underway.

1.5.7 Commerce and Religion: Trading by Religious Charities

Charities have always relied upon income, from donations and other sources, to fund their work. In the past many have often had some level of recourse to commerce. Usually this has related to their mission (e.g. workshops for the blind)[51] and has often been time limited until they had raised the funds targeted for a planned initiative. Religious organisations have also engaged in fundraising commercial enterprises often through charging fees to access service, such as education.[52] This low profile approach has recently changed.

Government is increasingly looking to charities to take up the slack as it manages a decanting of responsibility for some areas of public benefit utilities and service provision. In relation to particular categories of service – mainly in education, health and social care – it is the religious organisations, with their centuries old track record of association with relevant areas of social disadvantage and experience of related provision, that are now being enlisted. Simultaneously, and for the same reasons of insufficient State revenues, government is reducing or removing the annual grants customarily given to charities. Both developments are driving charities into the marketplace either to compete for government service contracts or to engage in profitmaking commercial enterprises. This need for additional funds is exacerbated by the current economic recession which has had the effect of reducing the annual intake from public fundraising while increasing the demand for charity

[50] This wariness is not confined to instances where the Christian religion intrudes on public institutions. The founding of the Islamic Sharia Council in 1982, with its remit to address issues such as marriage breakdown, has also caused controversy. The 85 Sharia 'courts' have since processed many thousands of cases and there is concern that they may exercise an intimidating influence on Islamic communities: see, BBC's Panorama programme at: http://www.familylawweek.co.uk/site.aspx?i=ed112864.

[51] See, *Oxford Group v. Inland Revenue Commissioners* (1949) 2 All E.R. 537 for guidance as to when a purpose cannot be defined as "ancillary and incidental".

[52] See, for example, *Brighton Convent of the Blessed Sacrament v. Inland Revenue Commissioners* (1933) 18 TC 76, where a convent school that charged admission fees was held to be engaged in commercial trading.

support. Current investment in commercial opportunities is often neither short-term nor necessarily mission related. The result is an expanding area of boundary permeability between business and religion as evidenced in the spread of faith-based schools in the United States and the U.K., and the growing involvement of religious organizations in health care, nursing homes, and residential homes for the elderly, etc. These developments also indicate the subliminal capacity of religion to penetrate and become an integral part of commonplace social facilities.

1.5.8 Funding from Commercial Sources

The policy of transferring services from the public sector has had particularly important consequences for the State monopoly of education. Many of the thousands of schools leaving State control are doing so to become academies, trust schools or free schools and many so doing are, in the process, acquiring a faith based ethos, private sponsorship and charitable status. The Church of England, for example, is converting the majority of its almost 5,000 schools to 'academies' which will expand its opportunities for engaging in commerce.[53] As the privatization of health care and housing gathers momentum, further such opportunities will arise for the Church, other charities and religious organisations.

The problems that come with the involvement of charity, particularly a religious charity, in commerce are well known: the danger that a concern for profit margins will outweigh altruism and/or religious belief; and the possibility that some charities may exploit, or fail to appreciate the dominant effect of their status, to gain commercial advantage. The latter may become a significant issue in relation to the Church of England.

1.5.9 The Interface Between Religion and Anti-terrorism

International religiously based warfare is clearly nothing new: hostilities between Christianity and Islam, not to mention between Catholicism and Protestantism and within the latter, have a very long history. What has changed is the seemingly random and truly global nature of the modern conflict between militant Islamic factions and the developed Christian nations. Against that background, western governments have sought to 'guard against the enemy within' by monitoring the activities of domestic non-government organisations, particularly those with an overseas brief, some of which are religious charities.

Since 9/11 there has been a concerted international effort to increase government surveillance of charity funding streams. In response to the United Nations Security

---

[53] See, the *Chadwick Report* published by the Church of England (March 2012). This declared an aim to establish 200 more Anglican schools over the next 5 years.

Council Resolution 1373,[54] most common law nations and others have in recent years introduced anti-terrorism legislation which is having a chilling effect, not only on the overseas operations of some charities and on donor contributions to them, but also on the domestic operations of some charities. These impinge upon the domestic and international operations of all charities including the Church of England.

1.5.10 Domestic Religious Charities

New regulatory provisions require charities including religious charities to provide, in greater detail than previously, data regarding cash flows into and out of their organisations, and permit the covert surveillance of its funds, activities and staff. This can have serious consequences for such bodies. For example the Commission's oversight of the North London Central Mosque Trust, which operated the Finsbury Park Mosque from 1998 to 2003, resulted in an intervention that temporarily suspended its activities. On evidence that the Trust's activities were incompatible with its charitable status, the Commission froze Trust bank accounts and removed the radical cleric, Sheikh Abu Hamza Al-Masri, from his position within the Trust.[55]

1.5.11 Operating Overseas

Many domestic charities with an overseas brief are religious or have strong links with a religious organisation. Christian Aid, for example, has for several decades been engaged in both treating the effects and lobbying for action to change the causes of poverty in Africa. International concern regarding possible further terrorist activity has undoubtedly led to constraints being imposed on such charities. There are now sophisticated international arrangements in place enabling governments to share information and track the flow of charity funds across jurisdictions. Charities are left in no doubt that governments view them as constituting a possible weak link in the fight against international terrorism and that tighter regulatory controls will be imposed to require greater transparency and accountability regarding movement of funds.

---

[54] On 28/09/2001, the UN Security Council unanimously adopted a wide-ranging, comprehensive resolution with steps and strategies to combat international terrorism. Among other things, this resolution: directed all States to prevent and suppress the financing of terrorism, to criminalise the 'wilful' provision or collection of funds for such acts and to freeze the funds, assets and economic resources of those involved; and it required all States to ensure that no asylum seeker is granted refugee status until satisfied that such person had not planned, facilitated or participated in the commission of terrorist acts.

[55] See, Charity Commission of England and Wales, *North London Central Mosque Trust* (1 July 2003).

1.6 Conclusion

The 500 year history of Anglicanism began with the Reformation but it did so on Christian foundations laid down over previous centuries. Since then it has been neither wholly confined nor defined by its relationship with the State. Its development has been shaped to some extent by factors that preceded that seminal point in Church/State relations and by others that subsequently, from time to time, exercised a varying degree of influence. While, in the present context, space prevents due consideration being given to the relative impact of these ‘external factors’, it would be a mistake not to bear them in mind as the following chapters unfold.

What stands out, and not just for present purposes, is the central importance of family oriented morality to the religious beliefs and social role of the Church of England. This thread, once pursued with something approaching fanatical zeal, has been present throughout the history of the Church.

Chapter 2
Religion, Charity and the Law

2.1 Introduction

> The essential attributes of a legal charity are, in my opinion, that it shall be *unselfish* – ie for the benefit of persons other than the donor – that it shall be *public*, ie that those to be benefited shall form a class worthy, in numbers of importance, of consideration as a public object of generosity, and that it shall be *philanthropic* or *benevolent* – ie dictated by a desire to do good.

These and other core concepts, principles, precepts and related legal definitions associated with 'charity' and 'religion' are examined in this chapter. It explores: their shared origins in the 'pious use'; their positive values such as piety and altruism; and more negative shared attributes such as a tendency to deference, to ameliorate rather than cure, and conservatism. It examines missionary work and proselytism. It considers religion's subliminal nature and the reductionist tendency to measure its effect in secular terms. It discusses the potential for religious charities to be partisan, thereby emphasising differences and increasing social polarization; for social capital[1] to be of the 'bonding' rather than the 'bridging' form.

It notes that for centuries the essential components for a religious organization, or for a donation to such an organization, to be legally recognized as charitable, have been broadly the same in all common law nations: a belief in a "supreme being"; and a shared commitment to faith and worship. Further, to be charitable in the same nations, the organization or gift must 'advance' religion, meaning "to promote or maintain or practice it and increase belief in the supreme being or entity that is the object or focus of the religion",[2] and it must do so for the benefit of the public (except in some jurisdictions where private piety is also deemed charitable). It identifies and analyses those matters held to constitute 'public benefit', the core legal

[1] See, Putnam, R. 2000. *Bowling Alone*. New York: Simon & Schuster.

[2] See, Charity Commission, 'The Advancement of Religion for the Public Benefit', December 2008, at para. C3.

K. O'Halloran, *The Church of England - Charity Law and Human Rights*, Ius Gentium: Comparative Perspectives on Law and Justice 36, DOI 10.1007/978-3-319-04319-7_2,

concept which was clearly recognised more than a century ago in the above quote[3] as lying at the heart of charity, and the centrality of which has now been legislatively restored in this jurisdiction. It examines this concept in the context of religious purposes and considers the relative importance attached to the doctrines, liturgy and tenets of the religion concerned.

2.2 Concepts, Principles and Definitions

England is a multicultural and multifaith society. The rich variety of religions now accommodated within this jurisdiction present a quiet challenge to the settled orthodoxy represented by the established Church of England. Part of the cultural heritage, accompanying the latter into the twenty-first century, is the common law or, more specifically, the law of charity. From their shared origins in the Reformation, the Church, a Protestant monarchy and charity law have co-existed and shaped English culture for the past four centuries. The slow evolution of charity law, untroubled by legislative intervention, has grown by incremental judicial precedents in response to changing patterns of social need. Concepts, principles and definitions that emerged over four centuries of case law are now encoded, and very largely unchanged, in the Charities Act 2011. These, the basic building blocks of contemporary charity law, remain essentially as when first formed and faithfully reflect their cultural context. For the purposes of this book, there is no more important single factor.

2.2.1 Religion

A *sine qua non* of religion is that it requires a belief in matters not amenable to objective proof. This gives rise to legal and other difficulties when it comes to definitions, boundaries and disentangling private from public interests.

2.2.2 Beliefs and Rationality

The subjective commitment to, and experience of, religious belief is clearly private and personal; verifiable, if at all, only within the matrix employed by the individual concerned. It differs from other frames of reference in the importance it attaches to a spiritual dimension. For example, it differs from: philosophy and secularism, the former having an accompanying toolbox of distinct schools of thought each with its own set of logically deduced dialectics, while the latter is adamantly functional and

[3] See, *Re Cranston* [1898] IR 431.

objective; from politics, with its structural approach to society, and need for authority to bring order; and from moralists, whose values and ethics may support religious belief but from which they are distanced by an absence of spirituality. As Dillon J explained in *Re South Place Ethical Society*[4]:

> Religion, as I see it, is concerned with man's relations with God and ethics are concerned with man's relations with man. The two are not the same and are not made the same by sincere inquiry into the question – what is God? If reason leads people not to accept Christianity or any known religion but they do believe in the excellence of qualities such as truth, beauty, and love, or believe in the platonic concept of the ideal, their belief may be to them the equivalent of a religion but viewed objectively they are not a religion.

The belief, as Dillon J points out, is in god (or gods or a supreme being). In terms of the well-established religions, that belief is accompanied not only by acts of private offerings of prayer and devotion but also by public acts of solidarity with fellow adherents such as attendance at and participation in practices of worship and by other ancillary rituals. The latter collective aspect is most usually supported by tenets, creeds and doctrines, which together constitute the venerated body of material that governs the religious activities of all adherents. So, while the religious experience is personal, being a religious adherent requires a public and shared commitment to a set body of explicit beliefs. In the past this public aspect has enabled the law to recognise and differentiate religions and test the credence of religious adherents. Indeed, in this jurisdiction the established view of the judiciary and regulators has long been that religion, at least in a charity law context, cannot be merely a private matter: prayer is not charitable[5]; to be charitable religious practices cannot be private, or limited to a private class of individuals, or not extend to the public more generally.

2.2.3 Differences in Approach and Their Consequences

Religious beliefs have traditionally been recognised by their theistic orientation and differentiated primarily by their doctrines. The doctrines of transubstantiation, immaculate conception and of 'purgatory', for example, are specific to Roman Catholicism,[6] the Nicene Creed is a core Christian belief,[7] while a belief in predestination distinguishes Calvinism. However, many religions share beliefs such as the

[4] [1980] 1 W.L.R. 1565; (1980) 124 SJ 774; [1980] 3 All E.R. 918. Also, see, *Bowman v. Secular Society* [1917] A.C. 406 (HL).

[5] See, *Re Warre's Will Trusts* [1953] 1 WLR 725 for the proposition that the law takes no notice of any benefit which might come from prayer.

[6] The doctrine of purgatory was subsequently denounced in England as an example of 'superstitious uses' and condemned by the 1547 Act. See, further, Ridge, P. 2006. The legal regulation of religious giving. *Law and Justice* 157: 17–28.

[7] Formulated in AD 325 at the First Council of Nicaea, the Nicene Creed was based on Christian understanding of the Canonical Gospels, the letters of the New Testament and to a lesser extent the Old Testament. Affirmation of this creed, which describes the Trinity, is generally taken as a fundamental test of orthodoxy for most Christian denominations.

doctrine of the immortality of the soul, which is central to the Protestant religion but is also common to other Christian religions and is proclaimed by Buddhists, Jews and Muslims among others. Such beliefs belong only to those of religious faith, they cannot be computed by philosophers, secularists, politicians and moralists. In essence, however, all trade in much the same area of morality. Arguably, the same set of concepts – to do with personal responsibility, civic engagement, equity, equality and compassion for the suffering – are fairly evenly shared among these groups, but for the purposes of this book the most important area of difference lies between those with religious beliefs and secularists (see, further, Chaps. 2 and 7).

2.2.4 Christianity

Over many centuries, Christianity has prevailed as the primary religion in England and since the Reformation this has taken the form of Protestantism as represented chiefly by the Church of England. The range of religions that now co-exist with Christianity in this jurisdiction is considerable and probably indeterminate. Islam, Hinduism, Sikhism and Judaism have a well-established presence and others including Druids, the Bahá'í Faith and such distinctive cultural entities such as the Rastafarians are also present. In addition there are a large and fluctuating number of organisations with a varying quotient of religious characteristics of which Mormons, Scientologists, Druze and Zoroastrians are perhaps among the most notable. Those of the Christian faith,[8] however, continue to predominate and it is against the particular background of morality formed by Christian doctrines, canon law and secular activity that we must view contemporary issues of social equality: issues which, to some extent, can be seen in terms of a conflict of laws – canon law, charity law and human rights law.

2.2.5 Confraternities

Organizations, in the form of guilds[9] or confraternities[10] dedicated to putting Christian precepts into practice, have been in existence for at least the last millennium. Confraternities, as Flack explains, "were established for a variety of purposes but

[8] In the 2011 Census, Christianity was the largest religion, with 33.2 million people (59.3 % of the population). The second largest religious group were Muslims with 2.7 million people (4.8 % of the population). The proportion of the population who reported they have no religion has now reached one quarter. See, further, Office for National Statistics at: http://www.ons.gov.uk/ons/rel/census/2011-census/key-statistics-for-local-authorities-in-england-and-wales/rpt-religion.html.

[9] See, Westlake, *The Parish Gilds of Mediaeval England*, 1919, where mention is made of "the gild of the Blessed Virgin Mary in the parish church of St Botolph at Boston founded in 1260 gave a yearly distribution of bread and herrings to the poor in alms for the souls of its benefactors"; cited in Brady, J. 1975. *Religion and the law of charities in Ireland*, 14. Belfast: Northern Ireland Legal Quarterly.

[10] See, Flack, T. 2008. Insights into the origins of organised charity from the catholic tradition of confraternities. Occasional paper for Australian Centre of Philanthropy and Nonprofit Studies, Queensland University of Technology, Brisbane.

fundamentally they were about laymen and women joining a voluntary association to receive mutual encouragement to live pious lives".[11] He adds that they may have existed in both the Eastern and Holy Roman Empires even before the sack of Rome in 410. Some had charitable purposes such as one with a special devotion to the sick and diseased, which flourished in Constantinople in 336, and others in the West which looked after abandoned children as early as 400 AD. The earliest Catholic lay confraternities were probably formed in Italy as early as the third century, but were certainly well established by the mid tenth century.

2.2.6 *Christian Charitable Organisations in England*

In mediaeval England, many schools and hospitals were founded by religious organizations. These include King's School Canterbury, founded in 597 and reputed to be the oldest English charity, and St John's Hospital in Malmesbury which dates from the early tenth century. During this period, provision for the poor remained primarily a matter for the church, which provided shelter and succour for the needy, rather than the State (see, further, Chap. 2).

Historically and currently, the contribution of religious organisations to total charitable activity in this as in all common law jurisdictions is inestimable.[12] They have been most obviously prominent in activities which serve to advance religion, sometimes with contentious outcomes, but have also often been engaged in putting in place social infrastructure both in common law countries and in developing nations. Religious organizations laid much of the foundations for our present health and education systems and often provided the staff and resources for their functioning and maintenance.

2.2.7 *Canon Law and Christian Morality*

Canon law in this jurisdiction, with its origins in Catholicism and Papal authority, predates the Reformation by several centuries but has since then formed the body of law, rules and regulations made or adopted by the Church of England and administered by the Church's ecclesiastical courts. The latter's terms of reference enabled them to deal not only with Church related matters but, until the mid-nineteenth century, they also had exclusive authority in respect of marriage, divorce, wills, and defamation.[13] Leaving criminal issues to the secular courts, allowed the ecclesiastical

[11] Ibid.

[12] In November 2012, the Charity Commission estimated that nearly 20 % of charities then on the register were for the advancement of religion and many more charities had their roots in a faith ethos; of the religious charities, some 24,529 were Christian, 2,387 Jewish and 1,398 were Muslim.

[13] The 1603 canons, for example, included directives such as: No Sentence for Divorce to be given upon the sole Confession of the parties (no. 96); In all Sentences for Divorce Bond to be taken for not marrying during each others Life (no. 97).

courts to focus on those civil issues where immorality was most likely to be manifested and be amenable to policing in accordance with the Church canons and doctrine. This Christian shaping of secular law, both unsurprising and rigorous, was recently acknowledged by Laws LJ in *McFarlane v. Relate Avon Ltd.* when he commented that "the Judaeo-Christian tradition, stretching over many centuries, has no doubt exerted a profound influence upon the judgment of lawmakers as to the objective merits of this or that social policy".[14]

2.2.8 *Charity*

'Charity', as a social construct, has a broader meaning than its legal definition. Its origins lie in the doctrine common to all religions that only by doing good works in this life can eternal salvation be assured in the next. The links between charity and religion, meaning the Christian religion for the purposes of charity law, are inescapable. Indeed, to subscribe to the Christian faith entailed obeying the duty to love one's neighbour, an imperative requirement for the salvation of the soul.[15] In its initial religious context, charity was thus "more a means to the salvation of the soul of the benefactor than an endeavour to diagnose and alleviate the needs of the beneficiary".[16] Indeed, the soul, not just of the giver but that of those already deceased, could be saved by acts of generosity to the poor: masses offered for the dead being accompanied by alms for the poor of the parish; chantries[17] by endowments for the Church and monasteries; and guilds by bequests of property for the use of the Church.

2.2.9 *The Pious Use*

Gifts for pious uses, motivated by the concern of donors to ensure the redemption of their souls, were recognised as charitable gifts in the years prior to the Reformation. This 'use', the legal precursor of the 'trust', was a key concept developed in the

[14] [2010] IRLR 872; 29 BHRC 249 at para 23.

[15] Christianity was not unique in this respect: Buddhism teaches the love of mankind as the highest form of righteousness; Islam requires a tithe of one-tenth of income to be given to those in need; and the Jewish religion urges its followers to assist the poor and practice charity.

[16] See, *Report of the Committee on the Law and Practice relating to Charitable Trusts*, (Cmnd. 8710), HMSO, London, 1952, at para 36.

[17] A 'chantry' (from the Chanting of the Mass) was a religious service founded and endowed by a benefactor for the repose of the soul of one or more persons. It was an important institution of the mediaeval Church and very popular in the fourteenth and fifteenth centuries. See, Wood-Leigh, K., *Church Life under Edward III*, 1934, p. 91; cited in Brady, J, Religion and the Law of Charities in Ireland, op cit at p. 12.

fourteenth and fifteenth centuries which allowed feudal landowners to evade certain "incidents" (a form of property taxation) associated with the transfer of land on their death. Gradually, responsibility for the use[18] was assumed by the Court of Chancery, which provided the means for their enforcement,[19] until it was replaced by the trust as the means whereby a donor could impose a legal requirement upon a trustee or trustees to receive, retain and utilise a gift for purposes specified by the donor (see, also, Chap. 2).

2.2.10 Altruism

The single most important attribute of 'charity', as this term is known in all countries that share the common law tradition, is that it be unequivocally dedicated to the public benefit. Throughout the centuries the altruism[20] of the individual, generating the voluntary contribution of many for the public good, has always been held to be its vital and distinguishing characteristic.

2.2.11 Discretion

Donor discretion lies at the heart of charity and charity law. Any such exercise of discretion is necessarily accompanied by exclusionary criteria: the targeted beneficiaries are identified by a specification broad enough to be 'public' but sufficiently precise to exclude those outside donor intent. This exclusionary approach, exercised in favour of beneficiaries identified by their common affiliation to a specified religion, is clearly discriminatory in respect of all other religious and non-religious persons but has nonetheless attracted judicial endorsement. It is an approach that can only be accommodated with some difficulty in a human rights context (see, further, Chap. 7).

---

[18] It became the practice to convey land 'to A to the use of B'. While B had no legal estate in the lands which remained at common law the property of A, the Court of Chancery would recognise B's beneficial or 'equitable' ownership of the land.

[19] See, Jones, G. 1969. *History of the law of charity 1532–1827*, 3–4. Cambridge: Cambridge University Press.

[20] Meaning an unselfish concern for the welfare of others: a private act for public benefit. It was Comte's Philosophy of the Sciences (translated by George Lewes, 1890) that first introduced the word "altruism" (from the French "alteri huic") into the English language. See, further, Titmuss, R.A. 1970. *The gift relationship: From human blood to social policy*. London: Allen and Unwin.

2.3 Charity Law and Religion

Religion was not mentioned as a charitable purpose in the Statute of Charitable Uses 1601[21] probably for reasons to do with the politics of religion in the years before and after the Reformation, but there was never any doubt as to the legal inseparableness of charity and religion. This was confirmed by the decision in *Pemsel*[22] when Macnaghten LJ ruled that 'the advancement of religion' was a charitable purpose. Subsequently, the judiciary have added that for it to do so two conditions must be met[23]: the organisation or gift must contribute to the advancement of 'religion', as interpreted by the courts[24] and it must promote the religious instruction or education of the public[25]; a non-theistic organisation was initially held not to satisfy such conditions.[26] The prevailing legal presumption has traditionally been that such a charitable purpose is for the public benefit and this continues to be the case in all jurisdictions other than the UK where the presumption has been reversed since the completion of the charity law reform process (see, further, Chap. 6).

2.3.1 Charities and Charity Law

Charity in law has a technical meaning.[27] It is ancient, with its origins most probably lying in the *parens patriae*[28] responsibilities of the King (protecting the interests of charities, wards and lunatics), and over the past four centuries it continued to judicially evolve within the common law tradition with very little legislative interference. During this time it has taken root throughout nations, comprising the former British Empire, which have contributed to forming a body of jurisprudence that now, with varying emphases and subject to certain jurisdictional differences, constitutes charity

---

[21] Also known the Statute of Elizabeth; 43 Eliz 1, c 4.

[22] *The Commissioners for Special Purposes of the Income Tax v. Pemsel* [1879] AC 531.

[23] As explained in Warburton, J. 2003. *Tudor on charities*, 9th ed, 73. London: Sweet & Maxwell.

[24] See, *Dunne v. Byrne* [1912] AC 407.

[25] *Cocks v. Manners* (1871) LR 12 Eq. 574 at 585; *Yeap v. Cheah Neo v. One Cheng Neo* (1875) LR 6PC 381; *Re Joy* (1888) 60 LT 175; *Re Macduff* [1896] 2 Ch. 451; *Re Delaney* [1902] 2 Ch. 642 at 648; *Chesterman v. Federal Commissioners of Income Tax* [1926] AC 128; *Gilmour v. Coats* [1949] AC 426.

[26] See, for example, *Re Hummeltenberg* [1923] 1 Ch 237, when spiritualism was held not to meet the definition of 'religion' and *Bowman v. Secular Society Ltd* [1917] AC 406, where doubts were cast by Parker LJ on 'humanism'.

[27] See, *Income Tax Special Purposes Commissioners v. Pemsel op cit*, where Macnaghten LJ said of 'charity' "of all words in the English language bearing a popular as well as a legal signification I am not sure that there is one which more unmistakably has a technical meaning …" at p. 581.

[28] A parental jurisdiction inherently vested in the monarch, exercised by the Chancellor, delegated to the Court of Chancery and then administered by the High court and the Attorney General. See, Seymour, J. 1994. *Parens Patriae* and wardship powers: Their nature and origins. *Oxford Journal of Legal Studies* 14(2): 159–188.

law in the common law tradition. As understood within the terms of the Preamble to the 1601 Act, and as organised under the four *Pemsel*[29] heads, charity is an activity undertaken by bodies that vary greatly in type, size, legal form, longevity and in resources. The 1601 Act[30] has for four centuries provided a basic framework for the role and responsibilities of charity. The following purposes, identified in the Preamble as charitable, continue to provide the basis for modern charity law not only in this jurisdiction but across the common law world[31]:

> The relief of aged, impotent and poor people; the maintenance of sick and maimed soldiers and mariners, schools of learning, free schools and scholars of universities; the repair of bridges, havens, causeways, churches, sea banks and highways; the education and preferment of orphans; the relief, stock or maintenance of houses of correction; marriages of poor maids; supportation, aid and help of young tradesmen, handicraftsmen and persons decayed; the relief or redemption of prisoners or captives and the aid or ease of any poor inhabitants concerning payments of fifteens, setting out of soldiers, and other taxes.

During the ensuing centuries, this area of law has come to acquire a number of principles and rules that now characterize it in a common law context.

2.3.2 *Charitable Purposes*

Lord Macnaghten's[32] sparse statement of matters constituting charitable purposes fails to do justice to the immense volume and range of charities that have since been recognized as such by court and regulators, mostly under the 4th head with the aid of 'the spirit and intendment' rule.[33] It remains the case that to acquire or retain charitable status an entity must show that it can bring itself within the definition of "charitable purpose" and that its purpose (as stated in its governing documents) will be of "public benefit". While most religious organisations will seek charitable

---

[29] See, *Income Tax Special Purposes Commissioners v. Pemsel op cit*, where Macnaghten LJ first classified charitable purposes as follows:

> Charity in its legal sense comprises four principal divisions: trusts for the relief of poverty; trusts for the advancement of education; trusts for the advancement of religion; and trusts for other purposes beneficial to the community not falling under any of the preceding heads.

[30] A modified version of the Statute of Uses 1597 (39 Eliz. I, c.6).

[31] As noted in Tudor. 2003. *Charities*, 9th ed, 3. London: Sweet & Maxwell, the wording of the Preamble closely resembles a passage in *The vision of Piers Plowman* by William Langland.

[32] *The Commissioners for Special Purposes of the Income Tax v. Pemsel* [1879] AC 531 at p. 583. In recent years as a result of charity law reform, some jurisdictions have statutorily encoded these charitable purposes and a small number have gone further and added a *Pemsel* plus list (see, further, Chap. 6).

[33] As explained by Wilberforce L.J. in *Scottish Burial Reform and Cremation Society v. Glasgow Corporation* [1968] A.C. 138:

> The purposes in question to be charitable, must be shown to be for the benefit of the public, or the community, in a sense or manner within the intendment of the Preamble to the statute, 43 Eliz. 1 c.4.at p. 154.

registration under the 3rd *Pemsel* head, many engaged in secular activities such as in education, health or social care may register their subsidiary organisations under other heads.

2.3.3 Common Law Requirements

The well-established requirements for a charity to be recognised as such are that an entity must derive from charitable intent, be confined exclusively to charitable purposes, be for the public benefit, be independent, non-profit-distributing and non-political.

The first is deceptive: while motive is important, the presence or absence of charitable intent is not itself usually determinative. In most common law jurisdictions[34] the test judicially applied to ascertain a donor's intention is objective i.e. the fact that a donor believed when making the gift that it was charitable will not prevent the courts from ruling otherwise and vice versa because "the court cannot inquire into the motives of the donor if the gift is in its nature a charity".[35] No matter how charitable the donor's intention may be, this will not make charitable a gift which does not satisfy the common law definition of 'charity', has no intrinsic merit,[36] breaches the law or is contrary to public policy.

The second rule is that to be charitable a gift must be exclusively dedicated to charitable purposes. Where the courts find any ambiguity or equivocation in a donor's expressed intention or any possibility of a gift being used partially for non-charitable purposes then they will deny the gift charitable status. For example, a trust the income from which was paid to "any one or more religious charitable or educational institution or institutions operating for the public good", was held to be in breach of the exclusivity rule and therefore void: the term "public good" was wider than public benefit for charitable purposes and like "philanthropic" and "benevolent" could not therefore be construed as exclusively charitable.[37]

Thirdly, and most importantly, the gift must satisfy both arms of the 'public benefit test'; i.e. it must both confer an objectively verifiable 'benefit' and it must do so in favour of sufficient members of the 'public'. The test has traditionally been applied unevenly across the 4 *Pemsel* heads of charity: presumed satisfied per se in relation to religious purposes but falling most onerously upon all the relatively new purposes in the last category (see, further, below).

Fourthly, a charity is required under common law to be a free-standing, independent entity founded by and bound to fulfill the terms of the donor's gift. The duty resting on trustees to honour the terms of their trust and ensure that the objects of the charity prevail has always been seen as the primary means whereby the integrity of the donor's gift could be protected.

---

[34] Not in Ireland: see, for example, *In re the Worth Library* [1994] 1 ILRM 161, per Keane J at p. 193.

[35] See, *Hoare v. Osborne* (1866) LR 1 Eq. 585 *per* Kindersley VC at p. 588.

[36] *Re Pinion* [1965] Ch 85.

[37] *AG of the Cayman Islands v. Wahr – Hansen* [2000] 3 All E.R. 642.

Fifthly, while a charity does not compromise its status by making a profit, it will do so if any profit gained accrues to the benefit of individuals instead of being directed towards the fulfillment of the charity's objects. This can be problematic in the context of modern competitive trading practices in which many charities, including religious charities, are currently engaged. These profit-making enterprises are intended to raise funds for charitable purposes, but in practice the profits are often re-invested to 'grow' the business or increase market share, which can give rise to questions as to where the altruism and public benefit really lies.

Finally, the extent to which any political activity may be safely undertaken by a charity has long been fraught with uncertainty. The crucial issue is whether an organisation intends to pursue political activity as its principal objective or whether this is merely pursued ancillary to and in support of a main objective which is not itself political: the former is definitely incompatible with charitable status.[38] It is a rule that can inhibit assertive advocacy on behalf of the disadvantaged.

In determining whether a religion, a religious organization or a gift to such, can acquire or retain charitable status, all entities – including the Church of England – must satisfy these requirements.

2.3.4 Charity Law and the Definition of Religion

Religion, for the purposes of charity law, has been defined as "the promotion of spiritual teaching in a wide sense, and the maintenance of the doctrines on which it rests, and the observances that serve to promote and manifest it."[39] A body of case law precedents and related principles has accumulated to determine when religion, religious organisations and their activities meet the legal definition of 'charity'.

From the earliest beginnings of charity law, the necessity of a theistic component for this charitable purpose was regarded as a given: almost exclusively interpreted as monotheism in the traditional Judeo-Christian culture; and this has remained the case in all common law jurisdictions until comparatively recently (see, further, Chap. 6). For many generations and throughout the common law jurisdictions the basic indicators, employed by judiciary and regulators to define 'religion' and differentiate a religious body from other bodies, have been a belief in a "supreme being" together with a shared commitment to faith and worship.[40]

---

[38] See, for example, *Bowman v. Secular Society* [1917] A.C. 406, *National Anti-vivisection Society v. Inland Revenue Commissioners* [1948] A.C. 31 (HL) and *McGovern v. Attorney General* [1982] Ch. 321.

[39] *Keren Kayemeth Le Jisroel v. Inland Revenue Commissioners* (1931) 48 TLR 459 at p. 477. But also see *Thornton v. Howe* (1862), 54 ER, 1042, 31 Beav 14 where, in a doubtful ruling, the court held that a trust for the printing, publishing and propagation of the sacred writings of the late Joanna Southcote (who claimed to have been made pregnant by the Holy Ghost and was to give birth to the second Messiah) was a valid charitable trust for a religious purpose.

[40] See, Charity Commission, 'Analysis of the law underpinning *Public Benefit and the Advancement of Religion*', Feb 2008 at para.2.14 where the Commission concluded that the definition of a religion in English charity law was characterised by a belief in a supreme being and an expression of that belief through worship.

2.3.5 Belief in a Supreme Being

A religion will not gain judicial recognition as such unless its adherents at least profess belief in a "supreme being". The view that the legal definition of religion could be satisfied by a system of belief which did not involve faith in a god was explicitly rejected by Dillon J in *Re South Place Ethical Society*.[41] That case concerned a society the objects of which included "the study and the cultivation of a rational religious sentiment". Ultimately Dillon J held that the Society was a charity, but on the basis that it was established for the advancement of education and benefit to the community.

Belief in a supreme being, until relatively recently, was most usually interpreted in all common law countries to mean a Christian deity.[42] The judiciary, however, gradually extended recognition beyond the monotheistic Christian religions. In *R v. Registrar General ex p. Segerdal*,[43] for example, Lord Denning M.R. viewed the religion of Buddhism as an exception to the general requirement of religion that it should involve reverence to a deity and that "Buddhist temples are properly described as places of meeting for religious worship".[44]

The approach of the Charity Commission towards organisations such as the Church of Scientology has been to hold that religion for the purposes of charity law constitutes belief in a supreme being, an expression of that belief through worship, and an advancement or promotion of the religion. It has also required evidence that the organisation, by engaging with and being openly accessible to the local community, was satisfying the public benefit test. In that case the Commission refused registration on the grounds that the organisation's core practices of training and auditing (counselling) did not constitute worship of a supreme being,[45] even though it had been deemed charitable in the US,[46] and in Australia[47] though not in Canada.

2.3.6 Worship of a Supreme Being

In addition to belief in god or gods, members of a religion must practice a common form of worship and have a shared faith. Worship must have at least some of the

[41] [1980] 1 W.L.R. 1565; (1980) 124 SJ 774; [1980] 3 All E.R. 918.

[42] Although, in the US, the IRS took an early and clear view that charitable trusts could not be restricted to those that declared their belief in one 'Supreme Being'.

[43] [1970] Q.B. 697 (CA).

[44] Ibid, at p. 707.

[45] *Application for Registration as a Charity by the Church of Scientology (England and Wales)*, Charity Commissioners Decision, 17th November 1999 at p. 24.

[46] In 1993, the IRS recognized Scientology as a "non-profit charitable organization," and gave it the same legal protections and favourable tax treatment extended to other non-profit charitable organizations.

[47] *Church of the New Faith v. Commissioner for Pay Roll Tax* (1983) 49 ALR 65.

following characteristics: submission to the object worshipped, veneration of that object, praise, thanksgiving, prayer or intercession. As noted by Dillon J. in *South Place Ethical Society*[48] it would not seem possible to worship with reverence a mere ethical or philosophical ideal. The Charity Commission[49] more recently have added that a religion should have "a degree of cogency, cohesion, seriousness and importance; an identifiable positive, beneficial, moral or ethical framework."

2.3.7 Canon Law, Doctrines, Tenets etc.

Traditionally, the authority and integrity of a religion has been grounded in its particular corpus of laws, canons, ordinances and tenets. These comprise the essence of a religion: they commit and bind its members in collective adherence to an agreed interpretation of beliefs and rules. As stated in the Second Epistle of Peter, "no prophecy of the scripture is of any private interpretation". The point of religious doctrine is to assure members that the one true way is as ordained in their set of beliefs and require them to demonstrate this and seek to convince others. There is no room for compromise. For the religious individual as for the religious organisation, private piety and public conduct must be synonymous. As has been said[50]:

> It belongs to the religious convictions of a good many religious people in our society that they ought to base their decisions concerning fundamental issues of justice on their religious convictions. They do not view it as an option whether or not to do it.

Lord Halsbury once explained the importance of doctrines for religion in the following terms[51]:

> Speaking generally, one would say that the identity of a religious community described as a Church must consist in the unity of its doctrines. Its creeds, confessions, formularies, tests, and so forth are apparently intended to ensure the unity of the faith which its adherents profess, and certainly among all Christian Churches the essential idea of a creed or confession of faith appears to be the public acknowledgment of such and such religious views as the bond of union which binds them together as one Christian community.

The presence of a body of beliefs or teachings, to which an organisation or individual is fully committed, has always provided good supportive evidence of the nature of their commitment – that it is to a religion – although "a religion can be regarded as beneficial without it being necessary to assume that all its beliefs are

---

[48] [1980] 1 W.L.R. 1565; (1980) 124 SJ 774; [1980] 3 All E.R. 918 at p. 1573A.

[49] See, Charity Commission, "*Analysis of the law underpinning Public Benefit and the Advancement of Religion*", February 2008 at para C2.

[50] Woltersorrf, N. 1997. The role of religion in decision and discussion of political issues. In *Religion in the public square: The place of religious convictions in political debate*, ed. R. Audi and N. Woltersorrf. New York: Rowan and Littlefield.

[51] See, *Free Church of Scotland v. Overtoun* [1904] AC 515, HL (Sc), per Lord Halsbury LC at pp. 612–3.

true".[52] This point finds support in the corollary: a gift to a religious body will fail if in the meantime the congregation has so changed its tenets that it is no longer identifiable as the religion previously known to the donor.[53] The broad principle, as once stated in *Thornton v. Howe*,[54] – that a gift for the advancement of religion will be upheld unless the tenets of the society "inculcate doctrines adverse to the very foundations of all religion" – is in this jurisdiction now, more simply, subject to the public benefit test.

The significance of doctrines can be overstated. This was evident in *Re Allen*[55] when Birkett LJ warned that:

> when a testator uses the words 'a member of the Church of England', he must not be assumed to be speaking as a learned theologian or an ecclesiastical historian, with special meanings in his mind, or with refinements and reservations. He must be assumed to be an ordinary man using ordinary language.

Canon law is confined to the Catholic Church, the Greek Orthodox Church and the Anglican Church. Consisting of a body of 'canons' or rules that have been agreed and adopted by authority of the Church's ecclesiastical body over many centuries, canon law functions in much the same way as its civil counterpart.

2.3.8 Religions in General

The court or Commission will take judicial notice of the fact that certain bodies have acquired standing as established religions. A gift for the advancement of religion in general has been upheld as charitable.[56]

2.3.9 Differences Between Religions

The court or Commission will not inquire into the inherent validity of a particular religion nor does it examine the relative merits of different religions.[57] The broad principle was expressed by Walker L.C. in *O'Hanlon v. Logue*[58]:

> … a gift for the advancement of 'religion' is a charitable gift; and that in applying this principle, the Court does not enter into an inquiry as to the truth or soundness of any religious doctrine, provided it be not contrary to morals or contain nothing contrary to law …

[52] *Gilmour v. Coats and others* [1949] AC 426.

[53] *A-G v. Bunce* (1868) LR 6 Eq 563.

[54] (1862) 31 Beavan 14.

[55] [1953] Ch 116 at p. 834.

[56] See, for example, *Attorney-General v. Pearson* (1817) 3 Mer 353 per Eldon L.J. where he held that a bequest to maintain and propagate the worship of God was charitable at p. 409.

[57] *Thornton v. Howe* (1862), 31 Beav 14. Also, see, *Nelan v. Downes* (1917) 23 CLR 546.

[58] [1906] 1 I.R. 247 at pp. 259–260.

> Whether the subject of the gift be religious or for an educational purpose, the Court does not set up its own opinion. It is enough that it is not illegal, or contrary to public policy, or opposed to the settled principles of morality.

In practice it would seem improbable that the courts in this jurisdiction would now give special recognition to any one particular religion; even when that religion is 'established'. In the words of Cross LJ "as between different religions, the law stands neutral, but it assumes that any religion is at least better than none"[59]; though it may be that his latter proposition is now unsustainable in the light of the public benefit test and human rights considerations (see, further, Chap. 7).

2.3.10 Discrimination Between Religions

A gift will not fail to gain charitable status simply because it has been restricted to one specified religion. For example, in *Copinger v. Crehane*[60] a gift "for the advancement and benefit of the Roman Catholic religion" was upheld as charitable. In *In re Bonnet dec'd.; Johnston v. Langheld*[61] the court dealt with the question of general charitable intention of a gift to the Lutheran Church where the question was whether the gift was to the Lutheran Church or to the Protestant Church in general. As the testator had been a member of the Lutheran Church the court held that it had been her intention to confer a benefit on that body.

2.3.11 The Advancement of Religion

Charity law in a common law context requires an entity to be not only so constituted as to satisfy the legal definition of religion, by having objects or purposes of a religious nature, but its activities and gifts to it must also advance religion, meaning that they must "promote or maintain or practice it and increase belief in the Supreme Being or entity that is the object or focus of the religion".[62] That this is not always the case was demonstrated in *Berry v. St Marylebone*,[63] when the Theosophy Society sought exemption from rates as a charity. It was held that theosophy did not come within the third head of charity because it provided no answer to the question: "what religion does the society advance and how does it advance it?"

---

[59] *Neville Estates Ltd v. Madden* [1962] Ch. 832, at p. 853.

[60] (1877) L.R. 11 Eq. 429.

[61] [1983] I.L.R.M. 359.

[62] See, Charity Commission, "The Advancement of Religion for the Public Benefit", December 2008, at para C3.

[63] [1957] 3 All E.R. 677.

2.3.12 Advancement

As Denning LJ once remarked[64]:

> The word "advancement" connotes to my mind the concept of public benefit.... When a man says his prayers in the privacy of his own bedroom, he may truly be concerned with religion but not with 'the advancement of religion'.

To advance religion is to do something positive in the name of that religion and directly relevant to its beliefs. The entity must demonstrate that its activities are in fact linked to and actually further the essence of the religion: they must not be merely supplementary, tangential or in furtherance of an ancillary, non-charitable purpose. For example, in *Keren Kayrmeth Le Jisroel, Ltd v. Inland Revenue Commissioners*[65] the advancement of religion arose for consideration in relation to a company which had been established with the primary object of acquiring property in the Holy Land for the purpose of enabling the settlement of Jews. In that case, as in the more recent but not dissimilar application by a company called Good News for Israel, the Commission refused to grant charitable status.[66] The latter applicant organisation sought to advance the Jewish religion by (amongst other means) promoting the doctrine of Aliyah, being the promotion of the return of Jewish people to the land promised to them by God. The Commission considered that such activities, which sought to directly facilitate the settlement of Jewish people in Israel, had implications which went beyond the religious and spiritual. It was not, therefore, clear that these activities were solely directed to advancing religion.

Similarly, the members or staff of such a religious organisation will not be furthering that religion if they are engaged solely in activities that are of peripheral significance; a functional relationship of some importance for the accountability of those engaged, for example, as a caretaker or cleaner in a school run by a religious order. Indeed, as will become evident later, there are significant differences, with accompanying legal consequences, between: a religious adherent furthering their religion and giving effect to their religious beliefs through the terms and conditions of their chosen employment; such a person undertaking work in furtherance of a secular purpose; and a non-religious person undertaking work on behalf of a religious body (see, further, Chap. 7).

It is also the case that the beneficiaries must be appropriate. These are normally the followers or adherents, the wider church and the public generally, or, in the case of a charitable religious order, the beneficiaries are the members of that order

[64] *National Deposit Friendly Society Trustees v. Skegness UDC* [1958] 2 All ER 601.

[65] [1931] 2 KB 465; 100 LJKB 596; 145 LT 320; 47 TLR 461; *affirmed* [1932] AC 650 when Lord Hanworth M.R. observed:

> ... the promotion of religion means the promotion of the spiritual teaching in a wide sense, and the maintenance of the doctrines on which it rests, and the observance that serve to promote and manifest it.

[66] See, Charity Commission, "Decision on Application by the Good News for Israel ("GNFI") for Registration as a Charity", February 5, 2004.

and the wider public. In some cases, the 'wider public' can benefit by being able to participate in the rites and services of the religion, or by, for example, being the recipient of a charitable act undertaken by a follower or adherent as part of the practice of their religious belief.

2.3.13 Traditional Types of 'Advancement'

There is a long tradition of engaging in certain activities or making certain types of gift that are customarily upheld as being for the advancement of religion. The courts, for example, have had little difficulty in finding that missionary work serves this purpose. All bona fide missionary work is regarded as equally charitable: whether seeking to advance Christianity in general or the interests of a particular religion. As Donovan J. has advised[67]:

> To advance religion means to promote it, to spread the message ever wider among mankind; to take some positive steps to sustain and increase religious belief; and these things are done in a variety of ways which may be comprehensively described as pastoral and missionary.

Proselytizing or 'spreading the word', while naturally intrinsic to religious bodies, is associated also with the activities of religious charities and indeed provided the grounds for charity law's most famous case. *Commissioners for Special Purposes of the Income Tax Act v. Pemsel*[68] concerned the Moravian Church and its charitable purpose of "maintaining, supporting and advancing the missionary establishments among heathen nations". The key issue was whether proselytizing to the heathen in a distant land was charitable without having any other object such as relieving poverty or advancing education. It was the decision of the Commissioners to discontinue granting income tax exemption for this missionary work that brought John Pemsel before the court in his ultimately successful action.[69]

Christians have tended to regard proselytizing as part of their religious duties and this activity has been automatically granted charitable status within the common law jurisdictions. In *A-G v. Becher*,[70] for example, a gift to convert Catholics to the Church of England was upheld as charitable. However, proselytism is not without its problems: much depends on how it is manifested in practice. As has been pointed out[71]:

---

[67] See, *United Grand Lodge of Free and Accepted Masons of England and Wales v. Holborn Borough Council* [1957] 1 W.L.R. 1080; 121 J.P. 595; 101 S.J. 851; [1957] 3 All E.R. 281.

[68] [1891] AC 531 (H.L.).

[69] See, further, Bromley, K. 2000. The definition of religion in charity law in the age of fundamental human rights. Paper presented at ISTR conference, Dublin, .

[70] [1910] 2 IR 251.

[71] See, *Kokkinakis v. Greece* A 260-A (1993), 17 EHRR 397, per Pettitti J. In this context it is perhaps worth noting that websites now often provide a platform for proselytism; some may well be caught by the *Kokkinakis* caveat. The Islamic Sharia Council, for example, is a registered charity. On its website, the Islamic Sharia Council, among other things, encourages polygamous marriage,

> … a distinction has to be made between bearing Christian witness and improper proselytism. The former corresponds to true evangelism … The latter represents a corruption or deformation of it …

Moreover, it is important to bear in mind that proselytism acquired recognition as a charitable activity at a time when religious purposes benefited from a presumption that they were for the public benefit. It is difficult to see how court or Commission, when applying this test as they are now obliged to do, could possibly conclude that enducing someone to join a particular religion would be of benefit to the public.

In this jurisdiction, charitable status would most usually require the activities of religious organizations to have tangible public benefit outcomes. This could take the form of, for example, the followers or adherents putting the values of their religion into practice by taking positive actions to help others in society, such as visiting people who are distressed, sick or dying, or providing food and shelter to the homeless. The necessity to undertake secular activities is contentious: there is a view that it should be sufficient to satisfy the 'advancement' requirement that the members of religious organizations simply practice their faith in their daily life, demonstrating adherence to religious precepts; the virtuous lifestyle modelled by religious adherents being enough to advance that religion (see, further, below).[72] Any of the following are now generally accepted as advancing religion[73]:

1. the provision of sacred spaces, churches and worship services;
2. the provision of public rituals and ceremonies;
3. contributing to the spiritual and moral education of children;
4. contributing towards a better society for example by promoting social cohesion and social capital;
5. carrying out, as a practical expression of religious beliefs, other activities (such as advancing education or conflict resolution, or relieving poverty), which may also be charitable;
6. contributing to followers' or adherents' good mental and physical health; aiding the prevention of ill health, speeding recovery and fostering composure in the face of ill health;
7. providing comfort to the bereaved; and
8. healthcare and social care.

---

advises women to remain within violent marriages and advises that they do not have the right to refuse sex to their husbands. Where proselytism encourages conduct that is in breach of human rights and contrary to the law of the jurisdiction it cannot also be compatible with the public benefit. See, further, at:

http://www.islamic-sharia.org/marriage-fatwas-related-to-women/validity-of-polygynous-marriage-9.html

and

http://www.islamic-sharia.org/marriage-fatwas-related-to-women/denying-husbands-marital-rights-2.html.

[72] See, *Neville Estates Ltd v. Madden* [1962] 1 Ch 832.

[73] See, Charity Commission, *The Advancement of Religion for the Public Benefit*, December 2008, at para. D2.

In some jurisdictions, other than the UK, this list would extend to include gifts for private prayer,[74] private masses[75] and to closed religious orders.[76] It must of course be borne in mind that a religious body may decide to channel its charitable activity not directly into the advancement of religion but through an alternative charitable purpose such as the advancement of education or the relief of poverty.

2.4 Religion and Public Benefit

The Preamble can be seen as the initial statement by 'government' of matters it regarded as constituting the public benefit and responsibility for which it believed could be borne by charity. The charitable purposes listed therein are those that government identified as the core business of charity, its raison d'etre. This public benefit agenda comprises matters which continue to be of importance in all common law jurisdictions. The provision of health and social care services, training for employment, public utility provision and the physical maintenance of social infrastructure, are still very much the business of charities. Now as then, education, housing, the general alleviation of those in impoverished circumstances and the protection of citizens are also legally defined as contributing to the public benefit and therefore charitable. The capacity of charities to generate social capital, and the part played by religious organisations as providers of charity thereby reducing public spending, have ensured their support by government over the centuries and across the common law world.

2.4.1 The Public Benefit

The concept of public benefit lies at the heart of charity law: it serves to differentiate altruistic gifts intended for the benefit of strangers from private gifts intended to further the interests of the donor. Both the 'public' and the 'benefit' arms of the test must be satisfied. The challenge of marrying the concept of public benefit to the charitable purpose of advancing religion has, however, been considerably eased by the traditional legal presumption that gifts or trusts for this purpose are *ipso facto* for the public benefit.[77]

[74] See, *Re White* [1893] 2 Ch 41.

[75] See, *O'Hanlon v. Logue* [1906] 1 I.R. 247.

[76] See, *In re Macduff; Macduff v. Macduff* [1896] 2 Ch 451.

[77] See, *National Anti-Vivisection Society v. IRC* 1948] AC 31.

2.4.2 Public

Charitable status requires benefit to be provided to the public or, as the test is sometimes described, "an appreciably important class of the community".[78] While it does not impose an absolute bar on any private benefit accruing from a charitable gift, it does require that any private benefit conferred must be incidental. Where the access of potential beneficiaries to the benefits made available are in some way restricted this may compromise charitable status.[79]

Where the class of beneficiaries is defined by its faith then the courts construe this as a non-personal relationship nexus and therefore intrinsically public in nature.[80] Typically, a religious charity is entitled to restrict access to its place of worship to the followers or adherents of that religion. However, the well-known hypothetical instance cited by Simonds LJ, when he pointed out that a bridge restricted to impecunious Methodists would breach the 'public' requirement, nicely illustrates an underlying dilemma.[81] As he then noted, such a trust would fail the public requirement because the formally restricted class of beneficiaries means that the trust "does not serve the public purpose which its nature qualifies it to serve."[82] The point being that a bridge, unlike a place of worship, is clearly a public utility and to so restrict access to such a facility is to redefine it as 'private'. Such a restriction dooms the trust because "it is not for the benefit of the adherents of the religion themselves that the law confers charitable status, it is in the interest of the public."[83] A similar point was made in *Gilmour v. Coats* in which it was held that the spiritual benefit flowing to mankind from private piety does not fulfill this requirement – public benefit must be something which is "capable of legal proof".[84]

Access is also often restricted by fees which can again give rise to controversy. Fee-charging faith schools and hospitals may well be driven as much by considerations of profit as public benefit, but the fact that they nonetheless relieve pressure on the State, by diverting paying customers away from equivalent public services and so leaving greater service availability for others, can suffice to qualify for charitable status.[85] The growing involvement of charities, including religious charities, with commerce and profit is of some concern to courts and regulators in this jurisdiction (see, further, Chap. 8).

---

[78] *Verge v. Somerville* [1924] A.C. 496 at p. 499 (per Lord Wrenbury).

[79] The law is now uncertain in this regard, see *Independent Schools Council v. The Charity Commission* [2011] UKUT 421 (TCC) (13 October 2011).

[80] See, *IRC v. Baddeley* [1955] A.C. 572 and a class of "Methodists".

[81] Ibid at p. 592.

[82] Ibid at p. 592.

[83] *Holmes and others v. HM Attorney General* [1981] transcript.

[84] *Gilmour v. Coats* [1949] 1 All ER 848 (H.L.).

[85] *Re Resch's Will Trusts, Le Cras v. Perpetual Trustee Co Ltd* [1968] 1 AC 514 (PC). Also, see, *Joseph Rowntree Memorial Trust Housing Association Limited v. AG* [1983] Ch 159 (Ch).

2.4.3 Benefit

The requirement that organisations, or gifts to them, should also satisfy the benefit arm of the public benefit test has proven controversial. This is partly because in the words of Wright LJ, what is construed as 'benefit' in the charity law sense will "vary from generation to generation".[86] Mainly, however, in a religious context the difficulty lies in the extent to which private piety can be construed to be of public benefit. This has been particularly contentious in relation to gifts made to, or for the use of, a closed contemplative religious order,[87] for the saying of a private mass,[88] or for services in a private chapel[89] which, in some jurisdictions, have been found not to be charitable both because of their long association with superstitious uses (see, further, Chap. 3) and because intercessory prayers and the example set by leading pious lives were viewed as being too vague in terms of their benefit to the public.[90] The approach taken in this jurisdiction was summarized by Harman J. in *Re Warre's Will Trusts*, a case concerning a retreat house, when he said: "pious contemplation and prayer are, no doubt, good for the soul, and may be of benefit by some intercessory process, of which the law takes no notice, but they are not charitable activities."[91] In *Cocks v. Manners*[92] Sir Wickens V-C held that the Dominican Convent, a contemplative order of nuns, was not charitable. A view endorsed some years later by Rigby L.J. who made a similar finding in relation to the Dominican Convent which was not charitable as it abstained "even from good works as regards the outside public".[93] The judicial view that private piety in a convent does not tend, directly or indirectly, to edify the public was succinctly encapsulated in the ruling of Farwell J. who observed that there was no charity in attempting to save one's soul because charity, that is charity in law, was necessarily altruistic.[94] In *Gilmour v. Coats*,[95] the

---

[86] See, *National Anti-Vivisection Society v. IRC* [1948] A.C. 31 at p. 42.

[87] See, for example, *Cocks v. Manners* [1871] 12 Eq 574 where a contemplative order of nuns, was found to be not charitable in contrast to the Irish case *Maguire v. Attorney General* [1943] I.R. 238 when a similar convent was held to be a "spiritual powerhouse" and a bequest to it was charitable. However, note also the decisions of the Charity Commissioners in approving the charitable status of the Society of the Precious Blood (1989) 3, and the Catholic, Stanbrook Abbey in 2002 both contemplative orders but with a degree of outreach.

[88] See, for example, *Kehoe v. Wilson* (1880) 7 L.R. Ir. 10. Also, see, *Re Hetherington's Will Trusts* [1990] Ch. 1 where it was held that the celebration of a religious rite in private does not contain the necessary element of public benefit.

[89] *Hoare v. Hoare* (1886) 56 LT 147.

[90] *Gilmour v. Coates* [1949] AC 426. Also, see, *Trustees of the Congregation of Poor Clares of the Immaculate Conception v. The Commissioner of Valuation* [1971] NI 114 at p. 169, *per* Lowry LJ:an Order which has no other purpose other than to achieve its own sanctification by private prayer and contemplation is not an association with charitable objects.

[91] [1953] 1 WLR 725.

[92] [1871] 12 Eq 574.

[93] *In re Macduff; Macduff v. Macduff* [1896] 2 Ch. 451 at p. 474.

[94] *In re Delany: Conoley v. Quick* [1902] 2 Ch. 642 at p. 648.

[95] [1949] AC 426.

House of Lords placed their seal on this traditional interpretation, applied an objective test and ruled that a gift to a Carmelite priory was not charitable because of an absence of the requisite public benefit. However, unlike most charity law decisions emanating from this source, their lordships approach has not found favour everywhere: while the courts in Canada have shared their view, it has been rejected in both Ireland[96] and Australia.[97]

2.4.4 *Presumption of Public Benefit*

The principle that gifts generally expressed to be for the advancement of religion should be presumed to be for the public benefit was judicially recognised more than a century ago and has been accepted throughout the common law world. As was stated in *In re White*[98]:

> … a bequest to a religious institution, or for a religious purpose, is *prima facie* a bequest for a 'charitable' purpose, and that the law applicable to 'charitable' bequests, as distinguished from the law applicable to ordinary bequests, ought to be applied to a bequest to a religious institution, or for a religious purpose.

Once the court recognised a religious body as such then, unless the purpose of a gift was clearly in some way illegal or immoral it was generally presumed charitable. As Lord Langdale MR stated in *Baker v. Sutton* "all the cases, with one exception, go to support the proposition, that a religious purpose is a charitable purpose".[99] From an early stage, however, some judges were arguing that even religious purposes must demonstrate a public benefit[100]; an argument that centered on the above closed religious order conundrum. The justification then provided by Sir John Wickens for denying charitable status, though not accepted or followed in many other common law jurisdictions, was that[101]:

> It is said, in some of the cases, that religious purposes are charitable, but that can only be true as to religious services tending directly or indirectly towards the instruction or edification of the public…

In certain circumstances the presumption could always be rebutted and the gift then considered not to be of public benefit as, for example, if the organisation in

---

[96] See, for example, the ruling of Dixon J. in *Bank of Ireland Co Ltd v. Attorney General* [1957] IR 257 in which he confirmed the charitable status of an order of Discalced Carmelite nuns, engaged solely in a life of contemplation and prayer, living in cloistered solitude in their convent, having strictly limited contact with outside persons, and having no outside activities of any kind.

[97] See, Extension of Charitable Purposes Act 2004, s.5.

[98] [1893] 2 Ch. 41; followed in *In re Bain, Public Trustee v. Ross* [1930] 1 Ch. 224.

[99] *Baker v. Sutton* (1836) 1 Keen 224.

[100] See, for example, *Heath v. Chapman* (1854) 2 Drewry 417, 426; 61 ER 781, per Sir RT Kindersley VC at p. 784.

[101] *Cocks v. Manners* (1871) LR 12 Eq. 574, at p. 585, per Sir John Wickens VC.

question operated solely for profit, or if it employed oppressive psychological manipulation of its followers or potential followers.[102] Now, in this jurisdiction (and other UK jurisdictions, but nowhere else), the presumption has been reversed: since conclusion of the charity law reform process all bodies and gifts to them, dedicated to this charitable purpose, must demonstrate public benefit if they are to acquire or retain charitable status (see, further, Chap. 6).

2.4.5 Religion and Social Capital

The concept of 'social capital' has been coined to explain the motivation of individuals who engage in collective activity for altruistic purposes. It refers also to the environment of mutual trust, resulting from that engagement, which can be conducive to promoting public benefit by channeling collective activity into building the components of civil society.[103] Religion brings with it a capacity for social cohesion to which other groups can only aspire but it has proven to be challenging in the context of social capital because of its capacity, in differing circumstances, to generate either pluralism or polarization. To some extent this characteristic is one it shares with charity.

2.4.6 Social Capital and Charity

Government has a vested interest in facilitating the growth of charities. It can only gain from supporting entities that: generate a vibrant and diverse participative form of democracy; attract the involvement of volunteers; bolster a sense of social obligation and civic responsibility; thereby fostering the growth of social capital and consolidating civil society. Altruistic activity, a sufficient 'good' in itself, also acts as a model for others and can galvanize local communities into more responsible citizenship through bonding activities that accrue to the common good.

The larger charities, because of their institutional nature, pastoral concerns and longevity, are well positioned to reinforce and continue established social norms: some, such as religious or faith based organisations, are often accused of having a conservative if not reactionary influence and can have a strong investment in maintaining the status quo. Their longevity, coupled with financial and information resources, together with expertise and credibility established over generations of close engagement with vulnerable communities, place charities in a singularly strong position to provide the necessary continuity of concerned involvement to those communities with potential to threaten government stability. By absorbing the needs of minority groups, assuaging

[102] Ibid. Wickens V-C initially suggested that the "benefit" quotient of a religious organisation for the "public" lay in its moral and spiritual values which could be found in its beliefs, doctrines and practices (at p. 585).

[103] See, further, Putnam, R. 2000. *Bowling alone*, 19. New York: Simon & Schuster.

the dissatisfaction of the alienated, mediating on behalf of the socially excluded and involving armies of volunteers in community care activities, charities can make a unique contribution to maintaining social cohesion.

2.4.7 Religion, Charity and Social Capital

The debate regarding religion's contribution to or detraction from social capital has generated much academic comment.[104] It is a discussion not presently permitted due to lack of space but some points must be made at this stage, as it is a theme with considerable significance for this book (see, further, Chap. 8).

Religious, or faith based, organizations, mostly tend to be politically conservative – but not always. On the one hand, because of their institutional nature and longevity, such charitable entities can reinforce and sustain established social norms and may exercise a reactionary influence when faced with the prospect of political change.[105] On the other, their pastoral concerns, established over generations of close engagement with vulnerable communities, can prompt them to be at the forefront of such change particularly when religion itself is being politically suppressed.[106] Religion, charity and charitable religious organizations share an approach that leans towards deference, acceptance and fortitude which can be problematic in some social contexts.[107]

Religion and the charitable activities of religious organizations have an undoubted capacity to generate social capital. However, the controversy as to whether religion is primarily for member benefit or public benefit, more inclusive than exclusive, is probably as old as religion itself. There are those who take the view that religion, religious organisations, the activities of the latter and gifts to them, are all essentially member benefit driven: that "altruism" the defining characteristic of charity is absent as, fundamentally, the primary motivation of all concerned is the very private matter of personal salvation; and everything that constitutes the purpose of advancing religion is subsidiary to this personal purpose. Religion, while cementing relationships between its adherents, preferences and sharply differentiates that religion from all others: the 'bonding' form of social capital provided by religion is at the price of the 'bridging' form.[108] The tendency for religious charities to be both very active and very partisan has served to emphasise differences, increase social polarization and raise tensions. This potential, for religion to be more malign than benign, was a

[104] See, for example: Hitchens, C. 2007. *God is not great: The case against religion*. London: Atlantic Books; and

Mendieta, E., and J. Van Antwerpen (eds.). 2011. *The power of religion in the public sphere*. New York: Columbia University Press.

[105] As occurred in some South American countries in the last half of the twentieth century.

[106] As occurred in Poland towards the end of the twentieth century.

[107] Such as the use of contraceptives to combat the spread of AIDS in Africa and to lift communities out of poverty by controlling population growth.

[108] Ibid.

matter of concern to Lord Scott of Foscote who spoke for the House of Lords in *Gallagher v. Church of Jesus Christ of Latter-Day Saints*[109]:

> [S]tates may…recognise that, although religion may be beneficial both to individuals and to the community, it is capable also of being divisive and, sometimes, of becoming dangerously so. No one who lives in a country such as ours, with a community of diverse ethnic and racial origins and of diverse cultures and religions, can be unaware of this. Religion can bind communities together; but it can also emphasise their differences. In these circumstances secrecy in religious practices provides the soil in which suspicions and unfounded prejudices can take root and grow; openness in religious practices, on the other hand, can dispel suspicions and contradict prejudices.

2.5 Conclusion

For the love of God – was, in all probability, the first instinctual motivation for charity.[110] It has always been open to question whether this indicated a primary concern for self or for others: altruism or personal salvation: public interests or private? The blending of religion and charity in the charitable purpose of ‘for the advancement of religion’ has perpetuated that initial uncertainty.

The common law foundations for charity law, in this as in many other of the world's leading developed nations, lie in the Statute of Charitable Uses 1601, particularly in the wording of its Preamble, and in the judicial principles and precedents, most notably the decision in *Pemsel*, established over the following centuries. In the post-Reformation years ‘religion’ and ‘charity’ were defined and practiced in accordance with clear terms of reference, mutually agreed and jointly applied by Church and State, within a resolutely Protestant culture. For some centuries there was no uncertainty as to the duality of their social roles: a monotheistic deity was to be worshipped as required by Church of England doctrines; with related public and private morality issues policed by the ecclesiastical courts; and charity law administered accordingly. It was during this period that standards of public morality, particularly in regard to the sanctity of marriage together with the illegality and sinfulness of sexual relations outside it, became entrenched. Over time, as other religions became accepted and the interpretation of ‘charity’ broadened, the judiciary and the Charity Commission gave more consideration to the part to be played by the public benefit principle as a determinant of charitable status.

Of all the concepts and principles underpinning charity law none is now more important than the requirement that charity must contribute to the ‘public benefit’; this is its governing and distinguishing principle. The chapters that follow will examine just how religion and charity have coexisted and consider the importance and effectiveness of the public benefit principle as the arbitrator between public and private interests.

---

[109] *Gallagher v. Church of Jesus Christ of Latter-Day Saints* [2008] 1 WLR 1852, 1867 at para 51.

[110] Equally, of course, it also provided the motivation for the Crusades (led by the Knights Templar, a charity) and for many wars ever since.

Chapter 3
Establishing the Church of England

3.1 Introduction

> Be it enacted by authority of this present Parliament that the King our sovereign lord, his heirs and successors kings of this realm, shall be taken, accepted and reputed the only supreme head in earth of the Church of England called *Anglicana Ecclesia*, and shall have and enjoy annexed and united to the imperial crown of this realm as well the title and style thereof, as all honours, dignities, pre-eminences, jurisdictions, privileges, authorities, immunities, profits and commodities, to the said dignity of supreme head of the same church belonging and appertaining.

So declared the Act of Supremacy 1534,[1] launching the Church of England on what to-date has been its 500 year journey as the established national Church.

This chapter begins by outlining the developmental history of the Church of England, explaining its emergence, its special constitutional standing, and the theocratic realities of an evolving Church/State relationship. It considers the rise of Protestantism, the preferential standing of Anglicanism as the established Church and the consequent suppression of all dissent – religious and secular – and noting that charity law has its origins in this context of religious turmoil. It provides a brief history of the jurisdiction of the Ecclesiastical Courts and their former authority to decide matters such as disputes relating to marriage, divorce, wills, and defamation. The chapter then gives an account of the consolidation of the Anglican Church in England and in the British colonies, explaining the differences in the secular and ecclesiastic jurisdiction in respect of the overseas Anglican Church. In conclusion the chapter reflects on the legacy of the Church, in terms of the benchmarks for morality it has identified and asserted over many centuries. By tracing its formative steps, considering the nature of the Church/State relationship, and assessing the part it played in issues that proved critically important to its development, this chapter presents an historical context for the Church of England which is essential for any appreciation of the current role of this institution as it finds itself once again at the forefront of social change.

[1] 26 Henry VIII, c.1.

K. O'Halloran, *The Church of England - Charity Law and Human Rights*, Ius Gentium: Comparative Perspectives on Law and Justice 36, DOI 10.1007/978-3-319-04319-7_3,

3.2 The Church of England: Origins and Historical Background

Almost a full millennium of obedience to Papal supremacy and adherence to Catholicism[2] began to crumble when on 31st October 1517 Martin Luther nailed his thesis of 'protests' to the door of the Castle Church, in Wittenberg. Prolonged frustration with the corruption and excesses of Papal rule triggered finally by the blatant fraud involved in the 'sale of indulgences', sparked a rejection of the Catholic hierarchy and an assertion of doctrinal differences by breakaway religious groups.[3]

3.2.1 The Protestant Reformation

There can be no doubt that the English Reformation was essentially a part of the greater European upheaval that constituted the Protestant Reformation in the sixteenth century. This marked a political, religious and cultural watershed for all of Europe. For England, its monarchy and its citizens, the resulting suppression of Catholicism, confiscation of its abbeys, monasteries and their lands, conversion of its cathedrals and the return to a more austere piety, constituted a cathartic break with the extravagances of Rome. It was also the beginning of a more fundamental separation of the English Church from European Catholicism. The break with the Papacy freed Church and monarchy from a degree of subservience to a foreign power; a relationship that had become too costly in terms of revenues and political machinations to maintain. It would allow England to be wholly self-governing and set the island nation politically apart from mainland Europe for the next three centuries.[4]

3.2.2 The Influences from Continental Europe

To a very considerable extent, the doctrine and liturgy of English Protestantism originated in continental Europe. The Lutheran and Calvinistic movements on the Continent, particularly Calvinism, directly influenced the English schism with Rome and provided leadership for the resulting transplanting of Protestantism. Other sources of influence came from theologians such as Martin Bucer, Heinrich Bullinger, and Peter Martyr Vermigli and from such religious groups as the Anabaptists.

---

[2] It was in the sixth century AD that the first Papal emissary, St Augustine, was sent from Rome to evangelise the Angles and established the first Christian church in Canterbury where he was the first to hold the office of Archbishop.

[3] See, further, MacCulloch, D. 2004. *Europe's house divided: 1490–1700*. London: Penguin.

[4] See, further, Heal, F. 2002. *Reformation in Britain and Ireland*. Oxford: Oxford University Press.

While the reform movement arose out of dissatisfaction with the Papacy on a number of issues, it was partly concerned with a theological dispute that focused on matters such as the role of the Scriptures: with the reformers arguing that all matters of faith should be viewed as subordinate to and derived from the Scriptures. For Lutherans, all human beings are considered sinners and, because of original sin, can only hope to achieve salvation through faith alone. For Calvinists, the salvation of the soul was achievable if an individual could address the five points: total depravity (all are born in sin and cannot unaided escape from that state); unconditional election (only those chosen by God can hope to find eternal salvation); limited atonement (atonement is limited in that it is intended for some but not for all); irresistible grace (the saving grace of God will be applied to, and cannot be resisted by, those whom he has determined to save); and perseverance of the saints (as God is sovereign and his will cannot be frustrated by humans or anything else, those whom he has called will persevere in their faith). Calvinism[5] spread from Switzerland to many parts of continental Europe before being espoused and disseminated by the preachings of John Knox to become the religion of the majority in Scotland.

3.2.3 The Doctrinal Changes

Before the breach with Rome there was absolutely no doctrinal difference between the faith of Englishmen and the rest of Catholic Christendom. Following the break with Catholicism and the embracing of Protestantism the following core doctrinal changes were promptly asserted: rejection of the Papacy; denial of Church infallibility; justification by faith only; supremacy and sufficiency of Scripture as the rule of faith; the triple Eucharistic tenet (i.e. that the Eucharist is a communion or sacrament, and not a mass or sacrifice, save in the sense of praise or commemoration; the denial of transubstantiation and worship of the host; and the denial of the sacrificial office of the priesthood and the propitiatory character of the mass); the non-necessity of auricular confession; the rejection of the invocation of the Blessed Virgin and the saints; the rejection of purgatory and the omission of prayers for the dead; and the rejection of the doctrine of indulgences. In addition, the Reformation introduced: the giving of Communion in both kinds; the substitution of tables for altars; and the abolition of monastic vows and the celibacy of the clergy.[6]

Thereafter the *Ecclesia Anglicana* – previously signifying that part or region of the one Catholic Church under the jurisdiction of the Pope which was situated in England – would refer to the Protestant Church of England, wholly severed from its Catholic and Papal origins.

---

[5] See, for example, Horton, M. 2011. *For Calvinism*. Grand Rapids: Zondervan.

[6] Heal, F. 2002. *Reformation in Britain and Ireland*. Oxford: Oxford University Press.

3.2.4 Emergence of Anglicanism

The process of disentangling the English Church from Papal rule began in the latter part of the reign of King Henry VIII (1509–1547) and proceeded in a series of legislative steps as that most resolute of English monarchs firmly removed any remaining sources and symbols of Catholic power and influence and ensured their replacement by Protestantism. It was not a development that could have been foreseen in the early years of his reign when Henry had renounced the Lutherian thesis,[7] defended the Catholic doctrine of the sacraments and earned from Pope Leo X the title of "Defender of the Faith". By the close of his reign, however, the Catholic Church had been banished and the ascendancy of the new Church of England secured.

3.2.5 The Statutory Foundations

Both prior to and following the upheaval of the Reformation, governance in England was essentially theocratic in nature: before 1534 King Henry VIII ruled by divine right in support of Catholicism with Papal guidance and afterwards he did so in support of Protestantism without it; while matters deemed to be in breach of religious doctrine and therefore sinful continued to receive secular endorsement – being treated as crimes meriting rigorous punishment. It was a time, however, when autocratic rule had the support of Parliament and the majority of subjects. This enabled many statutes to be introduced within a short period and provided a sound foundation for the Protestant Reformation in England.

The Act in Restraint of Appeals 1533,[8] prohibited the presenting of appeals in ecclesiastical matters to Rome and thereby enabled Henry's divorce case to be decided by Archbishop Cranmer in England. The Act of Dispensations 1534[9] transferred to the monarchy the Papal authority to give dispensations from obeying a law of the Church. The Act for the Submission of the Clergy1534[10] confirmed the earlier surrender in 1532 of Convocation to the Crown. The bishops and clergy in convocation were forbidden to make canons except when the King, by his "Letters of Business", gave them permission to do so, and even then the canons so made were to have effect only when approved by the King. The Crown was vested with absolute control in the appointment of bishops. The chapters were required under penalty

[7] See, the "Assertio septem sacramentorum", the book written by Henry VIII to refute Luther.

[8] 25 Henry VIII, c.12.

[9] 25 Henry VIII, c.21.

[10] 25 Henry VIII, c.19 which provided that only the canon law as it then stood was to bind the clergy and laity, and only so far as it was not contrary to common and statute law ("be not contraryant nor repugnant to the lawes statutes and customes of this realm", s.7), excepting only the papal authority to alter the canon law, a power which ended in later the same year, when it was enacted that England was 'an Empire governed by one supreme head and king'.

to elect the person named by the King, and the Archbishop was similarly bound to consecrate the person so named within 20 days after receipt of the King's writ (Significavit) commanding him to do so.[11] The Heresy Act 1534[12] declared that denial of Papal supremacy was no longer to be treated in English law as a heresy and An Act for the Establishment of the King's Succession 1534[13] vested succession to the English throne in the heirs of Henry VIII and Anne Boleyn. The Act of Supremacy 1534,[14] which followed the Act of Succession, enabled Henry VIII to start the process of creating the Church of England. It declared that "the King's Majesty justly and rightfully is and oweth to be the supreme head of the Church of England, and so is recognised by the clergy of this realm in their Convocations". Moreover, the King, as "the only supreme head in earth of the Church of England called Anglicana Ecclesia … shall have full power and authority from time to time to visit, repress, redress, reform, order, correct, restrain, and amend all such errors, heresies, abuses, offences, contempt, enormities whatsoever they be which by any manner, spiritual authority or jurisdiction ought or may be lawfully reformed". While the actual ministry of preaching and the sacraments was left to the clergy, all powers of the ecclesiastical jurisdiction were claimed by the sovereign. Parliament then formally recognised Henry VIII as supreme head of the Church of England under constitutional arrangements which provided for the reigning monarch to be thereafter both its Supreme Governor and Head of State. Coke explained the nature of the relationship between the monarchy and the Church of England at the Reformation as follows[15]:

> By the ancient laws of this realm … England is an absolute empire and monarchy consisting of one head, which is the King, and of a body politic … which the law divideth into … the clergy and the laity, both of them next and immediately under God, subject and obedient to the head …

3.2.6 Ecclesiastical Foundations

The ecclesiastical foundations of the Church of England came to rest on canon law, together with the Thirty-nine Articles of Religion, the Book of Common Prayer and the Ordinal.

Canon law originated in the 151 canons, or directives, that constituted the Canons of 1603.[16] The canons largely preceded the founding of the Church of England but,

---

[11] This enactment remains in force.

[12] 25 Henry VIII, c. xx.

[13] 25 Henry VIII, c.22.

[14] 26 Henry VIII, c. i.

[15] See, *Cawdrey's* case, 1591, 77 *English Reports* 1, at p. 10.

[16] See, Jones, P. 1929. *Lynwood's Provinciale*, ed. Bullard, J.V. and C.H. Bell. London: Faith Press. The *Provinciale* was compiled by William Lynwood in about 1432 and is the principal source of canon law in England.

having gained approved at the Convocations of Canterbury and York, in 1604 and 1606 respectively, they were adopted by the Church and from the outset formed its most basic body of rules.[17] As Lord Chief Justice Sir Matthew Hale later commented[18]:

> the authority and force they [the civil and canon laws] have here is not founded on, or derived from, themselves … they bind no more with us than our laws bind in Rome or Italy … all the strength that either the papal or imperial laws have obtained in this kingdom, is only because they … are part of the statute laws of the kingdom or else by immemorial usage and custom in some particular cases and courts, and no otherwise.

While some of the Commissioners appointed to report upon the ecclesiastical courts claimed, in their report published in 1883, that these courts did not regard themselves as bound by the rules of canon law framed by the various papal decrees etc., the better view is that many canons were carried over from the pre-Reformation era and even subsequently respectful attention was paid to new rules issued by the Catholic Church (though clearly they were not adopted). Some additions and revisions occurred from time to time, authorised by Convocation, until new canons were issued in 1865.

The canons were and are a mixture of rules serving quite different functions.[19] Some, being of a 'good housekeeping' or disciplinary in nature, govern matters such as dress, behaviour, the keeping of parish registers, the distribution of bibles and prayer books and are not necessarily specific to the Church. Others address issues of morals and legal status. Marriage, for example, was something that had traditionally been within the remit of the Church and while now governed by the statute law of Parliament the canons regulate such legal aspects as ages of consent, prohibited degrees of relationship, publishing of banns etc. Drunkenness, defamation, alms for the poor were also the subject of canons. They often offer guidance rather than lay down prescriptive rules. Some, however, clearly sought to exercise real power over clergy and adherents so as to demonstrate the continuing role of the Church, perfected during the Tudor and Stuart eras, as a source of authority which was able to legislate and enforce its laws, in parallel with that exercised by Parliament. The ecclesiastical courts were available to hear and to punish such breaches of the law as were stated in the canons.

It was in 1538 that attention was first given to the Thirty Nine Articles when three German theologians came to London and held conferences with the Anglican bishops and clergy. They presented a number of Articles, based on the Lutheran Confession of Augsburg, as the proposed core of a governing document

[17] See, *Middleton v. Crofts* (1736) 26 English Reports 788, in which 'it was said the canons of 1603 might be enforced so far as they were declaratory of the established canon law before the Act of Submission [of 1533, i.e. before the Reformation]'.

[18] See, Hale, M. 1713. *History and analysis of the common law of England*, University of Chicago Press, 1 28–29.

[19] See, further, Helmholz, R.H. 2004. *The Oxford history of the laws of England: The canon law and ecclesiastical jurisdiction from 597 to the 1640s*. Oxford: Oxford University Press.

for the Church of England. In 1539 Henry passed the Act of Six Articles,[20] which laid down the beliefs of the Church of England and essentially continued the main elements of the Catholic religion.[21] However in that year he also authorised a new translation of the Bible and from 1545 English replaced Latin as the language of church services.

With assistance from the German theologians a draft outline of Articles was drawn up. The first 13 of these formed the doctrinal section, which owed much to the Confession of Augsburg and to the Confession of Wurtemberg, and were readily agreed by Henry VIII, the Archbishop and other leading clergy. The second part, the "Abuses" (viz., private Masses, celibacy of the Clergy, invocation of Saints) proved more difficult and eventually an intransigent King dissolved the conference. However, the 13 agreed Articles were upheld by Archbishops Cranmer and Parker and attestation to them became a precondition for any preacher wishing to be licensed. In 1553, a royal decree was issued requiring the bishops and clergy to subscribe to 42 Articles of Religion. These, to a large extent, represented a Calvinist reformulation of the previously agreed 13. In 1563 they were revised in Convocation under Archbishop Parker: some being added, others altered or omitted; and the number required reduced to 38. In 1571, the XXIXth Article was inserted, to the effect that the wicked do not eat the Body of Christ, after which all Thirty Nine Articles were duly ratified by Queen Elizabeth and then approved and issued by Convocation without any parliamentary involvement.

One of the cardinal principles of the Reformation, brought to the Church of England in 1538 by the German theologians, was the rejection of the Catholic interpretation of the Mass as a 'sacrifice'. Instead they insisted that "the Mass is nothing but a Communion or synaxis".[22] This conception of the Eucharist was incorporated by Edward VI into a new English Communion Service, to be inserted at the end of the Mass, and which required Communion to be given under both kinds.

A further significant contribution to shaping the doctrinal basis of the Church was made by Richard Hooker,[23] a sixteenth century cleric and theologian, who after 1660 was often seen as the founding father of Anglicanism. Hooker's description of Anglican authority as being derived primarily from Scripture, informed by reason (the intellect and the experience of God) and tradition (the practices and beliefs of the historical church), was a powerful influence on Anglican identity.

---

[20] 31 Hen. VIII c.14.

[21] The first article expressed the doctrine of transubstantiation. Those denying this were to be burnt. If the other five articles were impeached the penalties were, for the first offence, confiscation of property, for the second, execution as a felon. The five articles declared (2) that communion in both kinds was unnecessary; (3) that priests ought not to marry; (4) that the vows of chastity ought to be observed in both sexes; (5) that private masses were allowable; (6) that auricular confession was necessary.

[22] Tunstall's Summary, M. S. Cleop. E. V., 209.

[23] Richard Hooker (March 1554–3 November 1600), an Anglican priest and an influential theologian, whose best known work *Of the Lawes of Ecclesiastical Politie* was a study of the proper governance of churches and advanced the thesis that the Scriptures alone provided the rules necessary to ensure salvation.

The reign of Edward VI also saw the finalisation of the Book of Common Prayer, of which Archbishop Cranmer was the main author, it being approved by Parliament in 1549. On Sunday June 24 1559 the statutory Book of Common Prayer was first used. All people over the age of 16 were required to show their loyalty and obedience to God and to the Queen by attendance at the Book of Common Prayer service at their parish church on the 77 days of obligation in the year or be fined and be reported by ministers and churchwardens to the Ecclesiastical Courts.

A new Ordinal – or Order for making bishops, priests, and deacons – was compiled, from which all mention of the sacrificial office of the priesthood was rigorously excluded. It was approved by Parliament in 1552.

3.2.7 The Role of the Ecclesiastical Courts

From the time of the Reformation, ecclesiastical law as compiled and administered by the Church of England no longer drew from or was accountable to the see of Rome. Instead the law came from a mixture of domestic forums: from the rulings of the secular courts and the ecclesiastical courts, from the canons and guidance issued by Convocations/General Synod and from the statutes of Parliament. These sources of authority reveal a complex entanglement of Church and State interests, reflecting the need for institutional inter-dependency and mutual reinforcement. Specifically, the ecclesiastical courts had come to represent the cutting edge of Church/State functions in relation to the morality of English citizens. As was explained in *Cawdrey's* case[24]:

> The ecclesiastical law and the temporal law have several proceedings and to several ends: the one being temporal, to inflict punishment upon body, lands or goods: the other being spiritual pro salute animae ... to reform the inward [man]. [Thus] both ... jurisdictions ... do join in this: to have the whole man inwardly and outwardly reformed.

This clarifies the original purpose of the courts' ecclesiastical jurisdiction: the theocratic assumption was that the State, as well as the Church, had a responsibility for the souls of its subjects; English law at that time was as concerned with regulating the law relating to the salvation of souls as in the law relating to the disposal of property; and the business of saving souls required the State to agree with the Church the moral issues that were of such importance as to jeopardise the prospect of eternal salvation and to take such steps as may be necessary to uphold the relevant moral standards, reform the recalcitrant, and publicly punish those whose breaches jeopardised their souls and outraged public morality.

[24] (1591) 77 English Reports 1 at p. 7.

3.2.8 *Jurisdiction*

The network of some three or four hundred ecclesiastical courts that administered ecclesiastical law[25] from the Reformation held their authority from the Crown as ex-officio the Supreme Governor of the Church of England. These courts had jurisdiction over matters dealing with the rights and obligations of church members which, in effect, meant almost all English citizens during the reign of the Tudors and Stuarts. Although this jurisdiction later shrank a little in relation to English citizens, as the secular law relaxed to permit the recognition of non-Church of England citizens, it also grew exponentially in keeping with the Crown's growing overseas commitments; although whether or to what extent the writ of such courts ran in the colonies was always a matter of some uncertainty.

The range of offences that fell within the scope of the ecclesiastical courts in theory extended to all matters which could be construed as 'sinful', and therefore to a large extent they simply continued the brief they had assumed during the Middle Ages. Traditionally, these offences were in the nature of lewd/drunken/immoral behaviour, debts and defamation, sexual offences, infidelity and the law relating to marriage, affairs of probate etc.

3.3 Consolidation, Suppression and Charity

So effectively was the legislative basis for the Church of England entrenched during the reign of Henry VIII, as revived by Elizabeth and confirmed in subsequent reigns that, as Lord Campbell pointed out in his famous Gorham judgment,[26] in 1850, it served to locate in the Crown all that decisive jurisdiction which before the Reformation had been exercised by the Pope. The fact that Protestantism was safely established, and Catholicism together with fealty to the Pontiff just as surely ousted, did not prevent further action being taken to consolidate the changed religious regime. This was particularly evident in the latter part of the Elizabethan era as evidence mounted of domestic and overseas determination to reverse the changes made.

3.3.1 *Consolidating Protestantism*

In the years following the Reformation, Parliament passed a considerable number of statutes that intervened in the traditional jurisdiction of the ecclesiastical courts: the

[25] The ecclesiastical law of England consists of the general principles of the *ius commune ecclesiasticum:* see, further, *Ever v. Owen* Godbolt's Report 432, per Whitlock J.

[26] *Gorham v. Bishop of Exeter*, The Privy Council, March 9, 1850.

legislative intent perhaps being to criminalise conduct associated with lax morals; making any such breach an offence punishable by the common law courts not merely left to the ecclesiastical courts with their limited enforcement capacity. However, the ecclesiastical courts also broadened their remit and together with the crown courts the overall effect was to bring to bear the authority of Church and State to police a new and more austere public morality than had earlier prevailed.

3.3.2 *The Crown Courts*

Within a few decades after the Reformation, Parliament had introduced a range of statutes targeting the moral turpitude of English citizens. So, for example, bankruptcy (1571),[27] bastardy (1576),[28] bigamy (1603),[29] blasphemy (1605),[30] brawling in churchyards (1552),[31] buggery (1563),[32] abuse of charities (1601),[33] drunkenness (1606),[34] perjury (1563),[35] religious nonconformity (1571),[36] swearing (1624),[37] usury (1571)[38] and witchcraft (1563)[39] were all declared to be criminal offences.[40] Being so designated, however, did not necessarily oust Church jurisdiction, only where there was direct conflict between provisions of canon law and statute would the latter prevail.

3.3.3 *The Ecclesiastical Courts*

In addition to the offences that traditionally preoccupied these courts, their workload expanded considerably in the post-Reformation period. This was in part due to the closer ties between monarch and Church, at least until the civil war broke out, and to the extended jurisdiction that came with the many new statutes dealing with civil

---

[27] 13 Eliz. 1, c.7.

[28] 18 Eliz. 1, c.3.

[29] 1 Jac. 1, c.11.

[30] 3 Jac. 1, c.21.

[31] 5 & 6 Edw. VI, c.4.

[32] 5 Eliz. I, c.17.

[33] 39 Eliz. I, c.6 and 43 Eliz. I, c.4.

[34] 4 Jac. I, c.5.

[35] 5 Eliz. I, c.9.

[36] 13 Eliz. I, c.1.

[37] 21 Jac. I, c.20.

[38] 13 Eliz. I, c.8.

[39] 5 Eliz. I, c.16.

[40] As cited in Helmholz, R.H. 2004. *The Oxford history of the laws of England: The canon law and ecclesiastical jurisdiction from 597 to the 1640s*, 276. Oxford: Oxford University Press.

obedience coupled with new privileges enabling the ecclesiastical courts to invoke the powers of the crown courts to enforce its rulings in relation to offences such as 'contumacy'. It would seem that like their secular counterparts, the ecclesiastical courts felt empowered to exercise ever greater public intervention into the private lives of English citizens: behaviour indicative of lax morals was no longer to be addressed in a private confessional relationship with the minister but was to be treated as a public matter warranting proclamations and public acts of penance. As Helmholz has noted[41]:

> The Reformation did not bring to an end penitential relations between people and clergy in England, and conscience continued to serve as a legitimate arbiter of human conduct. But the courts had to judge by externals. The consequence was to make public 'trials' of what might once have been left to private settlement. The boundary line of the classical canon law – public penance for public offences, private penance for private offences – had always been a porous one. Here it admitted of distinct movement towards expansion in the number of disciplinary matters dealt with in the spiritual courts.

Although the jurisdiction of the ecclesiastical courts continued untroubled by the Reformation – except to the extent that matters relating to breaches of Catholic doctrine no longer formed part of their brief, nor would there be any further recourse to the Papal court – the actual volume of related litigation increased considerably in the late fifteenth century right through until the outbreak of civil war.[42]

Indeed, such was the theocratic nature of Church/State relations that the laws governing the Church of England were deemed to be part of the law of the England and were thus enforceable by the King's courts. Until the court reforms in the second half of the nineteenth century, the ecclesiastical jurisdiction extended over a wide spectrum of personal affairs including probate, marriage and divorce, tithes, defamation, and disciplinary prosecutions involving the laity. Arguably, these courts played a significant part in stabilising post-Reformation England during the Tudor/Stuart period. In so doing they also instilled an acceptance that the Church of England could be trusted to register and regulate matters deemed to constitute 'public morality' in English society.

3.3.4 Assertion of Church/State Protestant Partnership

The Reformation did not pass unchallenged. There were times when the threats of a resurgent Catholicism – from internal, external, or from a combination of both sources – endangered the continued survival of the Church of England as the

[41] Helmholz, R.H. 2004. *The Oxford history of the laws of England: The canon law and ecclesiastical jurisdiction from 597 to the 1640s*, 286. Oxford: Oxford University Press.

[42] See, for example: Owen, D. 1971. *A catalogue of the records of the Bishop and Archdeacon of Ely*; Anglin, J. 1972. The Essex Puritan Movement and the "Bawdy" courts 1577–94. In *Tudor men and institutions: Studies in English law and government*, ed. Slavin, J. Baton Rouge: Louisiana State University Press; and Hill, C. 1997. *Society and Puritanism in pre-revolutionary England*. New York: St. Martin's Press.

national religion. There were risks also in the differing approaches taken by successive monarchs.

The short but bloody reign of the Catholic Queen Mary (1553–1558) saw the English Church reunited with Rome,[43] the persecution and execution of many Catholics and the banning of English translations of the Bible. The Elizabethan era began confidently and with some accommodation afforded to Catholics and other nonconformists. However, after the issue of a Papal Bull by Pope Pius V in 1570, declaring Elizabeth a heretic and sanctioning insurrection to depose her, she authorised the suppression of Catholicism. This intensified in the face of organised Catholic threats: the Spanish Inquisition; the spread of Catholic missionaries and Jesuits; the Spanish Armada and plots involving Mary Queen of Scots, both of which threatened to overthrow her throne and Protestantism and were duly neutralised. The legislative foundations of the Church of England were restored and consolidated by Elizabeth I (1558–1603), following the two short reigns of Edward VI (1547–1553) and Queen Mary I (1553–1558) that intervened after the death of her father Henry VIII. The Act of Royal Supremacy 1534, repealed by Queen Mary, was reinstated by Elizabeth in 1558 but with an "Admonition" in which she renounced all claim to "power of ministry of divine offices in the Church".[44] In the same year, the Act of Uniformity revived the 1552 Prayer book of Edward VI, making the English Church Protestant in doctrine but more traditional in its form of worship. Elizabeth reasserted Henry VIII's authority in respect of ecclesiastical matters, but also cultivated a broad base of support. Her reign is particularly significant for this book as it produced the founding statute for charity in England, later extended to the rest of the common law world: the Statute of Charitable Uses 1601.[45]

Elizabeth's approach was undone by that of her successor James I (1603–25) who believed his rule to be by the "Divine Right of Kings" (under which he was considered appointed by God and not answerable to men). This autocracy continued into the reign of Charles I (1625–49) who in 1628 prefixed a royal declaration to the Thirty Nine Articles, which declared that it belonged to the kingly office "to conserve and maintain the Church committed to our charge, in unity of religion and the bond of peace". It then demanded that the Articles be understood literally and threatened punitive action in respect of any person who should presume to re-interpret them in any way. It stated "no man hereafter shall either print or preach, to draw the Article aside any way, but shall submit to it in the plain and Full meaning thereof: and shall not put his own sense or comment to be the meaning of the Article, but shall take it in the literal and grammatical sense." This stamped the Articles, the core beliefs of the Church of England, with both the status of religious dogma and of royal command. It also fuelled Protestant

[43] As it was again under the brief reign of James II (1685–88).

[44] The Act of Supremacy 1558 restored the arrogation of ecclesiastical authority to the monarchy, confirmed Elizabeth I as Supreme Governor of the Church of England, and required any person taking public or church office to swear allegiance to her. In response, the Roman Catholic Church excommunicated Elizabeth in 1570.

[45] A modified version of the Statute of Uses 1597 (39 Eliz. I, c.6).

dissent and the resentment of an increasingly marginalised Parliament culminating in civil war.

However, the mid-seventeenth century was a time when Parliament was seeking to assert its independence from the dual institutions of Church and monarchy. So when in 1640 Archbishop Laud had a series of canons drawn up in Convocation and published, the House of Commons passed a resolution unanimously declaring that "the Clergy in Convocation assembled has no power to make any canons or constitutions whatsoever in matters of doctrine, discipline or otherwise to bind the Clergy and laity of the land without the common consent in Parliament".[46] This resolution remained in effect until 1833, with the Crown exercising its jurisdiction through a special body called the Court of Delegates, when it was abolished, and its powers were transferred to the King in Council.

3.3.5 Suppression of Other Religions

After various unsuccessful challenges from Catholicism, regime efforts became vested in a determined drive to establish a national Protestant religion regulated by statute; other religions would be suppressed.[47] As Rivers has pointed out,[48] up until at least the early eighteenth century religious minorities were barely tolerated by the State. Alongside the perceived external threat of other religions, the Church of England was constantly challenged by schisms giving rise to the possibility of internal fragmentation.

3.3.6 Persecution of Catholics and Dissenters

Adherents of the former national religion were in a different category to other religious believers and one that was seriously compromised in post-Reformation England. Because their faith required obedience to Papal pronouncements they could with some justification be accused of being the subjects of a foreign power. This interpretation allowed many prominent Catholics to be politically defined as enemies of the State. Others who simply dissented from the Church of England doctrines were also liable to find themselves prosecuted for sedition. An expedient method of prosecuting such offenders was by equating sins with crimes which served both to bind Church and State together in a consistent policy of prosecution and also permitted the use of extreme forms of punishment. The secular

[46] Resolution, 16 December, 1640.

[47] See, for example, Coffey, J. 2000. *Persecution and toleration in protestant England 1558–1689*. London: Longman.

[48] Rivers, J. 2010. *The law of organized religions: Between establishment and secularism*, 16. Oxford: Oxford University Press.

enforcement of religious doctrine was through the designation of a range of conduct as 'profane', being both criminal and sinful, Consequently, many prosecutions for such profanities as apostasy, heresy[49] and blasphemy[50] were conducted and mediaeval punishments applied.

Blackstone, in dealing with offences against religion, refers to the heinous offence "of blasphemy against the Almighty, by denying his being or providence; or by contumelious reproaches of our Saviour Christ … These are offences punishable at common law by fine and imprisonment, or other infamous corporal punishment: for Christianity is part of the laws of England."[51] The gravity of the offence was demonstrated in the prosecutions of both Atwood in 1618 and Taylor in1676. In the first, although the offensive language was aimed chiefly at the established mode of worship, the court upheld the indictment because "these words are seditious words against the State of our Church and against the peace of the realm, and although they are spiritual words, still they draw after them a temporal consequence, namely, the disturbance of the peace."[52] In the second, the language used was much coarser causing Hale C. J. to proclaim that:

> Such words are not only a sin, but a crime. It may be they are punishable in the ecclesiastical Court; but they are also punishable in a temporal Court; for they tend to subvert the established order of things, of which Christianity is a part, and are therefore dangerous to the State. They are, in fact, seditious.

As Hale C.J. put it, "Christianity is parcel of the laws of England; and therefore to reproach the Christian religion is to speak in subversion of the law".

The Restoration in 1660 triggered a new and sustained bout of persecutions that targeted first dissenters and later Catholics. The Episcopal Church government was reinstated and the backlash against the Puritanism of Cromwell's Commonwealth (1649–1653) saw the Prayer Book, which had been suppressed during the Commonwealth, restored to favour and made compulsory by the Act of Uniformity 1662. It was subjected to revision in Convocation and Parliament but the eventual amendments were mainly confined to emphasising the Episcopal character of Anglicanism in contrast with Presbyterianism. In that year the opportunity to reject Puritanism and reassert the founding principles of the Reformation was seized: the new liturgy returned to the doctrinal basis of the Reformation: the Lord's Supper was defined as a Sacrament or Communion, and not as a Sacrifice; and all indications of any sacrificial dimension to the Eucharist were expunged. The resulting Anglican Articles and liturgy continued virtually intact into the twenty-first century. Then in 1678, following the scare over the Popish Plot, the second Test Act was introduced which included the

[49] The last heretics to be burned at the stake in England were Legate at Smithfield in 1612 upon a writ *de haeretico comburendo*, and Wightman at Lichfield about the same time.

[50] See, the trials of Atwood 1618 (Cro. Jac. 421; 2 Roll. Abr. 78,) and Taylor 1676 (1 Ventris 293; 3 Kebble 607; 2 Strange 789).

[51] See, Blackstone, *Commentaries on the Laws of England*, (Book 4, c.4, s. iv), Yale Law School, at: http://avalon.law.yale.edu/18th_century/blackstone_bk4ch14.asp.

[52] 2 Bolle's Abridgment, 78.

declaration laid down in the 1673 Act abjuring transubstantiation, worship of the Virgin Mary and the celebration of mass.

The execution of Oliver Plunkett in 1681 was the last 'martyrdom' of a Catholic on English soil. A Scottish student hanged for blasphemy in 1697 was the last person in the British Isles to be executed for his religious views. However, the persecution of Protestant by Protestant in England after the Restoration was possibly unequalled anywhere in seventeenth century Europe.[53] This was a period when the Church of England showed resolute determination in its efforts to prevent fellow Protestants weakening its position. The Clarendon Code, a composite series of statutes, was in particular designed to keep other Protestants from holding office in the institutions of Church or State.[54] It also served to deny any liberty to form associations, unless this was in furtherance of the interests of the established Church, by making it an offence for five or more persons to be present at "any assembly, coventicle or meeting, under colour or pretence of any exercise of religion, in any other manner than according to the liturgy and practice of the Church of England".[55] This policy of shoring up the position of the Church of England was evident also at the coronation of William and Mary in 1689 when they were required to swear the following oath:

> Will you solemnly promise and swear to govern the people of this kingdom of England, and the dominions thereto belonging, according to the statutes in Parliament agreed on, and the laws and customs of the same? Will you to the utmost of your power maintain the laws of God, the true profession of the gospel and the protestant reformed religion established by law? And will you preserve unto the bishops and clergy of this realm, and to the churches there committed to their charge, all such rights and privileges as by law do or shall appertain unto them, or any of them?

3.3.7 Charity Law and the Church/State Hegemony

The Statute of Charitable Uses 1601 inaugurated charity law in England. From there it was shipped, as so defined, with the armies of the Crown to virtually replicate English charity law in all major parts of the British Empire. It was a statute very much of its time and both reflected, and was deployed to serve, the interests of the State in managing charity and religion.[56]

[53] See, Coffey, J. 2000. *Persecution and toleration in protestant England 1558–1689*. London: Longman.

[54] Consisting of statutes such as: the Corporation Act of 1661 (prohibited from public office all who had not taken the Sacrament of the Lord's Supper in accordance with the rites of the Church of England); The Act of Uniformity 1662 (made it illegal to assent to anything outside of the Book of Common Prayer); and the Test Act 1973 (made it illegal for persons to hold public office without first "receiving the Sacrament of the Lord's Supper according to the usage of the Church of England").

[55] See, the Conventicles Act 1670 (22 Car II c 1), s.1, preceded by the Conventicles Act 1593 and 1664. This set of statutes all sought to compel attendance at the Church of England and penalise any other form of association for religious purposes: an ironic accompaniment to the Statute of Charitable Uses 1601 which, in providing the foundations for charity law, is often viewed as the legislative catalyst for initiating associational activity and generating what is now known as the nonprofit sector.

[56] See, further, Bromley, B. 2002. 1601 preamble: The State's Agenda for charity. *Charity Law & Practice Review* 17(3): 176–211.

The Preamble sets out the matters deemed to be charitable. Following as it did immediately after the Act for the Relief of the Poor 1601,[57] the legislative intent was to ensure that the responsibility and cost for relieving poverty, for other designated charitable purposes, and for restoring social order, would be borne by the Church and by those in local communities with sufficient wealth and goodwill to undertake tasks that would otherwise fall to a hard pressed monarchy. The listed charitable purposes omit any mention of religion. The reason for this must be to do with the fact that for Elizabeth I religion was defined exclusively as meaning the Church of England: Church and State were united in a theocratic relationship; all other religions were outside the law; to acknowledge their existence might encourage acts of sedition.

This interpretation is borne out by the discriminatory application of charity law to all religious purposes, other than those associated with the Church of England, for centuries after the introduction of the 1601 Act. Religion was politically defined and, by extension, so was charity when it was applied to further religious purposes. The only permissible object of a religious charity was an endowment for the national Church; all other gifts or purposes intended for religious ends were not only not charitable, they were illegal.

From an early stage in the Elizabethan era, discrimination in favour of charitable trusts for the benefit of Protestant causes was very apparent.[58] In 1606, for example, a trust to support students studying for the Roman Catholic priesthood was disallowed[59] while, in 1639, one for the purpose of maintaining a preaching minister was upheld.[60] State suppression of the Roman Catholic Church led to the systematic judicial voiding of many trusts that would have previously been found charitable including trusts to maintain popish priests,[61] and gifts dedicated to the advancement of any religion other than that of the established Church.[62] The provisions of the above-mentioned Conventicles Act 1670 further reinforced the ties between the Church, State and charity by prohibiting the forming of any religious organisation and of any associated religious activity that was not exclusively dedicated to and controlled by the Church of England. Suppression was not restricted to Catholicism as was evident in the similar judicial approach to trusts for the purposes of assisting Judaism or its adherents and in relation to support for non-conformist ministers.[63] In *AG v. Eades*[64] doubts were still being expressed as to whether a gift to poor Anabaptists was a good charity. Even later, gifts for religious purposes that were not associated with Protestantism in general, or the Church of England in particular,

---

[57] 43 Elizabeth I, c.2. See, Jones, G. 1969. *History of the law of charity 1552–1827*. Cambridge: Cambridge University Press.

[58] See, further, Picarda, H. 2010. *The law and practice relating to charities*, 90. 4th ed. London: Bloomsbury Professional.

[59] See, for example, *Croft v. Evetts* (1606) Moore KB 784.

[60] *Pember v. Inhabitants of Knighton* (1639), 1 Eq. Cas. 95.

[61] See, for example, *A-G v. Baxter* (1684) 1 Vern 248.

[62] *De Costa v. De Paz* (1754) 2 Swan 487n; *Cary v. Abbot* (1802) 7 Ves 490.

[63] See, for example, *Gates v. Jones* (1690), cited in 2 Vern 266.

[64] (1713), unreported; see *AG v. Cock* (1751) 2 Ves Sen 273, 28 ER 177, at 274.

were held to be invalid (see, further, Chap. 4). There could be no doubting the political investment in controlling religion and its relationship to charity: the interests of the Church of England, and by proxy the application of charity law to religion, would be closely watched by the State.

3.4 Toleration at Home and Expansion Overseas

The task of consolidating a society long ravaged by civil war and religious division probably began around the time of the Toleration Act 1689. Thereafter there was a perceptible loosening of the Church of England's controlling position as the State religion: a recognition that in practice a more pluralistic view would be conducive to forestalling further schisms in Protestantism and quell social unrest, began to take hold. This change in the religious/political climate was assisted by the ongoing draining of the pool of domestic dissent by the number of Catholics and other oppressed minority groups granted safe passage to join in the grand imperial project of building England's overseas colonies.

3.4.1 Some Toleration

Only gradually, following the crowning of William and Mary and the introduction of the Toleration Act 1689[65] (which extended freedom of worship rights to some religions but not to Catholicism), did the sustained persecution of those having religious beliefs different from the Church of England begin to ease. Strictly speaking, the provisions of this statute were not intended for the benefit of other Protestants anymore than for the benefit of Catholics: the objective was to enforce religious uniformity (as previously demonstrated in the Act of Uniformity 1662 by which use of the Book of Common Prayer was made compulsory).

3.4.2 Act of Settlement

At the turn of the eighteenth century a sequence of statutes stabilised the Church/State relationship, including the Bill of Rights 1688, the Act of Settlement 1700, the Act of Succession 1701 and the Act of Union 1706. Designed to secure the Protestant succession, this set of provisions required the monarch to join in communion with the Church of England, declare him or herself to be a Protestant,[66] swear to maintain

[65] 1 Will. & Mar. c.18.

[66] This taking the form of a specific doctrinal commitment:

> I doe solemnely and sincerely in the presence of God professe testifie and declare that I do believe that in the sacrament of the Lords Supper there is not any transubstantiation of the elements of bread and wine into the body and blood of Christ at or after the consecration

the established churches in England and Scotland and take the coronation oath. If he or she wished to attain or retain title to the throne they were required to abjure the prospect of marriage to a Roman Catholic, and any such marriage automatically excluded that person from the line of succession; conditions that continue to prevail in the twenty-first century. The determination to assert the primacy of Protestantism was clearly established in the opening words of the Bill of Rights:

> ... it hath beene found by experience that it is inconsistent with the safety and welfaire of this protestant kingdome to be governed by a popish prince or by any King or Queene marrying a papist the said lords spirituall and temporall and commons doe further pray that it may be enacted that all and every person and persons that is are or shall be reconciled to or shall hold communion with the see or church of Rome or shall professe the popish religion or shall marry a papist shall be excluded and be for ever uncapeable to inherit possesse or enjoy the crowne and government of this realme and Ireland and the dominions thereunto belonging or any part of the same or to have use or exercise any regall power authoritie or jurisdiction within the same ...

From that time the unequivocal, legislatively sealed, unification of monarchy and Church of England has remained unchallenged.

3.4.3 Limitations

Toleration would not be extended to the likes of anti-Trinitarians, Anabaptists and Jews nor to those who had promoted schisms within Protestantism such as Baptists and Puritans, and certainly not to those such as the Levellers, Diggers and atheists perceived as posing a more basic threat to institutions. A point emphasised in *Regina v. Woolston*,[67] where it was held "to say that an attempt to subvert the established religion is not punishable by those laws upon which it is established is an absurdity".

However, and despite appearances, this was arguably a period when the restored Anglican monopoly of political and social life allowed the ruling classes to behave with some flexibility towards those who posed no real threat. In the latter half of the seventeenth century concessions sufficient to avoid any further schisms in Protestantism were being made and some tentative steps towards a more pluralistic society were, perhaps,

---

> thereof by any person whatsoever; and that the invocation or adoration of die Virgin Mary or any other saint, and the sacrifice of the masses as they are now used in the Church of Rome are superstitious and idolatrous, and I doe solenmely in the presence of God professe testifie and declare that I doe make this declaration and every part thereof in the plaine and ordinary sense of the words read unto me as they are commonly understood by English Protestants without any evasion, equivocation or mentall reservation whatsoever and without any dispensation already granted me for this purpose by the Pope or any other authority or person whatsoever or without any hope of any such dispensation from any person or authority whatsoever or without thinking that I am or can be acquitted before God or man or absolved of this declaration or any part thereof although the Pope or any other person or persons or power whatsoever should dispense with or annull the same, or declare that it was null and void from the beginning.

[67] 1729 (Fitz-G. 64; 1 Barn. Ch. 162, 266; 2 Stra. 832).

being cultivated. The efforts of William III, to extend legal toleration of religious worship to Catholics, were not wholly unsuccessful as in practice Catholics were able to benefit from the simple fact that church attendance could no longer be made compulsory and they could discretely establish their own places of worship. By the early eighteenth century, practical toleration of most religious dissent was well advanced and this accelerated when, towards the end of that century, the Papists Act 1778 was introduced to address legal discrimination against Roman Catholics.

3.4.4 Post-waterloo

The early decades of the nineteenth century was a period when the position of the Church of England in the public life of England reflected the strength of its other institutions: Parliament and the nation's armed forces were very much in the ascendancy at home and abroad respectively. The settled social scene has been depicted as follows[68]:

> The established Church of England, richly endowed and privileged, had in 1815 at least the external support of almost the whole of the upper class, and, in most country districts, of the greater part of the population. There was a small Roman Catholic minority, denied full civil rights, but living quietly and without political importance. Irish immigration increased the number of Roman Catholics, but most of these immigrants were poor people whose troubles were economic rather than political. There was a much larger minority of protestant dissenters, also without full civil rights, though less hampered in practice by disabilities than the Roman Catholics. In Wales, and in some parts of England, there were more dissenters than churchmen; in Scotland, Presbyterianism was far stronger than any other denomination. Except in the west of England and parts of East Anglia and the north, the nonconformists belonged mainly to the shopkeeping and lower middle class of the towns.

In the years following the victory at Waterloo, the nation's relief at having finally brought to an end a draining continental war seemed to permit Church and State to relax and allow a process of creeping emancipation to ease the oppression long imposed upon its minorities. The Clarendon Code, which for the past century and more had prevented dissenters and non-conformists from engaging in much of civic life, was now in abeyance (though not repealed). The Unitarian Relief Act 1813, the Roman Catholic Charities Act 1832 and the Roman Catholic Relief Act 1829 greatly relaxed legal restrictions and non-Anglicans were beginning to hold municipal offices, university posts, and participate in Parliamentary elections. The Religious Disabilities Act 1846 provided that in respect of schools, places of religious worship, educational and charitable purposes and property held by them, Jews shall be subject to the same laws as Protestants who dissent from the Church of England. This did not stop the courts from enforcing the explicitly discriminatory intentions of testators in an endless list of cases that confirmed the right of donors to attach religious conditions prejudicial to non-Protestants. These cases included:

[68] See, Woodward, E.L. 1938. *The age of reform, 1815–1870*. Oxford: Clarendon Press.

Blathwayt v. Lord Cawley,[69] condition prohibiting becoming a Roman Catholic; *In re May, Eggar v. May,*[70] condition prohibiting practice of Roman Catholicism; *In re Morrison's Will Trusts, Walsingham v. Blathwayt,*[71] condition against becoming or marrying a Roman Catholic; *Clavering v. Ellison,*[72] condition requiring education in Protestant religion; and *In re Allen,*[73] condition of membership in and adherence to doctrines of Church of England.

3.4.5 The Church of England: Loosening Ties with the Overseas Anglican Church

Repression at home provided a strong incentive for emigration. Initially it was Catholics who left an intolerant England to build a more congenial community in America. In due course they were joined by Presbyterians, Jews, Quakers, Anabaptists and many other groups, fleeing from persecution perpetrated not only in England but also in the countries of continental Europe. Commerce was also a factor in the drive to colonise the 'New World'. As the major influx was from England and as the Church of England was a leading institution of the State, accustomed to acting alongside Parliament and the Crown, its representatives accompanied the forces of the Crown to its dominions overseas.

3.4.6 The Colonies

In 1606, King James I signed the first of three charters giving the Virginia Company the right to control an area extending 50 miles north, 50 miles south, and 100 miles west of the settlement on the east coast of America. The second charter in 1609 granted the Virginia Company an "able and absolute governor" and extended the boundaries of Virginia from those set in the 1606 charter. In 1612, a third charter incorporated Bermuda and established lotteries for the purpose of raising funds and in 1629 Charles I granted a Charter to the Massachusetts Bay Company for the settlement of New England. Others followed as England's policy of colonizing America, largely with recalcitrant religious minorities, gathered momentum. Not until 1788 did the settlement of Australia begin, with a penal colony in what is now New South Wales, to be followed by five more colonies during the first half of the nineteenth century.

---

[69] [1976] 1 A.C. 397 (H.L.).

[70] [1932] 1 Ch. 99.

[71] [1940] Ch. 102.

[72] (1859) 7 HLC 282.

[73] [1953] 1 Ch. 810.

The Maryland colony, commenced in 1634, was an experiment in religious toleration. Founded by the Roman Catholic Lord Baltimore, the colony was envisioned as offering freedom of conscience and economic opportunity to Roman Catholics and other religious dissidents from England and eventually elsewhere in Europe. However, the colony proved to have little immunity to the religious struggles which had given it birth, and in 1689 the colony became subject to Protestant control. This was a pattern repeated in other, but not all, colonies as the establishment structure of the 'motherland' was transplanted throughout its expanding empire. With the founding of overseas colonies came the creation of Church of England congregations with their chaplains and a governor who was obliged to enforce the laws of England. Thus, to an extent, the Church of England was transplanted as the 'established' religion to at least some of the Thirteen Colonies in North America and the West Indies in the seventeenth century; a development that ended with the War of Independence (1775–1789) and the loss of the First British Empire.

At least initially, the laws governing the colonies were those that applied in England[74]:

> What if there be a new and uninhabited country found out by *English* subjects, as the law is the birthright of every subject so, wherever they go, they carry their laws with them, and therefore such new found country is to be governed by the laws of England.

As the laws governing the Church of England formed part of the law of the England they would be enforced as such in the King's courts: church rules and practices would be enforceable in the colonial courts; with a right of appeal to the Privy Council in London. The duties of a colonial governor included enforcing the observance of religion and to take steps to ensure the celebration of public worship.

3.4.7 *The Status of the Church of England in the Colonies*

By the mid-nineteenth century, the status of the Anglican Church overseas was as follows[75]:

> In the mid-nineteenth century, the Anglican Church, established by law in England, Wales and Ireland,[76] was widely believed to be similarly privileged throughout the empire. Whether it was in fact ever legally established, and hence part of the structure of the state, was something of a moot point; but in the late eighteenth century and the early decades of the nineteenth century, there was scarcely any dispute about it. The few colonial bishops

[74] See, *Memorandum* (1722) 2 Peere Williams 75; 24 ER 464 (PC).

[75] See, Daw, E.D. 1977. *Church and state in the empire: The evolution of imperial policy 1846–1856*. Canberra: Faculty of Military Studies, UNSW (as cited by Tong, R. 2012. *Judicial intervention in the affairs of unincorporated religious associations in New South Wales*, 125. Unpublished thesis submitted for degree of Doctor of Juridical Science, Faculty of Law, QUT, Brisbane).

[76] The Act of Union 1800, article 5, united the Church of England and the Church of Ireland into "one protestant episcopal church, to be called, the united Church of England and Ireland".

who were sent out prior to 1840 were appointed, however reluctantly, by the imperial government, just as their brethren of the English episcopate were. They were treated as officers of the state, given status as such, and were generally supported financially by it. And yet, there was no adequate definition of the relations between church and state in the empire. Any such definition would have had to clarify the situation without separating the colonial church from the mother church; without encroaching upon apparent royal prerogatives; and without interfering in the colonies in matters of purely local concern.

By the second half of the nineteenth century the colonies had matured into quite settled entities, populated by people no longer necessarily originating from England, that had achieved varying measures of self-reliance; more so in America where the Thirteen Colonies had been separated from Great Britain since 1776. The nature of any continuing constitutional and other legal ties between colonies and the homeland was being openly questioned. Not until then did issues arise to challenge the assumption that the Church of England and canon law were vested with the same status in the colonies as they retained in the homeland.[77]

Coupled with this was the issue of whether the colonial Church had access to the Privy Council as the final court of appeal. The jurisdiction of the Privy Council originated in the prerogative powers of the King. The ecclesiastical aspect of this jurisdiction embraced any ecclesiastical matters in dispute which, prior to the Act for the Submission of the Clergy 1534,[78] would have been referred to the Pope, and any subsequently raised on appeal through his courts. In theory, the prerogative powers enabled the King, acting through the Privy Council, to hear any ecclesiastical matters in dispute in any colony on appeal from a colonial court. In England, the Church had been accustomed to turning towards the Privy Council when doctrinal issues needed to be resolved and increasingly its colonial counterpart now needed to know whether, as a last resort, the same avenue of appeal was equally available when doctrinal disputes arose within a colony or between a colony and England.

A series of cases then examined these matters, the first of which was *Gorham v. Bishop of Exeter.*[79] This case concerned Gorham, a clergyman, suspected by the Bishop of Exeter of not holding the correct doctrine on baptism and indicted for heresy. When found guilty by an ecclesiastical court he appealed to the Judicial Committee of the Privy Council and was acquitted, the Archbishops of Canterbury and York, sitting as Assessors, concurring. This decision caused considerable controversy as it questioned the autonomy of the Church of England and its capacity to determine its own doctrine and laws. The second case, *Williams v. Salisbury (Bp)*[80] concerned a matter of doctrine. In 1860 a volume of essays was published by seven prominent members of the Church of England the content of which was deemed by the bishops to constitute a breach of the 39 Articles of Religion. This finding was

[77] See, Helmholtz, R. 2004. *The Oxford history of the common laws of England: The canon law and ecclesiastical jurisdiction from 597 to the 1640s*. Oxford: Oxford University Press.

[78] 25 Henry VIII. C.19.

[79] (1850) Moore's Special Reports 462.

[80] (1863) 2 Moo PCCNS 375, PC.

upheld by an ecclesiastical court but overturned on appeal by the Privy Council which, again, gave rise to the question whether the Church had jurisdiction to determine doctrinal issues. In the third, *In re Lord Bishop of Natal,*[81] the judgment clarified the standing of ecclesiastical law in the colonies[82]:

> It cannot be said that any Ecclesiastical tribunal or jurisdiction is required in any Colony or Settlement where there is no Established Church, and in the case of a settled colony the Ecclesiastical Law of England cannot, for the same reason be treated as part of the law which the settlers carried with them from the Mother-country.

The last case in this series was *Forbes v. Eden*[83] in which Forbes alleged that the 1863 amendments to the 39 Articles were ultra vires the powers of the General Synod. He contended that as he had been ordained under the canons of 1838 he was therefore entitled to exercise the functions of a clergyman of the Episcopal Church of Scotland according to the doctrine and practice established by those canons and was not bound by new canons of 1863. The Lord Chancellor ruled that the issue was one which lay outside the jurisdiction of the civil courts as "it was a mere abstract question involving religious dogmas and resulting in no civil consequences which could justify the interposition of a Civil Court."[84] However, there was a further and crucial reason for non-interference. As Lord Colonsay put it, the court[85]:

> will not interfere with the rules of a voluntary association unless to protect some civil right or interest which is said to be infringed by their operation. Least of all, will it enter into questions of disputed doctrine, when not necessary to do so in reference to civil interests.

The civil courts were barred from interfering, not so much because matters of doctrine were outside the remit of a secular court, but because the standing of the Church itself – being outside the geographical jurisdiction of England – was judged not to have the 'established' characteristics of the Church based within that jurisdiction. Without the protection of 'establishment' it was in law simply just another voluntary association. In all cases the decisions told the same story, as far as the English courts were concerned: the Anglican church outside the physical territory of England did not enjoy the same legal status as the Established Church within it; and consequently they were required to treat the Established Church and overseas Anglican churches quite differently. By 1880 it had become clear that[86]:

> The *status* of the Anglican Church in the British colonies is one of ecclesiastical independence. This was the natural and inevitable outcome of the decision of the Privy Council in 1865, in the case of Bishop Colenso, and of the judgment of the House of Lords in 1867, in

[81] (1864) 3 Moo PCC NS 115, 148, 152; 16 ER 43. Also, see, *The Queen v. the Provost and Fellows of Eton College* 27 Law J Reports (NS)QB 132; (1857) 120 ER 228.

[82] Ibid at p. 57.

[83] (1867) LR 1 Sc & Div 568.

[84] Ibid, at p. 576.

[85] Ibid, at p. 588.

[86] See, Todd, A. 1880. *Parliamentary government in the British colonies*, 415. London: Longmans & Co.

Forbes v. Eden.[87] This case has been termed the charter of colonial church independence. It establishes and defines the powers of general synods, as being supreme in all matters over which civil courts have no jurisdiction.

3.4.8 The Church of England: Becoming More 'Established' at Home

In a domestic context, religion continued to be synonymous with the Church of England. As Parson Thwackum expressed it in 1749:[88]

> When I mention 'religion', I mean the Christian religion; and not only the Christian religion, but the Protestant religion; and not only the Protestant religion, but the Church of England.

While overseas the fortunes of the 'established' Church of England fluctuated in accordance with the British Empire, at home its position consolidated. Unlike the imperial apparatus of administration, however, when the empire shrank the Anglican Church still continued to grow. Along with other remnants of empire (e.g. language, infrastructure, institutions and charity law) the Church remained and, having put down its roots, began the lengthy process of working out a more pragmatic relationship with the motherland. Throughout the commonwealth, the Anglican Church now still maintains a presence – often with vibrant and growing congregations (see, further, Chap. 5).

3.4.9 Status

While the relationship between the Church of England and its colonial counterparts began to change from the middle of the nineteenth century, that between Church and State remained as steadfastly sealed a century and a half earlier by the Act of Settlement and ancillary legislation. Since then its disestablishment in Ireland, Scotland and Wales, has restricted its jurisdiction to the territorial boundaries of England.

In practical terms its status allows members of the Church of England to have full recourse to the civil courts to resolve internal issues. For that reason it has never had any courts or tribunals for determining disputes between members in relation to secular matters; it has always been assumed that members of the Church will be able to obtain justice in the State's courts. While it had a separate ecclesiastical jurisdiction, in which it retained an independent source of authority enabling it to exercise powers that pre-dated the Reformation, the Church had no need of a separate secular jurisdiction as its secular legal interests where wholly subsumed into and protected by the State (see, further, Chap. 4).

[87] (1867) LR 1 Sc & Div 568.

[88] See, Fielding, H., *The History of Tom Jones: A Foundling*, Modern Library, New York, at p. 84.

As the religion of the State, the Church of England has primacy over all other religions. Although this aspect of its status has been steadily relaxed, since the exclusiveness it mostly enjoyed through the reign of the Tudors and Stuarts, judgments upholding the primacy of the national religion continued well into the twentieth century. In 1917 Sumner LJ, in *Bowman v. Secular Society Limited,*[89] felt able to declare that: "Ours is, and always has been, a Christian State. The English family is built on Christian ideas", while even in 1943 the House of Lords could confidently rule that 'Jewish faith' was so uncertain a term as to render a will void.[90]

3.4.10 The Ecclesiastical Courts, Christian Values and Anglicanism

As Lord Finlay LC commented in *Bowman* when reflecting on previous centuries of case law[91]:

> It has been repeatedly laid down by the Courts that Christianity is part of the law of the land, and it is the fact that our civil polity is to a large extent based upon the Christian religion. This is notably so with regard to the law of marriage and the law affecting the family.[92]

These sentiments echoed those expressed a few years earlier by the Master of the Rolls when, in *R v. Dibdin,*[93] he emphasised that there was no difference between Church and State in relation to the law of marriage[94]:

> Marriage ... is one and the same thing whether the contract is made in church with religious vows superadded, or whether it is made in a Nonconformist chapel with religious ceremonies, or whether it is made before a consul abroad, or before a registrar, without any religious ceremonies. So far as I am aware the Established Church has never refused to recognise any marriage which by our law is valid as being otherwise than a good marriage for ecclesiastical purposes.

The jurisdiction and judgments of the ecclesiastical courts have undoubtedly made a significant contribution to shaping the Christian values that informed the established Church and were transmitted by it across the many countries that now

[89] [1917] AC 406. See, also, *Bird v. Holbrook* (1828) 4 Bing. 628 where it was pronounced that "there is no act which Christianity forbids, that the law will not reach: if it were otherwise, Christianity would not be, as it has always been held to be, part of the law of England", *per* Best CJ at p. 641.

[90] *Clayton v. Ramsden* [1943] AC 320 (HL). See, also, *Re Moss's Will Trusts* [1945] 1 All ER 207 where Vaisey J was of the opinion that "*the Jewish faith*, whatever be the sense in which the words are used, is an expression of complete uncertainty" at p. 209.

[91] [1917] AC 406 (H.L.).

[92] Ibid, citing: *Briggs v. Hartley* (1850) 19 L. J. (Ch.) 416; *Cowan v. Milbourn* (1867) L. R. 2 Ex. 230; *De Costa v. De Paz* (1754) 2 Swanst, 487; and *In re Bedford Charity* (1819) 2 Swanst. 470, 527.

[93] *R* v. *Dibdin* [1910] P 57, CA.

[94] Ibid at p. 109.

constitute the commonwealth.[95] The legacy of values and morality, incubated through centuries of adjudication in the courts of Church and State under the aegis of the Church of England, arguably, laid the foundations for contemporary law and social policy in England and much further affield.

3.5 Conclusion

Establishing Anglicanism as the national Church of England commenced, whether as cause or effect, with England breaking its ties to the Papacy and more generally to Catholic Europe. The Reformation reset boundaries: Papal permission was no longer required to consider the significance of breaches in religious doctrine and related social implications. England learned to look wholly inward for authority to arbitrate on matters of religion and morality.

As the 'established' Church of England for half a millennium, Anglicanism has of necessity been hugely influential in shaping the secular laws of the State while the influence from other quarters has been correspondingly reduced. England has not been alone in that respect. Other nations have also developed cultures dominated by symbiotic Church/State relationships, some overtly theocratic or only recently emerging from such a fusion of authority. A feature of that process in this jurisdiction, which would have implications for the future, was the rigour with which Church and State policed the agreed benchmarks of morality through the secular and the ecclesiastical courts. This was accompanied by determined efforts to suppress other religions, dissenters, nonconformists and safeguard against the undermining effects of schisms by deporting those who posed a threat to the established Church.

The alliance of Church and State has been one which has proved remarkably enduring and productive in terms of all that it has contributed to contemporary civilisation. The post-Reformation period saw the launching of charity law throughout the many nations now known as the commonwealth, which is important for present purposes, but it also saw the common law and parliamentary democracy similarly developed and similarly transferred to form the foundations of many of our contemporary developed nations. Indeed the bigger picture is the one of the British Empire. It was within that context, with all the reality of power and extensive geographic reach implied by imperialism, that both Anglicanism and charity law found the protection necessary to secure their permeation into the culture of this and other common law nations.

[95] A long catalogue of cases beginning with *De Costa v. De Paz* (1754) 2 Swans 487, Chancery, including *Lawrence v. Smith, Murray v. Benbow* (1822) The Times 2 Feb. 1822, *Briggs v. Hartley* (1850) 19 L. J. (Ch.) 416, and ending with *Pare v. Clegg* (1861) 29 Beav 589, 54 ER 756, established that "the Courts will not help in the promotion of objects contrary to the Christian religion".

Chapter 4
The Established Church: Governance, Organisational Structure and Theology

4.1 Introduction

> The ecclesiastical law of England is as much the law of the land as any other part of the law. It is grounded in both common and statute law, and is altered from time to time by statute or by Measure, a form of legislation initiated by the Church of England but requiring Parliamentary approval.[1]

This chapter concludes the historical journey of the Church of England, as outlined in Chap. 3, by depicting its contemporary structure, content and mission. In so doing, it sketches the background for Chap. 5 which then identifies and differentiates the formative milestones that have led the Church within this jurisdiction, and elsewhere in the Anglican communion, to the present impasse in regard to an agenda of equality issues.

In bridging that gap, this chapter examines the more salient features of the Church as it is today: explaining the system of mechanisms governing its functioning and the system of beliefs governing its approach to social issues. Beginning by exploring the 'established' nature of the Church, it probes the meaning of that term, relates it to an evolving charity law context, identifying and appraising the various indices that would seem to constitute such a status. It then outlines the Church's governance, organisational and administrative arrangements: these are complex and to some extent overlapping, comprising a mix of ancient inherited structures, modern management forums and an increased reliance on sophisticated investment portfolios. The modern role and remit of ecclesiastical law and the jurisdiction of its courts are considered and the accuracy of the above quote explained. The developments that have changed the role of ecclesiastical law, reflecting those in the Church/State relationship, are identified and assessed. The chapter concludes by summarising relevant aspects of the Church's doctrines, worship and liturgy and reflecting on the possible implications for presetting values and attitudes relating to current changes in family and society.

[1] *Tyler v. UK* (1994) European Commission on Human Rights, Determination 21283/93. As cited in Hill, M. 2001. *Ecclesiastical law*, 2nd ed, 677. Oxford: Oxford University Press.

K. O'Halloran, *The Church of England - Charity Law and Human Rights*, Ius Gentium: Comparative Perspectives on Law and Justice 36, DOI 10.1007/978-3-319-04319-7_4,

4.2 The Established Church

Barro and McCleary, in their 2000 survey of 188 countries, established that 40 %, or 75 countries, could then be classified as having a State religion[2]: 113 did not have a State supported religion; 29 did and were Muslim; 22 were Catholic; 10 Protestant; 4 Buddhist; 1 Hindu; and 1 Jewish. Those without included Ireland, Australia, New Zealand, Canada and the U.S. Catholicism was typically the State religion in southern Europe (Italy, Spain and Portugal) while in the U.K. it was Protestantism. The authors assert that establishing or maintaining a State religion enables a government "to favor the majority religion by subsidizing its practices and by restricting religious expression of minorities".[3]

The 'established' nature of the Church of England is not easily defined. The Act of Settlement 1700 refers to the "Church of England as by law established" and confirms and ratifies the laws "securing the established religion". The *Companion to Law*[4] suggests the description "a church legally recognised as the official church of the State or nation and having a special position in law". There are many other similarly non-definitive references in case law, Hansard and academic literature but it is perhaps more helpful to approach the matter by examining the status of the Church. In that context there are a number of indices of its status that cumulatively convey a generalised picture of what it means for Anglicanism to be the 'established' Church of England.

4.2.1 Locus Standi *of the Church*

The above descriptions of the Church/State relationship fail to indicate the source from which the Church has derived such authority as to convince the State that it should accept Anglicanism above all other religions as worthy of its special *locus standi*. Nor, of course, is any mention made of the specific services rendered by the Church that warrant State endorsement.

4.2.2 The Broad View

Briefly put, the Church is probably best viewed as part and parcel of the architecture of the State with the monarch as its head. This is shorthand for expressing a more complicated truth which, perhaps, has been somewhat prone to obfuscation.

[2] See, Barro, R.J., and R.M. McCleary. 2005. Which countries have state religions? *The Quarterly Journal of Economics* 120(4): 1331–1370.

[3] Ibid at p. 13. Also, see, Kettell, S. 2013. State religion and freedom: A comparative analysis. *Politics and Religion* 6(3): 538–569.

[4] Oxford University Press, Oxford, 1980.

The simple fact is that Anglicanism resulted from what was essentially a monarchical coup ousting the Papacy and Catholicism. The Reformation allowed Henry VIII to abruptly and thoroughly sever all links with what for centuries had been the head of *Anglicana Ecclesia*. In typical autocrat fashion, instead of then setting up an alternative independent structure within the jurisdiction, he basically vested Papal authority in the monarchy by seeing to it that all Church appointments, Church edicts and the role of the Church in society, would thereafter be subject to State approval. The subsequent absence of any initiative to institute a replacement for the ousted Papal line of authority, with its separate and independent capacity to determine all doctrinal and some secular matters, is worthy of note. Ever since it has been the Church of England, to the exclusion of all other religions, that for five centuries has had its doctrines, edicts, court rulings and property ownership sanctioned by State law throughout the kingdom.

4.2.3 Case Law

The unquestioned 'establishment' of the Church is reflected in the scarcity of relevant case law.

The most well known case, the facts of which are only tenuously related to the issue of the legal standing of the Church, but which nonetheless provided Lord Justice Phillimore with an opportunity to extemporise on the matter, was *Marshall v. Graham*.[5] This case concerned the prosecution of two fathers for withdrawing their children from school on Ascension Day. In their defence, the fathers successfully pleaded a statutory provision that permitted a child to be withdrawn from school 'on any day exclusively set apart for religious observance by the religious body to which its parent belongs'. Thus the statute did not refer to the Church of England specifically, but the fathers claimed to belong to the Church of England. Having declared that "the accepted legal doctrine is that the Church of England is a continuous body from its earliest establishment in Saxon times" Phillimore LJ went on to suggest that "establishment means that the State has accepted the Church as the religious body in its opinion truly teaching the Christian faith and given to it a certain legal position and to its decrees it rendered under certain legal conditions, certain civil sanctions".[6] He further and famously remarked that "a Church which is established is not thereby made a department of the State".[7] This would seem accurate to the extent that the Church is not on the same footing as say the Foreign Office, as it has not been created by the State specifically to give effect to its policies; nor do State processes, staffing procedures etc. entirely govern its functioning. However, the Church is nonetheless part of the State, because its laws and institutions are assimilated into those of the State.

---

[5] (1907) 2 King's Bench 112.

[6] Ibid at p. 126.

[7] Ibid.

The case of *R v. Chief Rabbi of the United Hebrew Congregations of Great Britain and the Commonwealth, Ex p Wachmann,*[8] concerned the jurisdiction of the court to review a decision of the Chief Rabbi to terminate a rabbi's employment on the grounds of the latter's immoral conduct. Finding that "this court is hardly in a position to regulate what is essentially a religious function – the determination whether someone is morally and religiously fit to carry out the spiritual and pastoral duties of his office", Simon Brown J went on to caution "the Court must inevitably be wary of entering so self-evidently sensitive an area, straying across the well – recognized divide between Church and State". He added:

> the State has not surrendered or delegated any of its functions or powers to the Church. None of the functions that the Church of England performs would have to be performed in its place by the State if the Church were to abdicate its responsibility. The relationship which the State has with the Church of England is one of recognition, not of the devolution to it of any of the powers or functions of government.

He held that the decision of the Chief Rabbi to terminate a rabbi's employment was not reviewable: to attract the court's supervisory jurisdiction, there must be "not merely a public but potentially a governmental interest in the decision-making power in question".[9]

More recently, in *Parochial Church Council of the Parish of Aston Cantlow and Wilmcote with Billesley, Warwickshire (Appellants) v. Wallbank and another (Respondents),*[10] Nicholls LJ noted on behalf of the House of Lords[11]:

> The Church of England as a whole has no legal status or personality. There is no Act of Parliament that purports to establish it as the Church of England.[12] What establishment in law means is that the State has incorporated its law into the law of the realm as a branch of its general law.

This, in summary, seems as close as it is possible to get to defining the legal standing of the Church of England and its relationship to the State.

Laws LJ, in *McFarlane v. Relate Avon Ltd.*,[13] has since added a postscript to this discussion by warning that the legal system would not tolerate any clerical attempt to influence judicial impartiality: not even from the 'established' Church; and not even from the head of that Church. This was a religious discrimination case concerning the charity Relate in which Lord Carey, the former Archbishop of Canterbury, sought to intervene. He made suggestions as to the desired composition of the court (deemed by Laws LJ to be "deeply inimical to the public interest"[14]) and also

[8] [1992] 1 WLR 1036, 1042A.

[9] Ibid at p. 1046.

[10] [2003] UKHL 37.

[11] See, *Parochial Church Council of the Parish of Aston Cantlow and Wilmcote with Billesley, Warwickshire (Appellants) v. Wallbank and another (Respondents)* [2003] UKHL 37, per Nicholls LJ at p. 61.

[12] Ibid, citing Sir Lewis Dibdin. 1932. *Establishment in England: Essays on church and state*, 111. London: Macmillan.

[13] [2010] IRLR 872; 29 BHRC 249.

[14] Ibid at para 26.

regarding the need to address what he perceived to be an alleged "lack of sensitivity to religious belief"[15] by the judiciary when dealing with such cases. While acknowledging that "the liturgy and practice of the established Church are to some extent prescribed by law", Laws LJ added "but the conferment of any legal protection or preference upon a particular substantive moral position on the ground only that it is espoused by the adherents of a particular faith, however long its tradition, however rich its culture, is deeply unprincipled".[16] In such a context, no special privileges would be extended to the Church.

4.2.4 The Established Church and Charity Law

The contemporary judicial view, as expressed by Laws J above, took some time to evolve. In the years leading up to the mid-nineteenth century the judicial approach to charitable gifts for religious purposes accurately reflected the prevailing political policy of protecting the primacy of the established Church. As can be seen below, traces of a less than even-handed weighing of the interests of different religions were evident in charity case law well into the twentieth century.

4.2.5 Religious Discrimination

For several centuries the Christian nature of the State was not to be questioned; no other religion would be granted equal legal status. As Lord Eldon C asserted[17]:

> I apprehend that it is the duty of every judge presiding in an English Court of Justice, when he is told that there is no difference between worshipping the Supreme Being in chapel, church, or synagogue, to recollect that Christianity is part of the law of England ... he is not at liberty to forget that Christianity is the law of the land.

Such views were commonly expressed by the judiciary[18] and rigorously enforced. Indeed, a long catalogue of cases beginning with *De Costa v. De Paz,*[19]

---

[15] Ibid at para 20.

[16] Ibid at para 23.

[17] See, *In re Masters of Bedford Charity* (1819) 2 Swanston 470, 36 ER 696 at p. 712 when he refused to include Jewish children as possible beneficiaries of a fund established for the education, apprenticeship and marriage of persons engaged in religious practice.

[18] See, for example: Best CJ "There is no act which Christianity forbids, that the law will not reach: if it were otherwise, Christianity would not be, as it has always been held to be, part of the law of England", in *Bird v. Holbrook* (1828) 4 Bing. 628 at p. 641; and Sumner LJ "Ours is, and always has been, a Christian State. The English family is built on Christian ideas", in *Bowman v. Secular Society Limited* [1917] AC 406.

[19] (1754) 2 Swans 487, Chancery.

including *Lawrence v. Smith, Murray v. Benbow,*[20] *Briggs v. Hartley,*[21] and ending with *Pare v.* Clegg[22] established that "the Courts will not help in the promotion of objects contrary to the Christian religion". Gifts intended to advance a religious purpose other than that of the established Church were almost routinely held to be non-charitable. These included gifts for the education of children in Roman Catholicism,[23] for assisting study in the Jewish religion[24] and for promoting the doctrine of papal infallibility.[25]

4.2.6 Towards Equality

Not until the early part of the nineteenth century did legislation[26] gradually allow the courts to endorse as charitable trusts made for the promotion of the religious purposes of Unitarians,[27] Roman Catholicism[28] and of the Jewish faith.[29] Other signs of greater tolerance came with the abandonment of parliamentary religious hegemony which had ensured that members were drawn solely from the established Church. This had remained undisrupted until 1828 and 1829 when the election of dissenters and Catholics to the House of Commons was then permitted. With the introduction of the Places of Religious Worship Registration Act 1855,[30] equal opportunities were finally provided for all religious bodies or denominations to establish their own places of meeting for religious worship and have these certified as such by the Registrar General. It was Sir John Romilly MR in *Thornton v.* Howe[31] who first authoratively ruled that the courts would no longer make any distinction between religions. He then expressed the view that[32]:

---

[20] (1822) The Times 2 Feb. 1822.

[21] (1850) 19 L. J. (Ch.) 416.

[22] (1861) 29 Beav 589, 54 ER 756.

[23] *Cary v. Abbot* (1802) 7 Ves 490; *A-G v. Power* (1809) 1 Ball & B 145.

[24] *Da Costa v. De Paz* (1754) Dick 249, 21 ER 268; Amb 228, 27 ER 150; 2 Swanston 532, 36 ER 715. See, further, Herman, D. 2011. *An unfortunate coincidence: Jews, Jewishness & English law*. Oxford: Oxford University Press.

[25] *De Themmines v. De Bonneval* (1828) 5 Russ 288.

[26] Unitarian Relief Act 1813; Roman Catholic Charities Act 1832; and the Religious Disabilities Act 1846.

[27] *Shore v. Wilson* (1842) 9 Cl & Fin 355; *Shrewsbury v. Hornby* (1846) 5 Hare 406.

[28] *Bradshaw v. Tasker* (1834) 2 My & K 221.

[29] *Straus v. Goldsmid* (1837) 8 Sim 614; *Re Braham* (1892) 36 Sol Jo 712.

[30] 1855 c.81 (Regnal. 18 and 19 Vict). Not until the House of Lords ruling in *Bourne v. Keane* [1919] AC 815 did gifts for the saying of masses again become legal.

[31] (1862), 31 Beav 14.

[32] Ibid at pp. 19–20. Also, see, *Re Michael's Trust* (1860) 28 Beav 39 when the same judge expressly ruled that no distinction could be made in law between the status of Jewish and Roman Catholic charities.

> the Court of Chancery makes no distinction between one sort of religion and another. They are equally bequests which are included in the general term of charitable bequests. Neither does the Court, in this respect, make any distinction between one sect and another.

Subsequently the courts ruled that they would not inquire into the inherent validity of any particular religion.[33] Even so, the courts were reluctant to embrace the ethos of equality. In 1943, for example, the House of Lords felt able to rule that 'Jewish faith' was so uncertain a term as to render a will void.[34]

4.2.7 *Indices of 'Establishment'*

There are various indicators of the pre-eminent significance of the Church of England in terms of its legal, constitutional and social standing as the 'established' religion. Most telling is the fact that no other religion has comparable standing and no initiative by government or Church has ever been taken to change that arrangement.

4.2.8 *Constitutional*

The fact that the monarch is the Supreme Governor of the Church provides one clear indicator of the latter's preferential standing. As stated in canon A7 'Of the Royal Supremacy': "We acknowledge that the Queen's excellent Majesty, acting according to the laws of the realm, is the highest power under God in this kingdom, and has supreme authority over all persons in all causes, as well ecclesiastical as civil". Associated with that role are a number of ceremonial rituals. On coronation, for example, the new monarch is blessed by the Anglican Archbishop – but only after taking an oath to be the 'Defender of the Faith' – and thereafter reigns as head of both State and Church. Moreover, succession to the throne is limited to those who are members of the Church, all others are excluded.[35] The Church, and only the Church, provides a chaplain to the monarch,[36] who also serves as chaplain to the House of Commons' Speaker in which capacity the chaplain leads members of parliament in daily prayers. The post of Chaplain-General, responsible for providing a

---

[33] See, *O'Hanlon v. Logue* [1906] 1 IR 247 where Lord Walker advised that "the Court does not enter into an inquiry as to the truth or soundness of any religious doctrine, provided it is not contrary to morals, or contain anything contrary to law" at p. 259.

[34] *Clayton v. Ramsden* [1943] AC 320 (HL). See, also, *Re Moss's Will Trusts* [1945] 1 All ER 207 where Vaisey J was of the opinion that "*the Jewish faith*, whatever be the sense in which the words are used, is an expression of complete uncertainty" at p. 209.

[35] See, for example, Doe, N. 1996. *The legal framework of the Church of England*, 9. Oxford: Clarendon Press.

[36] The occupant of that post is currently Ms Rose Hudson-Wilkin, the 79th such chaplain.

chaplaincy service to all prisons, is reserved exclusively to Church of England applicants; despite the fact that by far the majority of the prison population do not have any religious affiliation.

The monarch is also still required to approve the appointment of archbishops, bishops and deans (on the recommendation of the Prime Minister) and formally opens each new session of the General Synod. The Anglican Lords Spiritual continue in their constitutional role, to the exclusion of all other religious representatives, as they have done for many centuries: the only legislature in Europe to still allow religious representation; and doing so on an explicitly discriminatory basis. The Established Church continues to fulfil a prominent civic role: its bishops and priests are exclusively responsible for performing State weddings and funerals, acts of remembrances, memorial services as well as attending to coronations.

4.2.9 Political

In practice, it is the prime minister who chooses and appoints the Archbishop of Canterbury; a power demonstrated by Margaret Thatcher when she rejected the Archbishop of York as candidate and appointed instead the bishop of Bath and Wells. The fact that the appointment of the spiritual head of the nation is a political matter, and indeed party political, clearly indicates that the office is deeply part of the 'establishment'. While there is no suggestion that the appointee is thereafter politically beholden in any way to his party political masters, the political dimension is clearly there and it cannot always be a certainty that the Church, as represented by the Archbishop and the 26 bishops in the House of Lords, will always act with political impartiality when called upon to contribute to the determination of affairs of State. Moreover, the involvement of the Archbishop in contemporary politics also indicates a high degree of Church/State complementarity: Archbishop Justin Welby, for example, continues to hold his post as a member of the Parliamentary Commission on Banking Standards.

4.2.10 Religious

Essentially, the function of the Church is the administration of the Protestant religion, by word and sacrament, on a national basis. It does so through reference to its core resources – the King James Bible, the articles and the formularies, together with its cathedrals – which have long since entered the nation's collection of religious and cultural artefacts. Ecclesiastical law, as articulated through its doctrines and adjudicated in its courts, continues to regulate this function. The most important fact, however, is that it remains the case that the State chooses to license only the Church of England to act as the national vehicle for disseminating Christianity.

4.2.11 Legal

Anglican canon law has become assimilated into national law: it and the prayer book are part of the nation's body of statute law; and therefore Anglicanism, and Protestantism more broadly, continues to have a favoured legal status relative to all other religions. The Church also enjoys a stronger relationship with government: the hierarchy of Church officials hold their posts by government appointment rather than election; all 26 Anglican bishops (the Lords Spiritual) sit as of right in the House of Lords on the government benches; and in that capacity, from which all other religious representatives are excluded, they directly influence the framing of legislation. With that right comes the entitlement not just to contribute an ethical dimension to the shaping of government policy on matters such as family planning and child care, but to have a say in determining more secular matters such as banking and monetary policy. There are obvious issues here as to why, in an increasingly secular society, bishops should be so engaged and why, in a multi-cultural society, those bishops should be exclusively from the Church of England.

4.2.12 Social

Finally, it would be remiss to overlook the community of spirit that the Church has generated and sustained to give what others would see as a characteristically English feel to our society. So much of the social fabric of country villages and inner city areas are oriented around churches, halls and the activities therein. To be a Church member is to engage with a particular set of schooling, recreation and perhaps particular party political options, to embrace an holistic commitment to a sacred and secular package: subscribing to its beliefs and manner of worship; joining in the congregational singing of its hymns and psalms; and being proud of its architectural heritage. To belong to the Established Church suggests belonging to the 'establishment' but in a classless, even timeless, fashion. It provides an invitation to join in a pattern of social/religious activity that includes the role of 'godparents', the rites of matins and evensong, church bells morning and evening, witnessing the panoply of State ceremonial occasions, and presumes attendance at the most ancient and venerable churches – if often only at times of birth, marriage and death.

4.3 Governance and Management of the Church of England

In general terms, the Church's contemporary form of governance is inherited from and continues to resemble that given to it when it emerged from the Reformation. Unlike the Catholic Church, and probably in reaction to it, Anglicanism has never favoured the top-down hierarchical model where authority is largely vested in the head of the Church. Instead it has cultivated a more collegiate style, espousing a 'conciliar structure' – a model upheld by both Scripture and tradition in which the Church met in councils to consider and resolve theological and doctrinal issues. Mediaeval canon law, as Tierney has pointed out effected "a gradual extension and systematization of the rights of the members of the corporation in relation to its head".[37] The distinctive autonomy of English cathedrals is a legacy of that early policy but so also, as an inevitable corollary, is the reliance upon compromise and consensus rather than on leadership as the preferred way of forming and implementing policy.

4.3.1 Governing Legislation

Since the Reformation, the law regulating the Church's central activity of worship has been regulated by statute (the Acts of Uniformity and now the Worship and Doctrine Measure 1974). Even when the ecclesiastical courts were called upon to decide questions of worship and doctrine, their decisions were still subject to the overriding jurisdiction of the Privy Council.

4.3.2 Process

Because the Church of England is the established Church the legislation specific to it is passed by Parliament. However, legislation in the form of a 'measure'[38] can be drafted and agreed by the General Synod before being passed to the Ecclesiastical Committee of Parliament (made up of members of both the Commons and the Lords) which examines it and advises the Legislative Committee of the General Synod as to whether or not the measure should be made. If the Synod agrees then, as provided for in the Church of England Assembly (Powers) Act 1919,[39] the Measure can be laid before Parliament. If the Ecclesiastical Committee has objections then it is referred back to the General Synod which could, in theory, opt to bypass the Committee. Measures must be passed by both the House of Commons and the House of Lords before being presented for the Royal Assent. While Parliament is not bound to accept measures, and in principle may legislate directly, in practice the 1919 Act has been interpreted as giving the Synod the right to initiate legislation on matters wholly internal to the Church.

[37] Tierney, B. 1955. *Foundations of the conciliar theory*, 130. Cambridge: Cambridge University Press.

[38] As explained in the 1919 Act: "A measure may relate to any matter concerning the Church of England, and may extend to the amendment or repeal in whole or in part of any Act of Parliament, including this Act".

[39] (9 & 10 Geo. 5 c.76).

4.3.3 *Legislative History*

The history of the formative legislation with the most important and enduring effect on the Church of England is detailed elsewhere (see, Chap. 3). The 1919 Act can be seen as completing the process of a gradual division of powers which, in the mid-nineteenth century, had seen much of the Church's legal jurisdiction transferred to Parliament. By in effect granting the Church an independent legislative capacity, this statute further separated Church and State.

The Church, however, has not rushed to use its legislative powers: in many years no measures were created. Some of the more noteworthy have been: 1947, the Church Commissioners Measure, amalgamating Queen Anne's Bounty and the Ecclesiastical Commission; 1956, the Parochial Church Councils (Powers) Measure; 1969, the Synodical Government Measure (1969 No 2), instituting the General Synod; 1974, the Worship and Doctrine Measure providing a new dispensation and giving the Church almost complete control of its liturgy; 1988, similarly the Ecumenical Relations Measure 1988 and canons B43 and B44 constituting a new dispensation with regard to ecumenical worship and ministry; and in 1993, the Priests (Ordination of Women) Measure (1993 No 2), permitting the ordination of women to the priesthood.[40] In 2004, the Clergy Discipline Measure 2004 was issued which provides four grounds for alleging misconduct, the respondent has: acted in breach of ecclesiastical law; failed to do something which he or she should have done under ecclesiastical law; neglected to perform, or been inefficient in performing the duties, of his or her office; or engaged in conduct that is unbecoming or inappropriate for the clergy.

4.3.4 *Governors*

Episcopally led and synodically governed, the Church of England is a big organisation with 27 million members and many tiers and forums for policy making and management. While the present concern is for the Church as it is led and organised within the jurisdiction, it must also be borne in mind that the Church has strong links with and responsibilities to the extensive Anglican overseas communities (see, further, Chap. 5).

4.3.5 *The Monarch*

As mentioned above, the monarch is the Supreme Governor of the Church of England and appoints archbishops, bishops and deans of cathedrals on the advice of the Prime Minister. As declared in the canons: "We acknowledge that the Queen's

[40] See, further, Cranmer, F., Lucas, J., and Morris, B. 2006. *Church and state: A mapping exercise*. London: The Constitution Unit, UCL.

most excellent Majesty, acting according to the laws of the realm, is the highest power under God in this kingdom, and has supreme authority over all persons in all causes, as well ecclesiastical as civil". All clergy must first swear an oath of allegiance to the monarch before taking office.

4.3.6 The Archbishop of Canterbury

The direct authority of the Archbishop of Canterbury is confined to England where he is recognised as *primus inter pares*, or first amongst equals, and Primate of All England. In addition to the responsibilities of that office he is also: the diocesan bishop of Canterbury; the Metropolitan of the province of Canterbury; and carries a considerable weight of responsibility in relation to Anglican communities in the 36 overseas provinces (see, further, Chap. 5). Of necessity, he bears ultimate responsibility for the administration of the Church's vast estates and the repair and maintenance of its ancient architectural heritage. Primarily, however, he provides the nation's leading voice for Christianity on the moral issues of the day.[41]

The Archbishop of York, the second in command, is known as the Primate of England.

4.3.7 Organisational Structure

The Church of England ministry is delivered at three different levels: bishops, priests and deacons. There is no requirement for clerical celibacy. Within the jurisdiction, the geographical spread of the Church includes all of England, the Isle of Man, the Channel Islands, the Isles of Scilly and a small part of Wales.[42] That area is managed through the following hierarchical organisational structure.[43]

4.3.8 Primacy

The area governed by the Primate is known as the primacy. Canterbury and York are the two provinces that together constitute both the total geographical spread of the Church within these islands and the primacy, responsibility for which lies to its primate the Archbishop of Canterbury.

[41] See, further, Hurd, D. 2001. *To lead and to serve: The report of the review of the see of Canterbury*. London: Church House Publishing.

[42] The Church of Ireland and the Church in Wales separated from the Church of England in 1869 and 1920 respectively.

[43] See, further, Maseko, A.N. 2008. *Church schism & corruption*. Durban: Lulu.com.

4.3.9 Province

The Church of England is organised into two provinces: Canterbury for the Southern Province and York for the Northern; each led by an archbishop.

4.3.10 Diocese

The two domestic Church of England provinces comprise 43 dioceses, each of which is has its own cathedral, led by a bishop. Additionally, some dioceses have supplementary bishops, often known as 'suffragan bishops' who assist the diocesan bishop with his ministry, bringing the total number of bishops to 108. The appointment of diocesan bishops is the responsibility of the Crown Nominations Committee. It is not yet permissible for women to be ordained as bishops: in 2005 the Synod voted to 'set in train' the process of allowing the consecration of women as bishops; in 2008 it voted to approve their ordination as such; but in 2012 the General Synod rejected, by a narrow margin, a motion to finalise this process. The diocese, rather than the parish, is the smallest unit of management.[44]

Cathedral clergy are appointed either by the Crown, the bishop, or by the dean and chapter. The bishops work with an elected body of lay and ordained representatives in a Diocesan Synod to manage diocesan business.

4.3.11 Archdeaconry

This is an area comprised of a number of deaneries which together form the constituency of an archdeacon. The post of archdeacon can only be held by someone in priestly orders who has been ordained for at least 6 years.

4.3.12 Deanery

A dean is a priest who is the principal cleric of a cathedral or other collegiate church and the head of the chapter of canons. If the cathedral or collegiate church has its own parish, the dean is usually also rector of the parish. A number of parishes in a rural area will constitute a deanery for which a dean, drawn from the parish vicars, will be responsible. Each parish elects a representative to serve on the Deanery

[44] See, *Halsbury's Laws (5th ed.)*, vol 3A, 2011, where a diocese is defined as "a legal division of a province and the circuit of a bishop's jurisdiction" (citing Coke) at para 164.

Synod and they in turn have a vote in the election of representatives to the Diocesan Synod. Since 1861 women have been appointed as deacons but could not be ordained, nor could they fully function as deacons, until 1987.

4.3.13 Parish

Every diocese is divided into parishes, the most local part of the organisational structure, overseen by a parish priest (usually called a vicar or rector) known as 'the Incumbent' who has discretion to appoint curates. Again, women may be ordained as priests and many have been since this first became possible in 1993.[45] The Parochial Church Council, which consists of parish clergy and elected representatives from the congregation, assists the Incumbent in managing parish business.

4.3.14 Representative Bodies

The Church is not only a big organisation, with a wide range of responsibilities – from estate management to ecclesiastical law to matters of liturgy and worship – but it is also ancient and as such has inherited organisational structures and modes of governance that do not always provide the basis for a seamless and efficient management model. This would seem to lead to some overlap in functionality between representative and management bodies.

4.3.15 The Archbishops' Council

This body, chaired by the Archbishop of Canterbury, consists of bishops, clergy and lay members. It was established by the National Institutions Measure 1998, following the recommendations of the 1994 Turnbull Report, to "co-ordinate, promote, aid and further the work and mission of the Church of England".[46] Its 19 members and 7 directors aim to give a clear sense of direction to the Church nationally, support it locally, and provide it with a focus for leadership, executive responsibility and a forum for strategic thinking and planning. Within an overall vision for the Church set by the House of Bishops, the Council proposes an ordering of priorities in

[45] In 2010, for the first time in the history of the Church of England, more women than men were ordained as priests (290 women and 273 men).

[46] See, The Turnbull Report. 1999. *Internal control: Guidance for directors on the combined code*. London: The Institute of Chartered Accountants in England & Wales.

consultation with the House of Bishops and the General Synod and takes an overview of the Church's financial needs and resources. The Council's expenditure in 2008 was £73.2 million, which included £41.6 million of grants paid to the dioceses. The powers recently acquired by the Council, under the Ecclesiastical Offices (Terms of Service) Measure 2009, have equipped it to become an additional source of ecclesiastical law.

4.3.16 Church Commissioners

This body was formed in 1948, from the union of the Queen Anne's Bounty and the Ecclesiastical Commissioners, to support the work of the Church and facilitate implementation of the Dioceses, Pastoral & Mission Measure. Consisting of 33 Commissioners, its main task is to manage an investment portfolio so as to provide an income sufficient for the Church to undertake its main projects nationwide.

Their work is organised into three main areas: spending, the Commissioners' support for the church at national and local level includes funding towards the ministry of bishops and cathedrals and for mission at parish level and they also fund a large share of clergy pensions; administrative support for the Church, by helping dioceses and local churches deal with parish boundary reorganisation, parsonage and glebe matters, settle the future of churches that have been closed for public worship while also running the national clergy payroll and managing the publication of the Crockford's clerical directory; and managing investments. In fact, approximately 15 % (over £160 million) of Church income comes from the Church Commissioners who manage assets of £4.4 billion (at the end of 2008) on behalf of the Church.

4.3.17 The Church of England Pensions Board

This body was established in 1926 by the Church Assembly, as the Church of England's pensions authority, to provide retirement services on behalf of the Church of England for those who have served or worked for the Church. It manages pension and charitable fund assets of over £500 million and also operates seven retirement homes, a nursing home and provides housing assistance for retired clergy through mortgage assistance or for rent. It has more recently been given wide powers in respect of discretionary benefits and the provision of retirement accommodation to those retired from the stipendiary ministry and their dependents.[47]

---

[47] See, further, at: www.cepb.org.uk.

4.3.18 Management Bodies

The Church of England Assembly (Powers) Act 1919 conferred authority on the Church Assembly, a nationwide body, to prepare legislative Measures for Parliament; although the two Convocations of Canterbury and York retained their ancient power to legislate by canon. This body was wound up in 1970, when most of its responsibilities were assumed by the General Synod, and ever since the Church has been governed by the General Synod, the Convocations, the Ecclesiastical, Church Commissioners, and other representative institutions.

4.3.19 Convocations

By the beginning of the fifteenth century the Provinces of Canterbury and York each had a Convocation, or ecclesiastical assembly, the membership of which consisted of the archbishop and bishops, the abbots and priors, the deans and provosts of cathedrals and collegiate churches, the archdeacons, two proctors for the clergy of each diocese and one for the chapter of each collegiate church. The clergy formed the Lower House and the bishops the Upper House of each Convocation.

Each of the Convocations still consists of the same two Houses. The Upper House consists of all the diocesan bishops in the Province, the Bishop of Dover (in the case of the Convocation of Canterbury), bishops elected by the suffragan bishops of the Province, and any other bishops residing in the province who are members of the Archbishops' Council. The Archbishop presides. The Lower House comprises clergy (other than bishops) who have been elected, appointed or chosen in accordance with Canon H2 and the rules made under it (including deans, archdeacons, proctors from the dioceses and university constituencies and clerical members of religious communities) together with ex-officio members.

Although the Convocations continue to exist and they retain some residual rights, most of their powers have been transferred to the General Synod.

4.3.20 The General Synod

The General Synod is the national assembly of the Church of England. It came into being in 1970 under the Synodical Government Measure 1969, when the Convocations ceded their ancient power to legislate by canon to the newly constituted General Synod. It replaced an earlier body known as the Church Assembly. This body is the legislative arm of the Church of England and as such is empowered to create both measures and canons. Measures of Synod have to be approved, but cannot be amended by the Westminster Parliament, before receiving the royal assent. Canons require both royal licence and royal assent. Since the 1969 legislation, canons have become, in effect, the secondary legislation of 'parent' measures. This has produced much greater legislative coherence.

The General Synod is elected from the laity and clergy of each diocese. For the purposes of this book, it is relevant to point out that this body is not one that can be said to be very representative of its increasingly pluralistic constituency: in 2012, for example, only 15 of its 467 members were black or Asian. It meets in London or York at least twice annually to consider proposed legislative initiatives, formulate new forms of worship, debate matters of national and international importance, and approve the annual budget for the work of the Church at national level. The General Synod regulates the Church of England's relations with other churches and makes provisions for matters relating to worship and doctrine. It may approve, amend, continue or discontinue liturgies and make provision for any matter (except the publication of banns of marriage) to which rubrics of the Book of Common Prayer relate and to ensure that the forms of service contained in the Book of Common Prayer continue to be available for use in the Church of England. It can make provision by act of Synod, regulation or other instrument in cases where legislation by or under a measure or canon is unnecessary.

The General Synod comprises the Convocations of Canterbury and York, joined together in a House of Bishops and a House of Clergy, to which is added a House of Laity.

4.3.21 The House of Bishops

The House of Bishops constitutes one of the three Houses of the General Synod. It consists of all 44 Diocesan Bishops of the Church of England, plus the Bishop of Dover, and seven suffragan bishops elected from among the total number of suffragan bishops (four from the Province of Canterbury, and three from the Province of York). The three Provincial Episcopal Visitors can also attend and speak when the House meets separately, but they do not having voting rights unless they are elected to the House as a suffragan bishop.

In addition to meeting as part of the General Synod, the House of Bishops meets twice a year in private session prior to scheduled sessions of the General Synod, and a summary of its decisions are then circulated to brief the General Synod. The agenda of this House varies to reflect matters relating to the exercise of episcope in the Church, but it has a special role under Article 7 of the Constitution of the General Synod. This reserves to the House the right to determine all proposals for change in relation to church doctrine, rites and ceremonies, or the administration of the sacraments.

4.3.22 The House of Clergy

Membership of the House of Clergy comprises the Lower House of the Convocation of Canterbury and the Lower House of the Convocation of York. It consists of clergy (other than bishops) who have been elected, appointed or chosen in accordance with

Canon H2 and the rules made under it (including deans, proctors from the dioceses, armed forces and university constituencies, and clerical members of religious communities) together with ex officio members and up to five co-opted members.

4.3.23 The House of Laity

Those who serve on this body do so after election by deanery Synod members. It has been claimed that this system: delivers an unrepresentative membership; that very few congregations are aware of the process of election and very few members of congregations get involved in the elections. Consequently, in July 2011, the Synod voted to explore alternatives and report with recommendations in 2013.

4.4 Ecclesiastical Law and Jurisdiction of the Courts

The ecclesiastical courts (previously known as Doctor's Commons) are a system of courts, held by authority of the Crown, as the ruling monarch is also the Supreme Governor of the Church of England.[48] The courts have jurisdiction over matters dealing with the rights and obligations of Church members, although this is now limited to controversies in areas of church property and ecclesiastical disciplinary proceedings. In England these courts, unlike common law courts, are based upon and operate along civil law procedures and in accordance with canon law-based jurisprudence.[49] Offences against ecclesiastical laws are dealt with differently depending on whether the laws in question involve church doctrine.

4.4.1 Ecclesiastical Law

Defined by Lord Blackburn as "such canons and constitutions ecclesiastical as have been allowed by general consent and custom within the realm",[50] ecclesiastical law is derived from canon[51] and civil law. It is now to be found mainly in measures and

[48] For further information, see Jones, P. *Ecclesiastical law: Comments on English ecclesiastical law and related subjects*, at: http://ecclesiasticallaw.wordpress.com/category/ecclesiastical-law-and-canon-law/.

[49] See, Doe, N. 1996. *The legal framework of the Church of England*. Oxford: Clarendon Press.

[50] See, *Mackonochie v. Penzance* (1881) 6 Appeal Cases 424, at p. 446.

[51] See, Moore, G.E. 1993. *Introduction to English Canon Law*, 3rd ed. Oxford: Oxford University Press. Also, see, *Read v. Bishop of Lincoln* (1889) 14 Probate Division 88.

canons, and continues to be administered by the ecclesiastical courts[52] the jurisdiction of which is set by the canons.[53]

Until the mid-nineteenth century, this was a significant jurisdiction which was very relevant to the daily life of English citizens as it included matters relating to matrimonial causes, testate and intestate succession, defamation and lapses in the moral conduct of the laity. Wherever legal processes provided opportunities for moral laxity the Church had a long established responsibility to intervene to safeguard the immortal soul of a recalcitrant individual: indeed, the whole *raison d'etre* of ecclesiastical law was to regulate the relationship between citizen and God.

Proceedings would conclude with: sentences or decrees; excommunications; absolutions; damages and bills of costs; prohibitions, preventing further action in the ecclesiastical court; and the transfer of proceedings to the civil court. With the closure of Doctors' Commons, the courts became marginalised as sources of ecclesiastical law, as the initiative for generating legislative provisions passed to the Convocations, General Synod and Parliament. This mix of sources has been noted by Hill who distinguishes between "[ecclesiastical] laws … some imposed by the State, some made by the Church with the concurrence of the State, and others created internally by the Church".[54]

4.4.2 Law Reform in the Mid-nineteenth Century

In the mid-nineteenth century law reform impacted upon the ecclesiastical courts. This seemed to reflect a legislative intent to separate the administration of ecclesiastical law from matters of a more temporal nature – in effect a rudimentary division of the legal system along Church/State lines. It was a quite far-reaching programme of reform for its time: the defamation jurisdiction ended in 1855; the probate jurisdiction was transferred to the newly created Court of Probate in 1857; the matrimonial and divorce jurisdictions went to the newly-created Divorce Court; with further reforms being introduced by the Ecclesiastical Courts Jurisdiction Act 1860.

The judiciary also began to pointedly distance itself from the traditional concern to safeguard the soul of an offender: reform or rehabilitation might be a judicial consideration for reasons of restoring an offender to a useful social role for their good and that of society; but it could no longer be justified on the grounds of saving

[52] See, Adam, W. 1944. *Legal flexibility and the mission of the church: Dispensation and economy in ecclesiastical law*. Farnham: Ashgate Publishing. Also, see, Denning, L.J. 1944. The meaning of ecclesiastical law. *Law Quarterly Review* 60: 235.

[53] See, *Canons of the Church of England* (7th ed.), Section G, The Ecclesiastical Courts, G 1 of Ecclesiastical Courts and Commissions.

[54] See, Hill, M. 2001. *Ecclesiastical law*, 2nd ed, 1–2. Oxford: Oxford University Press.

his or her immortal soul. As noted in *Phillimore v. Machon*[55] "the punishment of the laity for the good of their souls by the ecclesiastical courts would not be in harmony with modern ideas".

After this tidying-up of boundaries it could be said that[56]:

> ... the ecclesiastical law – is simply part of the general law of England. There is one system of law in England – some of which is ecclesiastical and some of which is temporal in nature – and matters requiring a legal determination are dealt with in the courts that are best equipped to do so: the ecclesiastical courts in the case of ecclesiastical matters and the temporal courts in the case of temporal matters. That being so, the Church of England has not sought to duplicate the work of the temporal courts with tribunals of its own dealing with the same subject matter.

However, the line drawn to demarcate the business of Church from State was never going to be watertight. As secularism gained a stronger social and political foothold, so Parliament strayed further into areas previously deemed to lie within the jurisdiction of the Church. For example, the Marriage Act 1949 and the Chancel Repair Act 1932, regulating church marriage and the repair of places of worship respectively, were both introduced by Parliament rather than the Church. During the nineteenth and twentieth centuries, most ecclesiastical law was codified in statute.

4.4.3 The Court System: Non-doctrinal Cases

Every Church of England diocese has its own Consistory Court.[57] These have been in existence since shortly after the Norman conquest with a jurisdiction that continued essentially unaffected by the Reformation. Originally, their remit was very wide indeed and covered such matters as defamation, probate, and matrimonial causes as well as a general jurisdiction over both clergy and laity in relation to matters relating to church discipline and to morality more generally and to the use and control of consecrated church property within the diocese. The judge of the Consistory Court, appointed by the bishop, was the bishop's official principal and vicar-general of the diocese and became known in his judicial capacity by the title "chancellor". The law reforms of the mid-nineteenth century left the ecclesiastical courts dealing mainly with issues relating to the management of consecrated ecclesiastical property – essentially churches and their churchyards and certain other consecrated places such as municipal burial grounds. They also retained their disciplinary powers and criminal jurisdiction in relation to the clergy – i.e. their capacity to deal with allegations of ecclesiastical offences against the clergy (for example for immoral conduct, neglect of duty or in relation to doctrinal or ceremonial matters).

---

[55] (1876) 1 Probate Division 481 at p. 487. See, also, *Marshall v. Graham* (1907) 2 King's Bench 112.

[56] See, McGregor, A. 2009. *Church of England*, 3. Westminster: The Legal Office of the National Institutions of the Church of England.

[57] Ibid, for more information on the ecclesiastical courts.

However, and despite the decline in morality cases involving the laity since the late eighteenth century, there still remains a considerable hierarchy of courts to deal with non-doctrinal issues.

4.4.4 *The Archdeaconry Court*

This, the lowest level of court reserved for such cases, is presided over by the local Archdeacon. Peculiars Certain parishes, or groups of parishes usually independent of the local court of the archdeacon, were known as 'Peculiar Courts'.

4.4.5 *The Bishop's Court*

This is the next court in the hierarchy. In the diocese of Canterbury it is known as the Commissary Court and in other dioceses as the Consistory Court. The Commissary Court is presided over by a commissary-general; a Consistory Court is presided over by a chancellor.[58] The Clergy Discipline Measure 2003 transferred to this court the criminal jurisdiction over the clergy (other than in relation to matters of doctrine, ritual or ceremonial) with modern procedures and a revised scheme of statutory penalties. Its jurisdiction was further extended by the Pastoral Amendment Measure 2006 to include the determination of "any question relating to the interpretation or enforcement of any term of any lease granted under" the provisions of that Measure (which amended s.56 of the Pastoral Measure 1983 to enable leases to be granted of parts of churches and of land belonging to or annexed to a church).

Specialist courts in the Province of Canterbury are the Court of Faculties, the Court of Peculiars and the Court of the Vicar-General of the Province of Canterbury. In the northern province there is the Court of the Vicar-General of the Province of York.

4.4.6 *The Archbishop's Court*

The next step up is the Archbishop's Court, which in Canterbury is called the Arches Court, and in York the Chancery Court; formerly known as 'Prerogative Courts'. Each court includes five judges; one judge is common to both courts. The common judge is called the Dean of Arches in Canterbury and the Auditor in York; he or she is appointed jointly by both Archbishops with the approval of the Crown.[59]

---

[58] The chancellor or commissiary-general must be 30 years old and either have a 7-year general qualification under the Courts and Legal Services Act 1990, s.71, or have held high judicial office.

[59] They must either hold a 10-year High Court qualification under the Courts and Legal Services Act 1990, s.71, or have held high judicial office.

Two members of each court must be clergy appointed by the Prolocutor of the Lower House of the provincial Convocation. Two further members of each court are appointed by the Chairman of the House of Laity; these must possess such legal qualifications as the Lord High Chancellor requires.

Commissions of Convocation are appointed by the Upper House of the Convocation of Canterbury or of York to try a bishop for an offence (except for an offence of doctrine). Both Convocations make the appointment if an Archbishop is prosecuted. This would comprise four diocesan bishops and the Dean of the Arches.

4.4.7 Appeals

Appeals from the Arches Court and Chancery Court lie to the Queen-in-Council. In practice, the case is heard by the Judicial Committee of the Privy Council, which includes present and former Lords Chancellor, a number of Lords of Appeal and other high judicial officers.

4.4.8 The Court System: Doctrinal Cases

In cases involving church doctrine, ceremony or ritual, the abovementioned courts have no jurisdiction. As Eady J explained, in *HH Sant Baba Jeet Singh Ji Maharaj v. Eastern Media Group Limited and Hardeep Singh,*[60] in an action for defamation which was stayed by the High Court because of "the well-known principle of English law to the effect that the courts will not attempt to rule upon doctrinal issues or intervene in the regulation or governance of religious groups".

4.4.9 The Court of Ecclesiastical Causes Reserved

This court hears doctrinal cases. It was established by the Ecclesiastical Jurisdiction Measure 1963 which transferred to it the criminal jurisdiction over the clergy – where the case involved a question of doctrine, ritual or ceremonial – from the Consistory Court. It is composed of three diocesan bishops and two appellate judges: with jurisdiction over both of the provinces of Canterbury and York; but it only rarely convenes.

[60] [2010] EWHC (QB) 1294 (17 May 2010).

4.4.10 *Appeals*

Jurisdiction over doctrinal cases appealed from the Court of Ecclesiastical Causes Reserved, lie to an ad hoc Commission of Review, composed of two diocesan Bishops and three Lords of Appeal (who are also members of the Judicial Committee of the Privy Council).

4.4.11 *The Role and Jurisdiction of the Privy Council*

The Judicial Committee of the Privy Council is the Court of Final Appeal for the Church of England. It hears appeals from the Arches Court of Canterbury and the Chancery Court of York; except on matters of doctrine, ritual or ceremony, which go to the Court for Ecclesiastical Causes Reserved. By the Church Discipline Act 1840 and the Appellate Jurisdiction Act 1876 all archbishops and bishops of the Church of England became eligible to be members of the Judicial Committee. The composition and role of this secular body illustrates just how much of the ecclesiastical legal system has, ultimately, been subject to secular oversight.[61]

4.4.12 *Jurisdiction*

Appeals to the Privy Council are on civil, not ecclesiastical grounds as it claims no jurisdiction to decide matters of faith or doctrine. This has been evident from at least 1880 when it was noted that[62]:

> … the Privy Council expressly disclaims having any 'jurisdiction or authority to decide matters of faith or to determine what ought in any particular to be the doctrine of the Church of England. Its duty extends only to the consideration of that which is by law established to be the doctrine of the Church of England, upon the true and legal construction of her articles and formularies.

To the extent that ecclesiastical or doctrine questions must be answered, the Privy Council restricts itself to the 'true and legal' construction of the 'articles and formularies of the church'.[63] The determination of the Privy Council to resist any change to the accepted traditional interpretation of doctrinal matters was made

---

[61] See, for example, the Acts of Uniformity and the Worship and Doctrine Measure 1974.

[62] See, Todd, A. 1880. *Parliamentary government in the British colonies*, 415. London: Longmans & Co.

[63] The 'articles' refers to the *Thirty-Nine Articles of Religion*, and the 'formularies' refers to the *Book of Common Prayer* and the *Ordinal.* Usually, all three documents are published and bound together.

clear in *Martin v.* Mackonochie[64] when it categorically denied that bishops had power to depart from the 1662 regime: "In the performance of the services, rites and ceremonies ordered by the Prayer Book, the directions contained in it must be strictly observed: no omission and no addition can be permitted". This secular sanction was further reinforced by Parliament when it rejected the prayer book measures in 1927 and 1928.[65]

4.5 Doctrine, Worship and Liturgy

The characteristic elements, that have always been of fundamental importance to the Church of England, continue to be so. The doctrine of the Church is grounded in the Holy Scriptures, and is to be found in the Thirty-nine Articles of Religion, the Book of Common Prayer, and the Ordinal: together they still govern the life of the Church. While, over time, the Church has ceded much of its former jurisdiction in relation to family matters to the secular courts, as it has with regard to the morality of the laity more generally, in matters of worship and doctrine it has acquired considerable autonomy from the State.

4.5.1 The Middle Way

Anglicanism is often viewed as having forged a middle path between Catholicism, as defined and practiced in the sixteenth century, and the more extreme versions of Protestantism as represented by Calvinism and Lutheranism: not just in terms of doctrines and modes of worship, but also as regards organizational structure and forms of governance; it avoids the dangers of both a centralised, controlling curia and a fragmentary, federation of cathedral led congregations. It is seen as cultivating and delivering through its ministry its own interpretation of Christianity.

4.5.2 Religious Beliefs

The website for the Church of England offers the following synoptic summary of its theological position[66]:

[64] (1868) 2 Law Reports Privy Council 365 at pp. 382–3.

[65] The 1944 report *Dispensation in Practice and Theory*[1] was a response to Parliament's rejection of the revised Prayer Book and its stipulation that the Church adhere to the Act of Uniformity and Book of Common Prayer of 1662. The report proposed 'the revival or extension of the practice of dispensation' (p. 159). Individual bishops, or the bishops collectively, would be empowered to dispense with obsolescent ecclesiastical laws and inconvenient liturgical rubrics. However, not until the Worship and Doctrine Measure 1974 did the Church acquire almost complete control of its liturgy.

[66] See, further, at: www.churchofengland.org.

> Anglicanism, in its structures, theology and forms of worship, is understood as a distinct Christian tradition representing a middle ground between Roman Catholicism and Protestantism and, as such, is often referred to as being a *via media* (middle way), between these traditions. Anglicans uphold the Catholic and Apostolic faith and follow the teachings of Jesus Christ. In practice Anglicans believe this is revealed in Holy Scripture and the creeds and interpret these in light of Christian tradition, scholarship, reason and experience.

There are a number of core beliefs, characteristic of this religion, that continue to represent its doctrinal position in the twenty-first century. Foremost among these is the necessity for belief in the Scriptures: the 'authorised version' is held to be the 'word of God'; and everything necessary to secure the eternal salvation of the soul is to be found therein. Also necessary for salvation is a belief in the Bible (both the Old and New Testaments) and the Gospels, particularly in the two sacraments of Baptism and the Lord's Supper. The Book of Common Prayer is unique to Anglicanism and is held to contain the rules for practicing their belief and worship, and within it the three Creeds – the Apostles', the Nicene, and the Athanasian – are of special significance. The Thirty-nine Articles is the body of beliefs that most approximates a doctrinal creed, and they serve to establish the links with and differentiate the Church from the doctrines of Catholicism and other forms of Protestantism. The articles are no longer binding and the degree to which each has remained influential varies. Arguably, the most influential has been Article VI on the sufficiency of Scripture, which states that "Scripture containeth all things necessary to salvation: so that whatsoever is not read therein, nor may be proved thereby, is not to be required of any man, that it should be believed as an article of the Faith, or be thought requisite or necessary to salvation". Article XXV approves the First and Second Book of Homilies as containing "a godly and wholesome doctrine necessary for these times", and adjudges them to be read in churches "diligently and distinctly".

While embracing some themes of the Protestant Reformation, the Church also maintains Catholic traditions of the ancient church and teachings of the Church Fathers, unless these are considered contrary to Scripture. The Catholic heritage is perhaps most strongly evident in the importance Anglicanism continues to place on the sacraments and on salvation in its liturgy and doctrine. The Church accepts the decisions of the first four ecumenical councils concerning the Trinity and the Incarnation and holds that belief in the doctrine of Transubstantiation is essential. It also celebrates the traditional sacraments, with special emphasis being given to the Holy Eucharist (sometimes referred to as Holy Communion, the Lord's Supper or the Mass) which is regarded as central to worship for most Anglicans as a communal offering of prayer and praise. Finally, it holds to the traditional system of Church order focused on the ordained ministry of bishop, priest and deacon.

4.5.3 Anglican Identity

The Church of England is a broad church, representing a wide spectrum of theological thought and practice, sometimes expressed in terms of a scale running from 'High Church' to 'Low Church'. This, however, is a shorthand and misleadingly polite allusion to a blunt fact that carries difficult implications: in England Anglicanism dates back to the Reformation and the compromises then made which, although they largely succeeded in holding the Church together, never managed to wholly bridge the quite serious divisions within it.

4.5.4 Low Church

Low Church Anglicans, or those belonging to the evangelical school of Anglicanism, adhere most strongly to the Reformation principles that prompted the initial break and which most sharply differentiate Anglicanism from Catholicism. Within Anglicanism, it is the most stringently Protestant grouping in terms of both ceremony and theology, with its roots in Puritanism. For many Reformation Puritans the proper answer to any issue is in the Bible which provides the one legitimate source of truth for Christians: they are more prone to repudiate practices and interpretations of liturgy or doctrine that are at variance with tradition; schism is a legitimate means of preserving the integrity of Anglicanism. For some Low Church adherents the sixteenth-century reformed Thirty-Nine Articles form the basis of Anglican doctrine. They represent a deep-seated attachment to the principles of the Reformation on which the Anglican settlement was founded, and the determination to preserve the standards of belief and worship then established.

4.5.5 Broad Church

Also called the Latitudinarian school of Anglican religious thought, this grouping derives from a rationalist approach to Protestant dogma, and draws from the writings of Richard Hooker, who responded to the Reformation debates by reaffirming the role of reason. Hooker is best known for his balance of authorities: Scripture, reason and tradition; with no single authority regarded as an infallible source of truth; and where decision-making requires a range of authorities and a need to balance them against each other. Adherents tend to be numerous, learned, and influential with an aversion to all that is dogmatic, supernatural, or miraculous. They lean towards the middle of the road in terms of their ceremonial preferences.

4.5.6 High Church

This party places importance on the Church of England's continuity with the pre-Reformation Catholic Church, adherence to ancient liturgical usages and the sacerdotal nature of the priesthood. Its origins lie with the Anglican bishops and divines in the seventeenth and eighteenth centuries who, while bitterly opposed to Rome, and loyally Protestant, stood above the prevailing low level of churchmanship, and put forward higher and philocatholic views, in the matters of Church authority, belief, and worship.[67] For them the Book of Common Prayer is the key expression of Anglican doctrine: *lex orandi, lex credendi* (the law of prayer is the law of belief). Although comparatively few in number, this grouping has exercised a challenging and progressive influence on the Church. This so-called 'Anglican Revival' has continued to be a potent force within Anglicanism and is prompted to acquire, whenever practical, such aspects of Catholic doctrine, liturgy, and practice, church vestments or church furniture as, from time to time, seem appropriate.

4.6 Conclusion

The mid-nineteenth century saw much of the Church's legal jurisdiction transferred to Parliament. With the introduction of the 1919 Act the process of separating the powers of Church and State was taken a stage further but, arguably, any independent legislative capacity retained by the Church was and remains largely illusory. Such is the 'established' nature of the Church that, as presently constituted, it cannot in any true sense achieve meaningful independence from the State.

Stripping from the Church its centuries old jurisdiction in respect of certain matters (most notably defamation, probate, marriage and divorce), and entrusting these to parliament, has very tangibly secularised the legislation relating to core areas of morality. However, the Church in its 'established' role continues to influence at least policy and practice, particularly with regard to its central concern for morality in the context of family law: which most often focuses on defending the Nazarene model of the marital family unit; and attacking any permission given for sexual practices that are perceived to threaten it. The effectiveness of the Church in pursuing its traditional moral agenda is handicapped by its mode of governance, cumbersome tiers of management, estate preservation and cashflow concerns, and by the resistance it faces from an evermore pluralistic and secular society. Nonetheless, because of its 'established' status, it remains in a much stronger position to influence the shaping of the nation's laws, policy and practice than any other religion or any other group in our society. It is precisely this extra leverage that places a leadership onus on the Church of England to find a way of reconciling the differences between those who abide by its traditional moral agenda and those who push for a more whole-hearted acceptance and implementation of human rights.

[67] See, in particular, Cardinal John Henry Newman (21 February 1801–11 August 1890) who, as leader of the Oxford Movement, sought to restore many Catholic beliefs and traditional forms of worship to the Church of England. A large number of those who took part in the movement, most notably its leader, became Catholics, while others, in remaining Anglicans, gave a new and pro-Catholic direction and impulse to Anglican thought and worship.

Chapter 5
Anglicanism at Home and Abroad

5.1 Introduction

> The concept of our established Church is occasionally misunderstood and, I believe, commonly underappreciated. Its role is not to defend Anglicanism to the exclusion of other religions. Instead the Church has a duty to protect the free practice of all faiths in this country ... the Church of England has created an environment for other faith communities and indeed people of no faith to live freely.

This defence of the Church of England was, appropriately, given by Queen Elizabeth at Lambeth Palace in 2012. While sincere and accurate, the sentiments expressed are perhaps more important because they indicate that its Supreme Governor felt the need to acknowledge that the Church is misunderstood and needs to be explained and defended.

This chapter begins with a contemporary profile of the Church. It sets out the main difficulties and discusses some of the opportunities it now faces; particular attention being given to the changes affecting the clergy and the inescapable logic and likely impact of demographic trends. It explains that the Church of England is part of the Anglican Communion, a worldwide family of churches in more than 160 different countries, and considers why and to what effect so many Anglicans from such a diverse mix of cultures have joined in their common purpose. It outlines the functions of the different 'instruments' which serve to unify the Communion. The chapter then sets out the route map by which the Communion arrived at its present impasse. It identifies the sequence of contentious issues, assesses how the various member nations coped and analyses the outcomes. The intrinsic nature of the series of 'moral imperatives' that caused difficulties for the Communion is considered. Of these red line issues, the most divisive have been the ordination of women, gay priests and the legislative introduction of gay marriage.

It also focuses more particularly on the Church's difficulties in relation to homosexuality. The Church has had a policy of allowing for the ordination of gay priests, as long as they are celibate, but the election of an openly gay bishop in America prompted a national and international examination on the rights of homosexual

K. O'Halloran, *The Church of England - Charity Law and Human Rights*, Ius Gentium: Comparative Perspectives on Law and Justice 36, DOI 10.1007/978-3-319-04319-7_5,

clergy. Along with the Church, the wider Anglican Communion has also been wrestling with whether to sanction same-sex blessings and the challenge presented by gay marriages. These issues are causing serious divisions within the Church and throughout the Anglican Communion.

5.2 Anglicanism at Home

As the second millennium gets underway, all indications point to this being a particularly challenging time for the Church of England. Partly this is a natural consequence of English society becoming so much more pluralistic and secular within a relatively short period: while society has changed, the Church has steadfastly struggled to remain consistent. The changing social context has inevitably given rise to questions regarding: the appropriateness of the Church's continuing 'established' role; its capacity to respond theologically and humanely to a range of equality issues now centering on matters such as the ordination of women[1] and gay marriage; and how to accommodate the deep divisions within the Church and defuse the growing threat of schism. It would be a mistake, however, to underestimate the Church's resilience.

5.2.1 The Church of England: A Contemporary Statistical Profile

As with most traditional religions, at least in western Europe, the customary trends relied upon to measure the vitality of the Church do not reveal any grounds for optimism: while, in numerical terms, the non-Christian and evangelical religions continue to grow, the Church of England has been in decline since the Second World War.

5.2.2 Church Membership and Participation

Currently, while there are an estimated 27 million baptized members of what continues to be the main religion in England, Sunday attendance figures amongst Anglicans have dropped by some 10 % over the last decade. In fact it has been estimated that over the 36 year period from 1971 to 2007 the Church of England declined by 43 % while the population of the UK grew by 9.37 % indicating that the

[1] It has been estimated that least 430 priests left the Church of England due to the ordination of women and the cost of compensation was £26 million (see, further, the Telegraph, 6th February 2004).

share of the population going to the Sunday service in the Church fell by 52 % between 1971 and 2007.[2] The Church's website[3] suggests that only 1.1 million people, some 2 % of the population, now attend church on a weekly basis, and only 1.7 million, or 3 %, once a month, despite the fact that around half the population still profess themselves Anglicans. Moreover the outlook is not good: church attenders are elderly, statistics show that few 15–30 year olds go to church; there is a steady decline in the numbers choosing a church marriage service; and baptisms have fallen from about 67 % in 1950 to now less than 20 %.

On the other hand, as is pointed out on the Church's website: approaching 3 million people participate in a Church of England service on Christmas Day or Christmas Eve; 35 % of the population attend a Christmas service of some sort, rising to 42 % in London, nationally, and 22 % among those of non-Christian faiths. The spread of an evangelical approach to worship is also generating something of a 'New Age' revival with some churches now experiencing larger, younger and more enthusiastic congregations.[4]

The Church continues to have the largest following of any denomination or faith in Britain today: more than 4 in 10 in England regard themselves as belonging to the Church of England, while 6 in 10 consider themselves Christian. Each year 3 in 10 are said to attend regular Sunday worship and more than 4 in 10 attend a wedding in their local church, while still more attend a funeral there. In 2009, 43 % of adults attended a church or place of worship for a memorial service for someone who had died, an increase of 22 % since 2001.

5.2.3 Maintenance of Church Infrastructure

The Church has an extensive architectural heritage to maintain: 14,500 places of worship in England are listed as being of special architectural or historic interest; and three church and cathedral locations are 'World Heritage Sites' (Durham Castle and Cathedral, Canterbury Cathedral, St Augustine's Abbey & St Martin's Church, and Westminster Abbey and St Margaret's Church). The costs are considerable: approximately £110 million per annum is currently spent on repairs to churches; while, in 2006, it was estimated that it would be necessary to spend £925 million for repairs over the following 5 years. As the number of parishes remains set at 13,000 and the total of Anglican churches is little altered at around 16,000, the burden of infrastructure maintenance costs is therefore falling on a shrinking Church membership and this is causing real concern regarding the future ability to retain and adequately maintain the Church's venerable building stock.

---

[2] See, further, at: http://www.whychurch.org.uk/shrinking_cofe.php.

[3] See, further, at: www.churchofengland.org.

[4] See, for example, the Holy Trinity, Brompton, Kensington and the broader impact of 'the Alpha course', at: www.htb.org.uk/alpha.

5.2.4 The Church of England: Changes in the Clergy

The controversy associated with the ordination of women has been deeply divisive for the Church, at least in the short-term, but it has also served to deflect attention from other significant developments.

5.2.5 Declining Numbers

In 2011 the total number of ordained clergy – stipendiary and non-stipendiary, male and female – reached 11,418, with women making up 31 % of the total. However, the decline in paid clergy has been quite rapid. On the Church's own statistics, the beginning of the new millennium has already seen a fall of over 20 % to barely 8,000; quite a number having left to join the Ordinariate. The inexorable pace of existing demographic trends continues to exact its own toll: many clergy and many parishes are combining under the ministry of one permanent priest and one retired; a great number of churches are virtually empty on Sundays and are falling into disuse; and there are now more people claiming a clergy pension than there are ordained stipendiary clergy.

5.2.6 The Ordination of Women

In 1992 the General Synod voted for the ordination of women as priests and, in 1994, the first 32 women were ordained. By 2011 there were 1,763 women in full time parochial appointments: a 50 % increase since 2000; accordingly, one in every five paid parish clergy in the Church of England are now female.[5] The figures also show that while 23 % of the total stipendiary clergy are female, women make up more than half (54 %) of non-stipendiary positions. Of the Church's 3,575 female clergy, 46 % are in unpaid positions, compared to only 18 % of 7,843 male clergy.

Although the prospect of women being ordained as priests was itself very contentious, the more recent prospect of their ordination as bishops aroused an even greater level of dissent among the clergy (see, further, below).

5.2.7 Gay Clergy

Perhaps the first formal proclamation of the Church's views, on what had been a simmering area of contention, came in 1994 with the House of Bishops publication *Issues in Human Sexuality*,[6] which stated: "the clergy cannot claim the liberty to enter into

[5] The number of female clergy in the Church of England has passed 3,500 according to the latest figures released by the Church of England. Women accounted for 49 % or 245 of 2011s 504 ordinations.

[6] See, *Issues in Human Sexuality, a Statement by the House of Bishops*, Church House Publishing, December 1994.

sexually active homophile relationships"; an approach endorsed in 1998 by the Lambeth conference in resolution 1–10.[7] Since then the broad Church that is Anglicanism had in practice allowed considerable local diversity in attitudes towards gay clergy and indeed towards LGBT membership. There the matter rested until Jeffrey John, a gay priest, was elected suffragan Bishop of Reading in May 2003 (from which post he was induced to withdraw), followed in June by the ordination of Gene Robinson, a gay priest, to the post of Bishop of New Hampshire in the U.S. A few months later, against that background, the government introduced the Civil Partnership Act 2004. From that point, when it became possible for gay clergy and their partners to achieve equality of legal and social status with their lay counterparts, it was inevitable that the Church's internal conflicts on this issue would become public and political.

5.2.8 The Clergy and the Civil Partnership Act 2004

This recognition of the legitimacy of gay partnerships was perhaps the first serious State/Church clash on a fundamental Church belief – that the only permissible sexual relationship was both heterosexual and confined to a marital relationship (with a subtext that its purpose was procreation) – and a measure of how far apart the views of Church and State had grown since *R v. Dibdin*.[8] There had, of course, been previous skirmishes (recourse to contraception and abortion, baptism of children of unmarried parents, marriage in a registry office, divorce, the marriage of divorcees) but this was a 'game-changer' for the Church.[9]

The new groundbreaking statute contained several religious caveats, concessions to the Church, which sought to distinguish partnership from marriage: it could not be entered into on religious premises; and no religious service could be used while the civil partnership registrar is officiating at the signing of a civil partnership document. Nonetheless its success can be judged by the take up: from its introduction in 2005 to the end of 2010, some 47,000 partnerships had been registered in the UK. Essentially, like marriages in registry offices, civil partnership ceremonies are devoid of any 'sacramental' element. However, in substance the legal incidents of a civil partnership relationship are almost identical to those of a marital relationship.[10] In December 2011 the resemblance increased when the ban on civil partnership ceremonies being conducted on religious premises was removed.

---

[7] See, Lambeth Conference 1998, Resolution 1.10 *Human Sexuality*, at: http://www.anglicancommunion.org/windsor2004/appendix/p3.6.cfm.

[8] *R* v. *Dibdin* [1910] P 57, CA (see, further, Chap. 3).

[9] See, for example, Humphreys, J. 2006. The civil partnership act 2004, same-sex marriage and the Church of England. *Ecclesiastical Law Journal* 8(38): 289 *et seq*.

[10] Ibid. Note that the effect of the Civil Partnership Act 2004 together with the Gender Recognition Act 2004 is to require a married couple wishing to maintain their relationship after one of the couple undergoes gender reassignment to have their marriage annulled or dissolved and enter a civil partnership. Similarly, civil partners wishing to maintain their relationship after one party undergoes gender reassignment will have to dissolve their partnership and enter into a marriage.

For the clergy, while there was nothing in the civil law prohibiting them from blessing a couple after a civil partnership had been finalized,[11] there remained the theological issue of thereby giving formal Church recognition to the legitimacy of such a relationship. In 2004, in an early warning of forthcoming difficulties, the Chairman of the Lambeth Commission, in his foreword to the *Windsor* Report[12] deplored "the authorising by a diocese of the Anglican Church of Canada of a public Rite of Blessing for same sex unions".[13] Subsequently, the House of Bishops' Pastoral Statement 'affirms' that clergy of the Church of England should not provide services of blessing for those who register a civil partnership.[14] It also confirmed that lay homosexuals who had entered into civil partnerships would still be eligible for the sacraments of baptism, confirmation, and communion.

5.2.9 *Joining the Ordinariate*

In November 2009, Benedict XVI established the Personal Ordinariate for Anglicans who wanted to join the Catholic Church. The Personal Ordinariate of Our Lady of Walsingham was subsequently established in the UK in 2011 to allow Anglicans to enter into the full communion of the Catholic Church whilst retaining much of their heritage and traditions.[15] This body, led by three former Anglican bishops, receives those, mainly High Church Anglicans who, guided by their beliefs, have turned away from the Church of England and towards Catholicism. Initially it welcomed the many clergy opposed to women priests. Indeed, the rules on divorce and family led to a wave of about 600 Anglicans officially leaving the Church of England in early 2011 in protest at the move towards the ordination of women as bishops.

On New Year's Day, 2013, half of the Anglican nuns in the Community of St Mary the Virgin at Wantage in Oxfordshire (founded in the nineteenth century), joined the Ordinariate forming a new body to be known as the Sisters of the Blessed Virgin Mary. This was the biggest departure of nuns or monks since the first English woman priest was ordained in 1994. Currently the Ordinariate comprises about 1,500 people, 81 priests and some seminarians.

[11] Indeed, *Issues in Human Sexuality* 1991, provides that the Church must not reject lay people who sincerely believe that 'living in a loving and faithful homophile partnership, where mutual self-giving includes the physical expression of their attachment' (para 5.6).

[12] See, Eames, R. 2004. Archbishop of Armagh, Lambeth Commission on Communion. *The Windsor Report 2004*. London: The Anglican Communion Office, at: http://www.anglicancommunion.org/windsor2004/appendix/p3.6.cfm.

[13] In 2002, the Anglican Church of Canada, the diocese of New Westminster, had voted to allow the blessing of same-sex unions by those parishes choosing to do so.

[14] See, the House of Bishops' Pastoral Statement on civil partnerships (25 July 2005), para 17, at: www.churchofengland.org/media-centre/news/2005/07/pr5605.aspx.

[15] See, further, at: http://www.ordinariate.org.uk.

5.2.10 The Church of England: Public Benefit Service Provision

The Church's nationwide engagement in service provision takes various forms including: pastoral care for the sick, elderly, disabled and others in need; community activities centred around local church halls; some specialised housing; and such contracted provision as may be agreed with government departments. The involvement of many volunteers in Church service delivery not only defrays service expense, with additional user friendly benefits, but it also cultivates a more generalised healthy sense of civic responsibility and community cohesion.[16]

5.2.11 Education

The Church has, for some centuries, had a particular investment in schools. Currently, according to the Dept of Education, of the 6,814 faith based schools that now constitute 34 % of the maintained sector, approximately 67 % are Church of England.[17] While many of the country's most exclusive private schools (e.g. Westminster School and King's School Canterbury) are wholly owned by the Church so also, according to the latest available statistics, are one in four primary schools and one in 16 secondary schools. In total, approaching one million pupils are now being educated within the Church of England system of schools which consists of: more than 4,484 primary and middle schools; 193 secondary schools; and 50 sponsored and 217 converted academies. In the *Chadwick Report,*[18] published in 2012, the Church of England declared an intention to establish 200 more Anglican schools over the next 5 years and estimates that 70 % (3,360) of its 4,700 state schools will become academies within that period. Access to the services of the nation's largest and most effective education provider[19] is highly prized and filtered through the use of faith-based selection tests and church attendance rates. However, whether structured as 'foundation or trust schools', 'academies' or 'free schools' the Church's schools will almost always have: charitable status; government grants (of up to 90 % of the total cost) towards capital costs of the buildings and 100 % of running costs (including teachers' salaries); and be allowed to impose faith restrictions on staff employment, admissions, curriculum

[16] See, further, Church of England, *Resourcing Christian Community Action,* at: http://how2help.churchofengland.org/home.

[17] See, further at http://www.education.gov.uk/aboutdfe/foi/disclosuresaboutschools/a0065446/maintained-faith-schools.

[18] See, further, at: http://www.churchofengland.org/media/1418393/the%20church%20school%20of%20the%20future%20review%20-%20march%202012[1].pdf.

[19] Three-quarters of its schools are judged 'good' or 'outstanding' by Ofsted (the government regulatory body for education) as opposed to 57 % of all State schools.

content and on school worship. This heavily subsidised control of a large portion of the nation's schools has given rise to controversy. At the end of January 2013, on the eve of his appointment as Archbishop and in contrast to previously stated government policy,[20] Justin Welby proclaimed: "in the country as a whole the Church of England alone educates a million children every day … are we going to take the opportunities that are there for the grasping to bring people to know and love Jesus Christ?".[21] The British Humanist Association promptly condemned what it perceived to be a declaration of intent to use the schools as an expedient platform for proselytism.[22]

5.3 The Anglican Communion

The Anglican Communion, or Anglican Episcopal family, is said to consist of an estimated 85 million members spread across some 165 countries: approximately one-third are members of the Church of England; the 11 provinces in Africa have some 36.7 million members; while the North American provinces – the Episcopal Church in the U.S. with maybe 2.4 million members, and the Anglican Church of Canada with perhaps 740,000 members – represent only 4 % of Anglicans worldwide. They belong to 38 provinces, including the two in England,[23] and coalesce around four United Churches and six other churches: provinces may take the form of national churches (such as in Canada, Uganda or Japan) or a collection of nations (such as the West Indies, Central Africa or Southeast Asia). Each province is autonomous, with its own doctrine and liturgy derived from Anglicanism as it is known in England, and with its own system of governance headed by a primate. While united by mutual agreement on essential Anglican doctrines and a wish to further

[20] See, Secretary for the Communities and Local Government Department, in response to a question in the House of Commons following the introduction of the government White Paper *Communities in control: real people, real power*, when he explained: "I am concerned to ensure that if faith groups become involved, they do so on a proper footing – not by evangelising or proselytising, but by providing services in a non-discriminatory way to the whole community" (July 2008). Also, note, Office for Democratic Institutions and Human Rights, Advisory Council, 'Toledo Guiding Principles on Teaching about Religion and Beliefs in Public Schools', OSCE Office for Democratic Institutions and Human Rights (ODIHR), Warsaw, 2007.

[21] See, further, British Humanist Association, at: http://humanism.org.uk/2013/02/04/concerns-over-new-archbishops-desire-for-church-role-in-welfare-services/.

[22] Andrew Copson, the chief executive of the British Humanist Association, commented: "80 % of Britons are not members of the Archbishop's church and research shows that even those who consider themselves Christian do not wish a role for the Church in areas of public policy and service delivery. Transferring previously secular public services to the Church of England and other religious bodies, which have an agenda to convert people and the legal powers to discriminate in employment and service delivery, is sectarian and short-sighted".

[23] Note that the Church of Ireland and the Church in Wales separated from the Church of England in 1869 and 1920 respectively and are autonomous churches in the Anglican Communion.

develop their fellowship,[24] the Communion is currently facing considerable divisive pressures. As has been said[25]:

> There remains a very real danger that we will not choose to walk together. Should the call to halt and find ways of continuing in our present communion not be heeded, then we shall have to begin to learn to walk apart.

5.3.1 Definition

Halsbury[26] describes the Anglican Communion as 'a fellowship of churches historically associated with the British Isles which have certain characteristics in common, including standards of faith and doctrine and, to some extent, forms of worship'. The reference to 'communion' indicates that membership is for those who feel able to make mutual and full participation in the sacramental life of their Church available to all communicant Anglicans. Another phrase which is commonly found in recent Anglican documents to describe the relations between national Anglican Churches is 'bonds of affection'.

5.3.2 Interpretation

In practice this amorphous body of loosely defined 'Anglicans' is essentially bound together by a common wish to steer a moderate Protestant path between Catholicism on one side and the more extreme Lutheran/Calvinist factions of Protestantism on the other: to hold to 'the middle way'. Together all members of the Anglican Communion share a commitment to the same set of basic beliefs: in the Bible, both the Old and New Testaments; in the Nicene and Apostles' Creeds; in the sacraments of Baptism and Holy Communion; and in the traditional Christian Episcopate with the bishop at the centre. This 'quadrilateral', drawn up in the nineteenth century, is one of the definitions of Anglican faith and ministry. Another is a style of worship which has its roots in the Ordinal and the Book of Common Prayer: indeed the latter, unique to Anglicanism although subject to many revisions and to a degree of customization in some countries, is still the touchstone for Anglicanism in many very different cultures and is acknowledged to be one of the binding ties of the Anglican Communion. Other rites shared in common among the Communion include Confirmation, Reconciliation, Marriage, Anointing of the Sick, and Ordination.

---

[24] See, further, Anglican Communion website at: http://www.anglicancommunion.org/tour/index.cfm.

[25] See, The Lambeth Commission on Communion. 2004. *The Windsor Report 2004*. London: The Anglican Communion Office, at para 157.

[26] Hailsham, L.D. 1975. *Halsbury's laws of England*, vol. 14, 4th ed, 313. London: Butterworths.

It must be borne in mind, however, that only in Britain does Anglicanism date back to the Reformation: the theological compromises then made, which have carried forward into the context of current social change, are not shared (at least not to the same extent) by others in the Communion and are entirely absent from many. In that respect, the Church is differently situated from its overseas Anglican counterparts in relation to the theological implications arising from the same agenda of contentious social issues.

5.3.3 Brief Historical Background

The Anglican Communion has its origins in the British Empire: as the latter expanded so did the spread of Anglicanism; but as it contracted and British colonies became independent from England, the churches also gained independence. Thereafter Anglicanism continued to take hold and flourish in many nations despite the collapse of empire or, as in countries such as Japan, entirely regardless of that fact. The expansion brought with it a growing awareness of religious commonality and a need to construct mechanisms to express and facilitate that sense of unity.[27]

5.3.4 Imperial Beginnings

The first permanent English settlement in North America was in Virginia in 1607, and from 1610 official provision was made for worship according to the doctrines of the Church of England. There were penalties for non-attendance at services, parish structures were created and the 1604 Ecclesiastical Canons applied to church life. The Church of England was designated the established church in Virginia in 1609, in New York in 1693, in Maryland in 1702, in South Carolina in 1706, in North Carolina in 1730, and in Georgia in 1758. At this time the ministers were episcopally ordained, and there were no bishops, but the Church of England was actively pursuing its mission of 'spreading the word of God'.[28] The colonial governor granted licences and exercised supervision. The American War of Independence (1775–1783) ended these arrangements.

Following the American Revolution, while the Thirteen Colonies were no longer under British rule the need for a bishop to minister to the needs of

[27] See, Tong, R. 2012. *Judicial intervention in the affairs of unincorporated religious associations in New South Wales*. Unpublished thesis submitted for degree of Doctor of Juridical Science, Faculty of Law, QUT, Brisbane. The author acknowledges with thanks the historical outline material drawn from this thesis.

[28] The Anglican Communion can trace much of its growth to the older mission organisations of the Church of England such as the Society for Promoting Christian Knowledge (founded 1698), the Society for the Propagation of the Gospel in Foreign (founded 1701) and the Church Missionary Society (founded 1799).

Anglican congregations remained, so they formed their own dioceses and national church – the Episcopal Church in the United States of America – which declared its independence from the Church of England. In 1789 it became "the first Anglican Province outside the British Isles."[29]

In time it became natural to group other dioceses into provinces and a metropolitan bishop was then duly appointed to each.[30] In 1784 a bishop was consecrated for America, followed by two more in 1787 and a third in 1790. Additional colonial dioceses were erected in Quebec, in 1793; Calcutta, in 1814 (comprising all the area governed by the British East India Company); Barbados and Jamaica, in 1824; Australia in 1836; and New Zealand and Cape Town in 1847. By 1840 there were still only ten colonial bishops for the Church of England; but even this small beginning greatly facilitated the growth of Anglicanism around the world.

5.3.5 *Non-established Anglicanism*

Initially it had been tacitly understood that the transplanting of Anglicanism overseas had brought with it the status of 'established' Church. However, in the mid-nineteenth century, a series of cases clarified this issue: except where specifically established, the Church of England overseas had just the same legal standing as any other church (see, further, Chap. 3). By 1880, the leading constitutional historian, Alpheus Todd, could summarise the situation as follows[31]:

> It is unlikely that the Imperial Parliament will entertain any further proposals for legislation affecting ecclesiastical questions in the colonies. The *status* of the Anglican Church in the British colonies is one of ecclesiastical independence. This was the natural and inevitable outcome of the decision of the Privy Council in 1865, in the case of Bishop Colenso, and of the judgment of the House of Lords in 1867, in *Forbes v. Eden*.[32] This case has been termed the charter of colonial church independence. It establishes and defines the powers of general synods, as being supreme in all matters over which civil courts have no jurisdiction. It is confirmed in Upper Canada by the decision in the case of *Dunnet v Forneri*,[33] which declares that the court of chancery has no jurisdiction to inquire into the regularity of the excommunication of an individual, there being no question of property or civil rights involved.

Essentially, the Church in each colony would be left to make its own arrangements for self-management. Both in the United States and in Canada, the new

[29] See, *Episcopal Ministry: The Report of the Archbishops' Group on the Episcopate, 1990*, Church House Publishing, 1990, at p. 123. Followed by the creation of the Church of England in Canada in those North American colonies that remained under British control.

[30] The Consecration of Bishops Abroad Act 1786 allowed bishops to be consecrated for an American church, without the necessity for any allegiance to the British Crown.

[31] See, Todd, A. 1880. *Parliamentary government in the British colonies*, 415. London: Longmans & Co.

[32] (1867) LR 1 Sc & Div 568.

[33] 25 Grant Ch. Cas. 199.

autonomous Anglican churches with their own bishops proceeded to develop novel models of self-government, collective decision-making, and self-supported financing, consistent with the separation of religious and secular identities. In due course, this model was adopted by the many churches subsequently created in Africa, Australasia and the Pacific region. In the nineteenth century the term 'Anglicanism' was first coined to describe the common religious tradition of these churches in acknowledgement of the roots of their shared common identity.

5.3.6 Forging Formal Links

From the late 1840s, there was general interest in England in the reform of relationships with the colonies, including the relationship between the Church of England and the overseas Anglican communities. Attempts were made to have the imperial Parliament pass framework legislation to secure the position of the Church of England in the colonies and particularly in relation to the management of the internal affairs of the colonial churches. In 1841, the Colonial Bishoprics Council was established and soon many more dioceses were created.

It was the rapid extension of Anglicanism into non-English cultures, the growing diversity of prayer books, and the increasing interest in ecumenical dialogue, leading to questions regarding the parameters of the Anglican identity that resulted in the first Lambeth conference in 1868. At that conference Archbishop Longley, in words that now seem prescient, assured the assembled bishops that:

> It has never been contemplated that we should assume the functions of a general synod of all the churches in full communion with the Church of England, and take upon ourselves to enact canons that should be binding upon those here represented. We merely propose to discuss matters of practical interest, and pronounce what we deem expedient in resolutions which may serve as safe guides to future action.

Two years, later William Reed Huntington, an American Episcopal priest, published *The Church Idea, an Essay toward Unity.* The issues he raised regarding the grounds for attempting Church reunification triggered the Chicago-Lambeth Quadrilateral which is regarded by many Anglicans as having formulated the basic requirements for achieving a communal Anglican identity. The essential Huntington points were first wholly approved in a resolution of the House of Bishops of the American Episcopal Church, meeting in Chicago in 1886 before being endorsed in 1888 by the Quadrilateral in resolution 11. This scaled-back version of the resolution passed at Chicago read as follows:

> That, in the opinion of this Conference, the following Articles supply a basis on which approach may be by God's blessing made towards Home Reunion:
>
> (a) The Holy Scriptures of the Old and New Testaments, as "containing all things necessary to salvation," and as being the rule and ultimate standard of faith.
> (b) The Apostles' Creed, as the Baptismal Symbol; and the Nicene Creed, as the sufficient statement of the Christian faith.

(c) The two Sacraments ordained by Christ Himself – Baptism and the Supper of the Lord – ministered with unfailing use of Christ's Words of Institution, and of the elements ordained by Him.
(d) The Historic Episcopate, locally adapted in the methods of its administration to the varying needs of the nations and peoples called of God into the Unity of His Church.

The resolution, coming at a time of rapid expansion of the Anglican Communion, primarily in the territories of the British Empire, provided a basis for a shared ethos, and one that became increasingly important as colonial churches influenced by British culture and values, evolved into national ones influenced by local norms.

In 1908 a committee of the Lambeth Conference spoke of "the universal recognition in the Anglican Communion of the ancient precedence of the see of Canterbury". In 1924 it was proclaimed that it "owes its far-reaching influence to the spirit in which its experience and wisdom have been placed at the service of the Church in every province and diocese throughout the whole Anglican Communion". In the 1968 Lambeth Conference it was stated that "within the college of bishops it is evident that there must be a president. In the Anglican Communion this position is presently held by the occupant of the historic see of Canterbury, … this primacy is found to involve, in a particular way, that care for all the churches which is shared by all the bishops". Thereafter, further testimonies have been given to the value of the Communion and to the related importance of the Archbishop who has been described as "the focal point of our communion", and as the bishop who is "freely recognised as the focus of unity".

5.3.7 Organisational Structures: The 'Instruments of Communion'

The relationship between the Church of England and the overseas Anglican churches is not underpinned by a formal constitution or by international church law, but rather by a shared heritage, by ways of worshipping and by the relationships – the "bonds of affection" – between its members worldwide. It rests on a consensual understanding, that they can usefully share and work together on matters they have in common, rather than on any contractual agreement. Indisputably, the Archbishop of Canterbury functions as the head of the Anglican Communion as there can be no membership of the Communion without membership of Anglicanism, the governorship and spiritual leadership of which has always been vested in his office.

Insofar as there can be said to be formal structures that shape and give direction to the Communion these 'instruments' are the Lambeth Conference, the Anglican Consultative Council, and the Primates' Meeting. In addition, work has for some time been underway on what seemed destined to be in due course a fourth such 'instrument' – the Anglican Covenant. In the absence of any binding authority in the Communion, these international bodies have primarily served as vehicles for consultation and persuasion but are now increasingly being treated as forums for working out possible parameters for achieving conformity in certain areas of doctrine, discipline, worship, and ethics. The centrality of the office of the Archbishop of Canterbury is evident in that only he has the right to convene and oversee the Lambeth Conference and the Primates Meeting, and he is the President of the formally constituted Anglican Consultative Council.

5.3.8 *The Lambeth Conference*

This gathering of the bishops of the Anglican Communion is at the personal invitation of the Archbishop of Canterbury, and usually takes place every 10 years. The first was held in 1867 at Lambeth Palace. As numbers grew the Conference moved to Canterbury, and the last in 2008 involved more than 800 participant bishops. They have demonstrated that bishops of disparate churches can manifest the unity of the church in their episcopal collegiality despite the absence of universal legal ties. The Conference has always renounced any intent to legislate for change in Anglicanism and any intent to adopt the powers that would enable it to do so, but instead confines itself to passing advisory resolutions. It can, however, repeal its own resolutions (in 1939 it overturned its earlier ban on contraception).

More recently, and most importantly – for this book, for the Church and for the Anglican Communion – was the resolution that has become known as 'Lambeth 1.10'.[34] This resolution:

- commends to the Church the subsection report on human sexuality[35];
- in view of the teaching of Scripture, upholds faithfulness in marriage between a man and a woman in lifelong union, and believes that abstinence is right for those who are not called to marriage;
- recognises that there are among us persons who experience themselves as having a homosexual orientation. Many of these are members of the Church and are seeking the pastoral care, moral direction of the Church, and God's transforming power for the living of their lives and the ordering of relationships. We commit ourselves to listen to the experience of homosexual persons and we wish to assure them that they are loved by God and that all baptised, believing and faithful persons, regardless of sexual orientation, are full members of the Body of Christ;
- while rejecting homosexual practice as incompatible with Scripture, calls on all our people to minister pastorally and sensitively to all irrespective of sexual orientation and to condemn irrational fear of homosexuals, violence within marriage and any trivialisation and commercialisation of sex;

[34] See, Lambeth Commission on Communion. 2004. *The Windsor Report 2004*. London: The Anglican Communion Office, at: http://www.anglicancommunion.org/windsor2004/appendix/p3.6.cfm.

[35] Three-quarters of its schools are judged 'good' or 'outstanding' by Ofsted (the government regulatory body for education) as opposed to 57 % of all State schools.

- cannot advise the legitimising or blessing of same sex unions nor ordaining those involved in same gender unions;
- requests the Primates and the ACC to establish a means of monitoring the work done on the subject of human sexuality in the Communion and to share statements and resources among us;
- notes the significance of the Kuala Lumpur Statement on Human Sexuality and the concerns expressed in resolutions IV.26, V.1, V.10, V.23 and V.35 on the authority of Scripture in matters of marriage and sexuality and asks the Primates and the ACC to include them in their monitoring process.

The resolution was passed by the 1998 Lambeth Conference and has since been upheld by each of the other three instruments of Anglican unity. It renounced homosexual relationships, among other things, and affirmed the importance of marriage as traditionally defined. As the twenty-first century advanced, this benchmark of Anglican solidarity came to be seen as a watershed for traditionalists and, to some, as increasingly anachronistic.

In October 2003 the Archbishop of Canterbury established the Lambeth Commission to examine the life of the Anglican Communion. The following year the Commission submitted its *Windsor Report* outlining the state of the Anglican Communion with recommendations as to how to address divisive issues. It is noteworthy that, despite the many deeply felt opposing views, a large majority of the submissions received by the Commission were in support of the continuance of the Anglican Communion. This perhaps helped toughen the stance of the Archbishop as in 2009 he rejected calls from the Episcopal Church to reorder the Anglican Communion as a federation of churches. By the end of 2012, however, his resolve had dissolved and he expressed the view that Anglican Communion had become "corrupted" and should be considered no longer to be a communion of churches but a "community of communities."

5.3.9 The Anglican Consultative Council

The 1968 Lambeth Conference recommended that a new body be formed representative of all sections of the churches – laity, clergy and bishops – to co-ordinate aspects of international Anglican ecumenical and mission work. This resulted in the birth of the Anglican Consultative Council (ACC) in 1969, which meets approximately every 3 years, and has a permanent secretariat, the Anglican Communion Office, of which the Archbishop of Canterbury is president. The role of the Council is to facilitate the co-operative work of the churches of the Anglican Communion, exchange information between the Provinces and churches, and help co-ordinate common action. It advises on the organisation and structures of the Communion, and seeks to develop common policies with respect to the world mission of the Church, including ecumenical matters. The ACC membership includes from one to three persons from each province. Where there are three members, there is a bishop, a priest and a lay person. Where fewer members are appointed, preference is given to lay membership.[36]

The Standing Committee of the Anglican Communion is the executive arm of the ACC, charged with advancing its work between its 3-yearly plenary meetings on a worldwide basis. This is a 14-member group (15, if the Archbishop of Canterbury is present, as he is an ex officio member, as well as being its President), seven are elected by members of the ACC and five are members of the Primates' Standing Committee. The other two members are the Chair and Vice-Chair of the ACC, elected by the members in plenary session.[37]

5.3.10 The Primates' Meeting

As its name suggests, this body brings together the senior archbishops or bishops (or "moderators") of each Province for prayer and reflection, with the Archbishop of Canterbury as convenor, on theological, social and international matters. It was established in 1978 by Archbishop Donald Coggan (101st Archbishop of Canterbury), as an opportunity for "leisurely thought, prayer and deep consultation", and meetings have since taken place approximately every 2 years.[38]

A meeting held in October 2003 reaffirmed the Lambeth Conference 1998 resolution, and criticized the primates in the US and Canada, by suggesting that they 'could be perceived to alter unilaterally the teaching of the Anglican Communion'. The meeting authorized a Commission, which the following year produced the *Windsor Report* in which the hope was expressed that the Primates' Meeting 'should be a primary forum for the strengthening of the mutual life of the provinces, and be respected by individual primates and the provinces they lead as an instrument through which new developments may be honestly addressed'.[39]

5.3.11 The Anglican Covenant

The Covenant was initially proposed in the 2004 Windsor Report in response to the withdrawal of some North American provinces from the Anglican principles of consultation and interdependence in relation to the issue of women's ordination within the Communion. By Spring 2012, following its rejection by a majority of the Church's diocesan synods, this initiative had collapsed and the decision was taken that the matter would not return to the General Synod during the current quinquennium (see, further, below).

---

[36] See, further, at: http://www.anglicancommunion.org/communion/acc/about.cfm.

[37] See, further, at: http://www.anglicancommunion.org/communion/acc/scac/.

[38] See, further, at: www.anglicancommunion.org/communion/primates/.

[39] See, *The Windsor Report*, op cit, Appendix One, at para.5.

5.4 The Anglican Communion: Challenging Milestones

The Anglican Communion has no international juridical capacity. All its international bodies are consultative and collaborative, and their resolutions are not legally binding on its autonomous provinces. The Lambeth conferences came closest to providing such a function. These constitute an international forum for focusing clergy debates on the task of achieving conformity in certain areas of doctrine, discipline, worship, and ethics. The conferences had come to be seen as the place where policy could be negotiated, formulated, and proposed changes openly discussed. Over the years there had been areas of contention, some of which were theological (changes to the prayer book, gender and 'ministry', interpretation of the Eucharist, restrictions on the availability of the sacraments of 'baptism' and 'marriage') and some more social (use of birth control and abortion).[40]

However, the process by which certain matters, that were clearly the most contentious for the Communion, largely bypassed the conferences as member provinces took unilateral action, proved not only very damaging to the Communion ethos but also raised questions regarding the possible need for a body with stronger centralizing functions; contrary to the assurances given by Archbishop Longley at the first Lambeth conference in 1868. The most notable examples of this difficulty have been the resistance to the ordination of women and the objection of many provinces of the Communion (particularly in Africa and Asia) to the changing role of homosexuals in the North American churches.

5.4.1 Contention Regarding the Ordination of Women

While the ordination of women was, at the time, deeply divisive for the Church of England, it was less of an issue for the Communion as a whole and at least all nations had a long period in which to come to terms with the prospect. The first Anglican woman priest, Florence Li Tim-Oi was ordained in Hong Kong in 1944, followed by Jane Hwang and Joyce Bennett in 1971. From 1974 onwards other women were ordained, at first in the USA and Canada but soon afterwards elsewhere too. In 1970, the Anglican Consultative Council (ACC) passed a motion in favour of permitting the ordination of women and in 1978 the Lambeth Conference recognised 'the autonomy of each of its member Churches, acknowledging the legal right of each Church to make its own decision about the appropriateness of admitting women to Holy Orders'.

[40] In the 1970s, the Continuing Anglican Movement was established outside the Communion, in repudiation of concessions to change and to represent the more traditional aspects of Anglicanism.

5.4.2 Response of the Church of England

In England progress was noticeably slower and more contentious. In 1992 the General Synod voted to ordain women, but not everyone in the Church was in agreement. In 1993, in order to placate internal protests, it passed the Act of Synod setting up an official structure enabling parishes to refuse women's ministry and providing an alternative arrangement whereby a Provincial Episcopal Visitor or 'flying bishop' could officiate in dioceses which rejected women as priests. Arguably, this strategy solved one problem only to create a larger one: the Church was now exposed to the not unreasonable charge that it had institutionalised discrimination against women. For those male priests unable to accept the change, two other options were available: a scheme allowed men to leave the priesthood with appropriate financial support until they had resettled; and in 1993 the Roman Catholic Church allowed married (and non-married) Anglican priests to join its priesthood.

In 2004 the Windsor Report commented that the 2003 Lambeth Conference had 'addressed a situation where Hong Kong, Canada, the United States and New Zealand had all ordained women to the priesthood and eight other provinces had accepted the ordination of women in principle'. It was satisfied that the issue had been studied and debated within the Anglican Communion, and, based on scriptural evidence, it was deemed to be an issue upon which Christians might have legitimate differences within the bonds of the Anglican Communion. By then one in five of Church of England licensed priests were female and a working party, set up by General Synod, had published a theological study of women in the Episcopate and the impact such a move would have both on the Church of England and the wider Anglican Communion. By 2012, 28 of the 38 provinces of the Anglican Communion were ordaining women as priests and a total of almost 5,000 were in office.

5.4.3 Contention Regarding the Ordination of Gay Clergy

While priding themselves on belonging to a broad church, willing to accommodate many diverse views, the issue of the ordination of gay persons has in fact, since the 1990s, proved profoundly divisive for the Anglican Communion. In 1998, as mentioned above, the bishops of the Anglican Communion attending the Lambeth conference passed a resolution stating that homosexual acts are "incompatible with scripture" by a vote of 526–70. Since then the Communion has become steadily more fractured.

5.4.4 The U.S. and Canada

In North America there has been a move away from the Lambeth 1.10 position with some churches blessing same-sex unions and ordaining and consecrating gays and lesbians in same-sex relationships. The catalyst came in 2003 with the provision of a blessing service for same-sex partnerships by the Diocese of New Westminster, Canada, and the election of a partnered gay priest, Gene Robinson, to the post of Bishop of New Hampshire. This in turn has triggered a reaction that has seen some congregations leaving and setting up rival churches and organisations, such as the Convocation of Anglicans in North America, of a more traditional ethos. The American Episcopal Church has in particular been riven with internal divisions.

5.4.5 The Southern Hemisphere

For the majority of the provinces of the Communion, constituting three-quarters of all Anglicans, the sentiments of Lambeth 1.10 have found strong endorsement. This has been particularly the case in Africa, Asia and South America where strong objections have been expressed in relation to the actions taken by a minority of churches in the US and Canada; described as unscriptural, unilateral, and without the prior agreement of the Communion. In the late twentieth and early twenty-first centuries, some churches in Africa and elsewhere were established outside the Anglican Communion, largely because of their opposition to the ordination of openly homosexual bishops and other clergy. These have been referred to as belonging to the Anglican realignment movement, or as "orthodox" Anglicans, and they represent a clear point of reference for traditional Christian morality and a point of departure from Communion equivocation.

5.4.6 Response of the Church of England

Since 2002 there has been much controversy in the Church of England regarding the rights of homosexual priests. The Church, which had taken the position that it would allow the ordination of gay priests as long as they were celibate, found itself challenged in 2003 by the nomination of Canon Jeffrey John, who was in a homosexual relationship, as the new suffragan Bishop of Reading. Despite his ongoing relationship and his advocacy on behalf of gay couples living in faithful, permanent, stable relationships, he made it clear that he was celibate. Nonetheless, he was induced to withdraw his nomination. This resulted in considerable public debate, which intensified following the consecration of Gene Robinson as Bishop of New Hampshire, prompting the Chairman of the Lambeth Commission, to declare in his foreword to the *Windsor Report*[41]:

> The decision by the 74th General Convention of the Episcopal Church (USA) to give consent to the election of bishop Gene Robinson to the Diocese of New Hampshire, the authorising by a diocese of the Anglican Church of Canada of a public Rite of Blessing for

[41] See, Eames, R. 2004. Archbishop of Armagh, Lambeth Commission on Communion. The *Windsor Report 2004*. London: The Anglican Communion Office, at: http://www.anglicancommunion.org/windsor2004/appendix/p3.6.cfm.

same sex unions and the involvement in other provinces by bishops without the consent or approval of the incumbent bishop to perform episcopal functions have uncovered major divisions throughout the Anglican Communion.

Then came the introduction of the Civil Partnership Act 2004. In response to these events the House of Bishops in 2005 declared in a pastoral statement[42] that a celibate person of homosexual orientation would be eligible for ordination, even if that person had entered into a civil same-sex partnership and added that "the Church should not collude with the present assumptions of society that all close relationships necessarily include sexual activity."[43] This permitted clergy to enter chaste civil partnerships. A further step was taken with the ruling of the House of Bishops in December 2012 that gay men can be appointed bishops as long as they remain chaste and repent for any past sexual acts.

It would be difficult to overstate the divisive effect of the turmoil generated during the torturous process by which the Church accommodated, conditionally, the ordination of women and gay men: it will still not ordain sexually 'active' gays, or appoint such persons as bishops, nor will it bless same-sex partnerships. One consequence has been that considerable numbers of laity and clergy have left the Church.

5.4.7 Contention Regarding the Ordination of Women as Bishops

Given that the principle – 'ordination' and the responsibilities that go with it should be restricted to men – was addressed and resolved with the widespread acceptance of the ordination of women as priests (some 5,000 in total in the UK since 1994), it might have been predicted that the prospect of their consecration as bishops could not encounter any fundamental theological dispute. This would have been misguided. For Anglicans and other Christians, the ministry of a bishop is held to be of a different order to that of a priest. It is said to give rise to important questions regarding the capacity of the holder of the bishopric office to authentically fulfill the ministry of the word and sacraments: priests who do not accept the legitimacy of a female bishop may jeopardise or compromise the latter's ministry; and the currency of ordinations carried out by a female bishop may not hold their value among congregations in other provinces.

5.4.8 The U.S.

In 1989 Barbara Harris became the first woman bishop in the Anglican Communion when she was ordained suffragan bishop of Massachusetts. By November 2009

[42] See, further, at: http://www.churchofengland.org/media-centre/news/2005/07/pr5605.aspx.

[43] Church of England News, 'House of Bishops issues pastoral statement on Civil Partnerships', 25 July 2005.

the Episcopal Church had elected and consecrated 17 women as bishops in the face of organized opposition led by the now defunct Episcopal Synod of America. In November 2006, the Episcopal Church in the United States elected the Most Revd Katherine Jefferts Schori as the first woman primate and in 2010 the election of Bishop Glasspool, a lesbian who lives openly with her partner of 20 years, attracted particular controversy both in America and more widely throughout the Anglican Communion.

5.4.9 *Elsewhere in the Communion*

At the 1998 Lambeth conference a resolution was passed approving the consecration of women bishops by a 423–28 vote, with 19 abstentions. Since then, while women are not infrequently ordained as bishops in Canada, South Africa and New Zealand, only a few other provinces have followed their example (although the number of provinces where women bishops are canonically possible is much greater[44]). In November 2012, the Anglican Church of Southern Africa consecrated its first woman bishop in Swaziland by which time 17 of the 38 provinces of the Anglican Communion had removed all barriers to women becoming bishops.

5.4.10 *Response of the Church of England*

The protracted wrangling, torturous compromises and divisive dissent, that had accompanied the process by which women were eventually accepted as clergy in the Church, was continued in respect of their proposed ordination as bishops.

In 2005, 2006 and 2008 the General Synod voted in favour of removing the legal obstacles preventing women from becoming bishops. The task of taking this proposal further fell largely to a revision committee established by the Synod. When, in October 2009, this committee released a statement indicating its proposals would include a plan to vest some functions by law in male bishops who would provide oversight for those unable to receive ministry of women as bishops or priests, there was widespread concern both within and outside the Church of England about the appropriateness of such legislation. This strategy resonated with that adopted earlier to manage the dissent triggered by the ordination of women and seemed open to the same charge of institutionalizing discrimination against women. The committee subsequently abandoned the recommendation.

In July 2010 the Synod considered a measure that again endorsed the ordination of women as bishops. The measure included compromise provisions

[44] For example, both the Church of Ireland and the Scottish Episcopal Church have permitted the ordination of women as bishops since 1990 and 2003 respectively, but as yet none have been ordained.

(involving the creation of a mechanism providing for "co-ordinate jurisdiction" in parishes unable to receive the ministry of a female bishop whereby a male bishop would fulfill episcopal functions) was passed in all three houses and subsequently approved by 42 of the 44 dioceses, but an amendment by the House of Bishops, offering further concessions to opponents, meant that many proponents of the measure would have reluctantly voted it down, so the Synod adjourned the decision. When in November 2012, the proposed legislation for the ordination of women as bishops finally came before the General Synod it failed: after being passed by the House of Bishops and the House of Clergy, it was narrowly defeated in the House of Laity. As the Synod convenes at 5 year intervals, the prospect of pursuing this issue is effectively deferred until 1215 unless the Queen, as Supreme Governor General of the Church, is invited to dissolve the present Synod and allow the process to be speeded up. However, to resort to this option is not without risks as it will demonstrate the 'established' nature of the Church, the interdependency of politics and Protestantism and provoke controversy among other religious leaders.

5.4.11 Contention Regarding Same Sex Marriages

With the above clergy oriented controversies, clear fractures lines became discernible within the Communion. The laity oriented issue of 'gay marriage', however, has finally broken open those fractures, perhaps irreparably. While government had earlier sought to pre-empt confrontation with the Church by going to some lengths to distinguish civil partnership from marriage, it was now inescapable. Marriage – as a sacrament, as the cornerstone of family life, and as the legitimizing sanction for exclusively heterosexual relationships – has always been of central importance to the Church. This was well recognized by academics such as the German Lutheran theologian Wolfhart Pannenberg who, a number of years ago, expressed his much quoted view that 'gay marriage' was a 'first order issue'[45]:

> Here lies the boundary of a Christian church that knows itself to be bound by the authority of Scripture. Those who urge the church to change the norm of its teaching on this matter must know that they are promoting schism. If a church were to let itself be pushed to the point where it ceased to treat homosexual activity as a departure from the biblical norm, and recognized homosexual unions as a personal partnership of love equivalent to marriage, such a church would stand no longer on biblical ground but against the unequivocal witness of Scripture. A church that took this step would cease to be the one, holy, catholic, and apostolic church.

[45] See, Pannenberg, W. Should we support gay marriage? No. *Good News Magazine*, at: http://holytrinitynewrochelle.org/yourti92881.html.

His premonition that this would prove to be a red line issue has been borne out by the subsequent unfolding of events within the Communion.

5.4.12 The U.S. and Canada

In 1998, by passing resolution 1.10, the Lambeth conference had drawn what appeared to be a definite line in the sand. The Anglican Communion had resoundingly endorsed a motion that homosexual practice was "incompatible with Scripture" and rejected the blessing or ordaining of those in same-sex unions. Despite this, however, and allegedly without further consultation, some North American churches then breached the resolution.

In Canada, in 2002, the diocese of New Westminster, had voted to allow the blessing of same-sex unions, and a year later the Ontario Court of Appeal in *Halpern v. Canada (Attorney General)*[46] stated that "the dignity of persons in same-sex relationships is violated by the exclusion of same-sex couples from the institution of marriage" and consequently the "common-law definition of marriage as 'the voluntary union for life of one man and one women to the exclusion of all others' violates (human rights provisions in, *sic*) s.15(1) of the Charter." Consequently, the ensuing marriage law reform process concluded with the Civil Marriage Act 2005, a federal statute, which extended the legal capacity to marry for civil purposes to same-sex couples. In 2010, the General Synod of the Anglican Church of Canada issued a statement permitting local dioceses to decide whether to bless same-gender and currently three dioceses do so.

In the U.S.: in July 2009, the General Convention of the Episcopal Church adopted a resolution allowing individual bishops to choose whether or not to allow the blessing of same-sex unions; and in July 2012, the Episcopal Church passed a resolution approving an official liturgy for blessing same-sex unions. In their defence, the American Episcopal Church and the Anglican Church of Canada claimed they had acted: after lengthy scriptural and theological reflection; legally in accordance with their own canons and constitutions; and after extensive consultation with the provinces of the Communion. These actions proved to be a fair reflection of their cultural context: in the U.S., for example, by January 2013 nine states had legalized same-sex marriage, representing 15.7 % of the total population.[47]

---

[46] [2003] O.J. No. 2268, at para.108. Note, however, the 2012 court ruling that non-Canadian same sex couples cannot marry in Canada unless such a marriage would be lawful in their jurisdiction of origin. This would invalidate approx one-third of the 15,000 non-Canadian same sex couples who have married in Canada since the introduction of the Civil Marriage Act. The case has since been remanded to the Ontario Superior Court.

[47] In March 2013, a Reuters/Ipsos poll found that 63 % of Americans supported gay marriage or civil unions. See, further, at: http://newsandinsight.thomsonreuters.com/Legal/News/2013/03_-_March/Analysis__Silent_or_supportive,_conservatives_give_gay_marriage_momentum/.

5.4.13 Elsewhere in the Communion

In 2004, the Chairman of the Lambeth Commission, in his foreword to the *Windsor Report*[48] spoke for the majority of Communion members when he deplored "the authorising by a diocese of the Anglican Church of Canada of a public Rite of Blessing for same sex unions". The Commission called for a moratorium on such blessings and recommended that bishops who had authorised them "be invited to express regret that the proper constraints of the bonds of affection were breached by such authorisation." In response to the North American blessing of same-sex unions, bishops from Africa, Asia and Latin America and other provinces in the southern hemisphere, representing about half of all practicing Anglicans worldwide, broke off relationships with those dioceses. Some African provinces even consecrated missionary bishops for the United States (such missionaries have also been appointed by dioceses within the U.S.) in order to support the traditionalists and persuade the separatists.

The contrast within the Communion is stark. For example, in almost all African countries (excepting South Africa) gay or lesbian relationships are a criminal offence and in some it is punishable by the death penalty. The opposition of State and Church to homosexual relationships in countries such as Uganda is almost visceral. In November 2012 as the Westminster Parliament was preparing gay marriage legislation, the Ugandan Parliament was preparing a revised anti-homosexuality bill, providing for harsher penalties against suspected LGBT people and anyone who fails to report them to authorities, including long-term imprisonment and the death penalty.

Meanwhile, however, in other host countries of the Communion, same sex marriages were steadily gaining legal recognition. In New Zealand, as early as 1997, Tipping J had stated in *Quilter v. Attorney General*[49] "I see the inability of homosexual and lesbian couples to marry as involving (indirect) discrimination against them on the grounds of sexual orientation". Eventually the legislature concurred and in 2013, when the New Zealand parliament passed the Marriage (Definition of Marriage) Amendment Act 2013 enabling gay, bisexual, lesbian, transsexual and intersex marriages to be legal, it became the 13th country in the world to do so.

5.4.14 Response of the Church of England

The position of the Church on 'gay marriages' is essentially that the concept is incompatible with the way the legal institution of marriage has been defined by

[48] See, Eames, R. 2004. Archbishop of Armagh, chair of the Lambeth Commission on Communion. The *Windsor Report 2004*. London: The Anglican Communion Office, at: http://www.anglicancommunion.org/windsor2004/appendix/p3.6.cfm.

[49] [1997] 14 FRNZ 430 at pp. 575–6 (admittedly obiter).

Church and State in this country; it is a deviant interpretation. As the 'established' Church, the canon law of which had for centuries been assimilated into State law, it has fallen to the Church to affirm and uphold the legal characteristics of marriage as an institution. Central to canon law in this context is the tenet that marriage is confined exclusively to a heterosexual relationship; the 'sacrament' of marriage as administered through the ministry of the Church is wholly reliant upon the heterosexual nature of that relationship. State and Church had abided by this tenet in their approach to civil partnerships by carefully differentiating the legal status of that relationship from marriage. The established Church argues that it is not possible for it to either accommodate a new State variant of 'marriage' alongside the traditional form, nor for it to countenance an artificial distinction being drawn between a Church (or religious) service and a State (or secular) ceremony. Marriage must remain the legal institution and the sacrament as traditionally defined by canon law: jointly upheld by Church and State; administered by the former and registered by the latter.

However, in February 2013, following a public consultation, the Marriage (Same Sex Couples) Bill 2012–13 passed its second reading by a 400–175 vote and became law on receiving royal assent on 17th July 2013. This legislation allows same-sex marriage in England and Wales, makes provision regarding gender change by married persons and civil partners, and also provides an exemption for the conducting of same-sex marriage ceremonies for religious bodies whose doctrines oppose such relationships; no religious organisation or individual minister will be compelled to marry a same-sex couple or to permit this to happen on their premises. In an interesting initiative, presumably taken in recognition of the Church's 'established' status, the government has inserted a clause explicitly stating that it will be illegal for the Church of England to marry same-sex couples and that canon law, which bans same-sex weddings, will continue to apply: sympathetic clergy will be prevented from 'opting in' and either conducting marriage ceremonies or blessing the civil marriages of same sex couples.

5.5 The Covenant Crisis and Threat of Schism

In 2004 the Windsor Report proposed that a new Covenant should be drawn up to "make explicit and forceful the loyalty and bonds of affection which govern the relationships between the churches of the Communion"[50] bearing in mind that "it is our shared responsibility to have in place an agreed mechanism to enable and maintain life in communion, and to prevent and manage Communion disputes".[51] The Report was well received within the wider Communion and by all the Instruments of Communion. In March 2005, the Joint Standing Committee of the Primates and of the Anglican Consultative Council took the first step in implementing the Report's recommendation by commissioning a consultation paper, 'Towards an Anglican

[50] Ibid, at para 118.

[51] Ibid, at para 119.

Covenant'.[52] Given the consensual and non-directive nature of the Communion, in contrast to the depth and duration of the divisions as detailed above, all further steps were always going to be difficult.

5.5.1 *Launching the Covenant*

A Covenant Design Group was established under the chairmanship of Drexel Gomez, then Archbishop of the West Indies. Over a period of some years a number of different Covenant drafts were formulated: the Proposals for an Anglican Covenant in Appendix 2 of the Windsor Report (2005); the Nassau Draft (2007); the St Andrew's Draft (2008); and the Ridley-Cambridge Draft (2009). The latter, as amended by a committee set up by the Anglican Consultative Council (2009), was the final text which provinces were invited to sign.[53]

5.5.2 *Obstacles*

Perhaps the main obstacle to securing consensus has been that each member province highly prizes its autonomy, and the Communion as a whole has always prided itself on respecting that arrangement.[54] However, following recent difficulties, there is now a strong sense that a firmer framework is necessary to foster solidarity. This problem continues to find a primary focus in the fact that a significant minority of Anglican senior leaders oppose, both the stand taken by the Episcopal Church (U.S.) and the Anglican Church of Canada in relation to homosexuality, and the cultural assumptions that it embodies. While this represents the Rubicon for all Anglicans, the issues identified above are also relevant. In addition there is a technical difficulty for some provinces regarding their place within the legal structures of the countries they are based: for example, Hong Kong, the Churches of North and South India, and England at least, would all find it legally impossible to become a subordinate part of a larger, international body.

5.5.3 *Ongoing Communion Dissension*

Developments within the Episcopal Church[55] that triggered the Covenant initiative continue to provoke dissension both within that Church and within the Communion.

---

[52] See, further, at: http://www.anglicancommunion.org/commission/covenant/consultation/index.cfm.

[53] See, full text, at: http://www.anglicancommunion.org/commission/covenant/final/text.cfm/.

[54] See, further, at: http://noanglicancovenant.org/resources.html#120720aac.

[55] It is not without irony to note that this is the same Episcopal Church that was the first branch of the Anglican Communion to declare its independence from the Church of England, in 1789.

Some parishes and dioceses have withdrawn from the Episcopal Church, as have several hundred churches, and hundreds of individual Episcopalians are reputed to be leaving their Episcopal churches every week. Such congregational rifts have resulted in dissident members forming new Anglican churches, and/or joining with traditional Anglican churches or becoming affiliated with overseas provinces. There have already been a number of court cases over ownership of church property.[56] Not dissimilar developments are occurring in Canada, and to a lesser extent in Australia, New Zealand and in England.[57]

Many provinces, primarily from Africa and Asia and representing about half of the 80 million practicing Anglicans worldwide, have responded by declaring a state of impaired communion with relevant dioceses in the U.S. and elsewhere: in fact some 22 of the 38 provinces in the Anglican Communion have declared that they are in a state of broken, or impaired, communion with all or part of the Episcopal Church. Since 2000, some such provinces have appointed missionary bishops to the United States and Canada to provide pastoral oversight to disaffected Anglicans. This is considered by the Episcopal Church USA and the Anglican Church of Canada to be an illegitimate incursion into their territories. In 2005, the Primates' Meeting voted to request the two churches to withdraw their delegates from the meeting of the Anglican Consultative Council and in 2010 the U.S. was excluded from an ecumenical committee. In short, such change as there has been in recent years has seen a hardening of divisions. Many of the Covenant's original supporters now reject it because the final draft does not go far enough and consequently, in 2008, they formed the Fellowship of Confessing Anglicans (GAFCON).[58]

5.5.4 *The Covenant*

This brief nine-page document, consisting of a preamble, four substantive sections, and a concluding declaration, represents several years of work. The text: affirms basic Anglican beliefs and commitments; commits churches to a shared mission and service; establishes the authority of the four Instruments of Communion; and it then outlines a process for conflict resolution.[59]

[56] The resulting litigation regarding property ownership can cause great difficulties. Not that this is unusual in the Church's history which has seem many schisms followed by bitter court disputes over Church property. Lord Eldon is reputed to have identified this as one of the most difficult issues that faced him during his term in office as Lord Chancellor: see, *Foley v. Wontner* (1820) 2 Jac & W 245, 37 ER 621.

[57] These challenges are not, of course, confined to Anglicanism.

[58] The Global Anglican Future Conference (GAFCON) was an initiative led by several Global South Primates that ratified the 'Jerusalem Declaration' outlining principals of orthodox Anglicanism and also called for a Primatial Council to be formed of those Primates that agreed with the Jerusalem Declaration. The document also called for a new province in North America to be formed from the Common Cause Partnership.

[59] See, further, at: http://www.anglicancommunion.org/commission/covenant/final/text.cfm/.

5.5.5 Communion Solidarity

The Covenant focuses on how to keep the Communion united.[60] Churches must 'have regard for the common good of the Communion in the exercise of its autonomy', 'respect the constitutional autonomy of all of the Churches', 'spend time with openness and patience in matters of theological debate and reflection', 'seek a shared mind with other Churches', 'participate in mediated conversations', 'act with diligence, care and caution in respect of any action which may provoke controversy, which by its intensity, substance or extent could threaten the unity of the Communion', and 'uphold the highest degree of communion possible' at times of conflict. In 'matters of common concern', it requires that 'each Church will undertake wide consultation with the other Churches of the Anglican Communion and with the Instruments and Commissions of the Communion'.

By signing, provinces affirm that 'recognition of, and fidelity to, this Covenant, enable mutual recognition and communion'. Signatories thereby commit themselves to the view that the Covenant is 'foundational for the life of the Anglican Communion'. The strongest argument in favour of signing is that advanced by Fulcrum: [the Covenant] gives form to a vision of 'communion with autonomy and accountability' that has been central to the Communion's self-understanding and is a genuine Anglican *via media* avoiding the dangers of both a centralised, controlling Curia and a fragmenting, fractious federation; and it offers the best, perhaps the only, means of preventing further bitter fragmentation by enabling the highest degree of communion among Anglicans.[61]

5.5.6 Conflict Resolution

Section 4, the process for conflict resolution, is the controversial part. In the final version of the Covenant, the role of mediator is assigned to the Standing Committee of the Anglican Consultative Council (ACC) which is to be responsible for: administering the Covenant processes; determining whether an action is 'incompatible with the Covenant'; and for making recommendations to member Churches or (not 'and') the Instruments of Communion as to the 'relational consequences' that might follow. A 'relational consequence' would characteristically be to exclude a province from an international function (e.g. a province's bishops might be excluded from Lambeth conferences). It is argued that this still leaves churches free to make autonomous decisions, that there is no un-Anglican 'curial' structure and no church by signing the covenant will empower some extra-provincial body to overturn its

[60] Doe, N. 2008. *An Anglican Covenant: Theological and legal considerations for a global debate*. Norwich: Canterbury Press, hopes the Covenant will help tidy up Canon Law.

[61] See, Fulcrum, 'Churchgoer's Guide to the Anglican Communion Covenant', at: http://www.fulcrum-anglican.org.uk/page.cfm?ID=681.

own decisions. However, and undeniably, the role and responsibilities of the Standing Committee will interpose an oversight body into Community affairs, with powers and sanctions, where no such empowered body previously functioned.

5.5.7 *Current Status of the Covenant*

In December 2009 the churches of the Communion were asked by the Archbishop of Canterbury to adopt the "final text" of the Covenant and in response Mexico, Ireland, South East Asia, the West Indies, Myanmar, the Southern Cone of America and South Africa duly did so. However, the Church of England itself rejected the Covenant in March 2012, by a vote of 23 dioceses to 15, and the matter will not return to the General Synod during this quinquennium (2011–15). In June 2012, the Standing Committee of the Anglican Communion virtually abandoned the project when it decided that no timescale would be set for adoption of the Covenant.[62]

5.5.8 *Towards Schism*

It would seem that the net effect of launching the Covenant, and then failing to win the endorsement of its own provinces, has been that the Church of England has painted itself into a corner. Given that other provinces – in North America and in Africa/Asia – now similarly find themselves in corners of their own making, it is difficult at this stage to see by what processes of extraction the Communion can be restored.

Should this occur, and the Covenant be endorsed, the outcome, in effect, will be to establish a two-tier Communion: only those provinces sharing a traditional Anglican cultural commonality will sign and continue to represent mainstream Anglicanism; the others who either do not sign – or sign but become the subject of Standing Committee intervention, or sign but then reject a Standing Committee 'recommendation' – can only continue within the Communion with an inferior status.

5.5.9 *Schism*

It may, however, be the case that some or many provinces will opt not to sign but to instead establish a different and entirely separate body to represent their interpretation of 'Anglicanism' – then the Communion will have jumped directly into schism. If that were to occur, a three way split would seem probable: the GAFCON

[62] At the same time, the General Synod of the Scottish Episcopal Church voted similarly, followed in July by the Anglican Church in New Zealand and Polynesia.

contingent led largely by African and Asian provinces with their adherence to orthodox Anglicanism as represented by resolution 1.10 of the 1998 Lambeth conference; the minority of dioceses that follow the leadership and direction shown by the Episcopal Church in the US; and the considerable rump of Covenant adherents who hold to the middle way between both camps.

5.6 Conclusion

It is entirely possible that after 137 years of shared ecumenism, Anglicanism at home and abroad is on the verge of being wholly redefined. Whether or not the Covenant initiative ironically leads to schism, it is likely that there will be a strong move to separate the leadership of the Church of England from that of the Anglican Communion. In any event, the 'middle way' will prove to be a difficult road to take given the clash of theological beliefs and emerging cultural norms that now hedge in the options available to Anglicanism.

At home, leaving aside the above difficulties, the Church is set to encounter problems with its role in society. The questions regarding the continued viability of its standing as 'established' are not going to go away: particularly as its attendance figures fall and the general public become disenchanted by its discriminatory approach to women bishops and 'active' gay clergy; while Catholicism grows in numeric strength and Islam acquires a stronger voice; and as the political climate requires more levers to be pulled to facilitate pluralism. As its membership shrinks, the Church's annual outlay on maintaining its architectural heritage and its pension scheme for retired clergy is steadily increasing, a correlation that can only be problematic in the long term. Then there are also issues on the horizon in relation to its secular arm in education: whether such market dominance in schooling is tenable as the 'established' Church; and whether it is wholly compatible with equality and human rights principles may perhaps be open to question. It is against this background that the relevance for the Church of charity law reform together with the ongoing developments in human rights case law must now be considered.

Chapter 6
The Impact of Charity Law Reform

6.1 Introduction

> The aim of this reform is not to force churches to undertake community activities such as social services for older people or the sick, although many of course already do. Religious practice tends generally to contribute to the social and moral welfare of adherents. It is not proposed to change the principle that celebration of a religious rite which is open to the public should be regarded as providing public benefit. In accord with existing case law, the Charity Commission currently applies public benefit tests to religious bodies seeking registration. Removing the legal presumption will not affect this approach.

At the turn of the century a protracted period of charity law reform was launched. It began appropriately in England,[1] the progenitor jurisdiction of charity law, with a succession of reports culminating in a public consultation exercise launched by the *Private Action, Public Benefit* report from which the above quote is taken. Processes were then initiated in Canada,[2] Australia,[3] New Zealand,[4] the US,[5] the UK,[6]

[1] See, Cabinet Office, Strategy Unit Report, *Private Action, Public Benefit*, Consultation Paper, London, 2002, at para 4.33.

[2] See, Ontario Law Reform Commission, *Report on the Law of Charities*, Ontario, 1996.

[3] See, the Charity Law Reform Committee report *Inquiry into the Definition of Charities and Related Organisations*, Canberra, June 2001.

[4] See, the Working Party on Charities and Sporting Bodies, *Report on the Accountability of Charities & Sporting Bodies*, 1997.

[5] See, Panel on the Nonprofit Sector, *Strengthening Transparency, Governance, Accountability of Charitable Organisations*, final report to Congress and the Nonprofit Sector, Washington, 2005.

[6] See, for England and Wales: the National Council for Voluntary Organisations, *For the Public Benefit? A Consultation Document on Charity Law Reform*, London, 2001 and *Private Action, Public Benefit, a Review of Charities and the Wider Not-For-Profit Sector*, London, September 2002. See, for Scotland: the Scottish Charity Law Review Commission report, *Charity Scotland*, Edinburgh, 2001. See, for Northern Ireland: the Charities Branch, Voluntary & Community Unit, Department for Social Development *Consultation on the Review of Charities Administration and Legislation in Northern Ireland*, Belfast, 2005.

K. O'Halloran, *The Church of England - Charity Law and Human Rights*, Ius Gentium: Comparative Perspectives on Law and Justice 36, DOI 10.1007/978-3-319-04319-7_6,

Singapore[7] and Hong Kong.[8] Having now run its course in some of the leading developed nations, this programme of reform is destined to continue rippling across the common law world.

The reform outcomes so far achieved have been profoundly challenging for religion and religious organizations in all jurisdictions. For the Church of England, some changes introduced in post-reform legislation have come to test its most fundamental principles. Of those changes the most difficult for present purposes is the new requirement that the Church, in keeping with all other religions and religious organizations, demonstrate that it is benefiting the public. This gives rise to questions as to how this might be achieved, what measures should be used, should the benefit be gauged solely on secular terms or is there an integral value-added 'religious' component that must be taken into account? What bearing, if any, does the Church's status as 'established' have on its public benefit capacity?

This chapter begins by identifying the drivers for charity law reform, then explains the resulting changes and assesses their impact. It considers the nature and effect of changes to: the definition of 'religion' and 'belief'; the new definition of the public benefit test, the removal of the traditional presumption that religious purposes automatically satisfied the test and the consequences of its removal for those religious organisations which owe their charitable status to that presumption. These matters are analysed in terms of their application to religious purposes and the resulting consequences for the Church of England. It assesses the possible consequences for established charities, including religious organisations. It explains the post-reform remit of the Charity Commission, considers relevant recent guidance, case law and the growing acceptance by judiciary and regulator of the need for an additional 'activities test'. It evaluates the theological significance of subjecting religion to such tests: discussing the public benefit of private piety. It examines: the distinction now made between matters to be construed as 'religious' or, alternatively, as 'moral or ethical belief systems'; the necessity or otherwise, in charity law terms, for religion to have a body of liturgical and ecclesiastical teachings; and the judicial importance attached to the personal and subjective experience of religious belief. It notes the new definition and extension of charitable purposes, the absence of any reform relating to the requirements for charities engaging in trading and considers the implications arising for the ongoing involvement of the Church of England in service provision.

[7] See, for Singapore, the final report of the Inter-Ministry Committee on the *Regulation of Charities and Institutions of Public Character*, 2006.

[8] See, Hong Kong Law Reform Commission, *Consultation Paper on Charities*, 16 June 2011.

6.2 The Drivers and Outcomes of Charity Law Reform

That charity law reform occurred when it did, and then took the direction it did, were matters determined by a mix of domestic and international factors. While the governments of all jurisdictions involved were motivated by much the same set of incentives, in England and subsequently in the other UK jurisdictions a considerable focus of attention came to center upon religion, religious organizations and the advancement of religion as a charitable purpose: in no other reforming jurisdiction was there such an interest. The outcome, for all religions and faith-based bodies was unexpected and challenging but for the established Church of England it was particularly threatening.

6.2.1 Reform Drivers

The traditional common law approach, designed to address the social needs of Elizabethan England, no longer provided an appropriate or sufficient legal framework for charity in the twenty-first century.[9] The pace of socio-economic change in all developed western countries had left relatively untouched a range of long standing social problems and failed to prevent the emergence of many new ones. Charity, as traditionally defined, was no longer fit for purpose in terms of accommodating the many new and pressing social issues nor was the regulatory framework as efficient and effective as it needed to be in the post-9/11 world of global terrorism.

6.2.2 Regulatory Inadequacy

As the numbers of charities increased, so too did evidence of inadequacy in the mechanisms for ensuring relevance, accountability and transparency in relation to charitable activity.

For centuries the matching of charity law to patterns of social need had relied upon the common law capacity to provide judicial or other regulatory decisions in response to newly emerging problems: applying the law to new issues required charitable purposes to be judicially re-interpreted in a broad and creative manner sufficient to embrace the new manifestation of beneficiary need. This was wholly dependent upon a regular flow of cases through the courts. However, this flow had

[9] See, further, McGregor-Lowndes, M., and K. O'Halloran (eds.). 2010. *Modernising charity law: Recent developments and future directions*. Cheltenham: Elgar.

virtually dried up in all modern common law jurisdictions for reasons to do with the expense and time of court proceedings and the unwelcome media attention that such cases tended to attract. In some jurisdictions, such as Australia, decades passed without any significant charity law cases being heard in the higher courts. Reliance upon judicial intervention to ensure that the law developed in accordance with its evermore rapidly changing social context, a salient hallmark of the common law, had itself become a serious structural flaw in the charity law framework.

Moreover, in all jurisdictions except England, the regulatory agency assessing charitable purpose was the Revenue which was doing so for tax assessment purposes and was therefore not predisposed to interpret tax exempt charitable purposes generously. Only in England was there a charity specific lead regulatory body – the Charity Commission – that could focus on inspecting and supporting charities. So, the common law basis upon which the efficiency of charity law depended was failing.

There was also a general problem with the number of government agencies involved with charity matters.

The different areas of responsibility were distributed across different sets of statutes while government responsibility was diffused and alternated between several departments. There was a growing realisation that better systems were needed to identify, register and regulate charities, for the consolidation of legislative provisions relating to charities and their activities and for either a simplification or better co-ordination of the government departments and agencies involved. The widespread media coverage given to corporate scandals in the US (Enron[10] etc.) spread alarm elsewhere and awakened a general concern to ensure that adequate standards of propriety prevailed in corporate boardrooms. In all jurisdictions a primary reform incentive was to improve the scrutiny of charities and protect against abuse of charitable status, fraud and misuse of funds for terrorist purposes.

In England & Wales, the only common law jurisdiction with a charity specific regulator, the existing regulatory framework had the additional deficiency of excluding religious organisations. The Charity Commission had an established practice of categorising such entities as 'excepted' from the standard requirement that all charities should submit to the registration and supervisory regime.[11]

After years of various inquiries rejecting a statutory definitional reform of the definition of charity, the above quoted 2002 Strategy Unit Report[12] had recommended wide ranging definitional and regulatory reform for the law of charities. This included

[10] The Enron scandal, revealed in October 2001, eventually led to the bankruptcy of the Enron Corporation, an American energy company based in Houston, Texas. This, the largest bankruptcy reorganization in American history at that time, was attributed to audit failure.

[11] See, Charity Commission, 'Changes to the Regulation of Excepted and Exempt Charities', August 2011, at: http://www.charitycommission.gov.uk/start_up_a_charity/do_i_need_to_register/regreq.aspx.

[12] See, Cabinet Office Strategy Unit, *Private Action, Public Benefit: A Review of Charities and the Wider Not-For-Profit Sector*, London, 2002.

recommendations for a modernisation and restatement of charitable purposes, reform of the Charity Commission and the establishment of a Charity Tribunal.

6.2.3 Charitable Purpose Inadequacy

The four heads of *Pemsel*,[13] which had for centuries defined the spectrum of charitable purposes available to address social need, were no longer adequate.[14] They were failing to provide an appropriate and sufficient classification of purposes for the burgeoning range of charitable activity that was evolving in response to contemporary patterns of social need; in effect, the law was constricting the development of more relevant charitable purposes.

Certain matters urgently required attention. The definition of "charitable purposes" needed to be broadened so as to permit charities to undertake new forms of activity, and enable organisations with such activities to acquire charitable status. Immigration had introduced not just a larger workforce and a more multi-cultural society but also the "asylum seekers" phenomenon, racism, and new variants of inequity. Charities now had to be encouraged to develop innovative pluralistic methods of social intervention. Climate change, global threats to health, the degrading of the environment and a host of emerging social challenges needed corresponding recognition in charity law if organizations and gifts to them were to acquire charitable status and their resources channeled to address an ever expanding spectrum of need.

The legal problems relating to charitable purposes were not confined to their limited range. The bearing of the 'public benefit test' on charitable purposes was also problematic. Satisfying this test, a mandatory pre-condition for attaining or retaining charitable status, imposed a burden that varied according to the charitable purpose being pursued by an organization. A legal presumption held that an organization or gift dedicated to a purpose that fell within the legal definition of one of the first three heads (poverty relief, trust the advancement of education or the advancement of religion) would be deemed to satisfy the test; although this presumption could be rebutted. This differential in the burden borne by organisations seeking charitable status was viewed by many as iniquitous; there was a 'level playing field' argument that all charities be subject to a uniform public benefit test. In that event, there were questions as to how the test might be applied to religious purposes: definitional issues relating to 'religion' and theism had to be addressed.

Such questions prompted the Church of England and other bodies to resist the proposal that the presumption of public benefit compliance favouring religious

[13] *Commissioners for Special Purposes of Income Tax v. Pemsel* [1891] AC 531.

[14] Ibid. As Lord Macnaghten then ruled:

> 'Charity' in its legal sense comprises four principal divisions: trusts for the relief of poverty; trusts for the advancement of education; trusts for the advancement of religion; and trusts beneficial to the community not falling under any of the preceding heads' at p. 583.

organisations should be removed. The Church of England warned that Christian charities in particular were in danger of political interference from such changes to the public benefit rules. It expressed concern that a charity existing exclusively to promote traditional Christian views in a particular area – such as marriage and sexual ethics – could have its charitable status threatened. It took the view that the Commission's intention to assess – membership criteria, evangelism methods, doctrinal interpretation, and public opinion – seriously exceeded the Commission's powers and competence. It also pointed out that religious groups providing pastoral care were already under pressure in other areas to suppress their religious character and distinctive attributes.[15]

6.2.4 Human Rights Compliancy

Charity law reform was also pushed along by the concern of both government and charity to ensure that a future regulatory regime would be able to Convention-proof law and practice. The common law principles and parameters that had for so long determined charitable activity were, by the end of the twentieth century, being impacted by developments in the law relating to matters such as human rights, equity, equality and discrimination. Following the incorporation of the European Convention on Human Rights (ECHR) into UK law through the Human Rights Act 1998, all 'public bodies' including courts, local authorities and the Charity Commission, had been required to ensure that their processes and decisions were Convention compliant[16] (see, further, Chap. 7). For the most part, following the introduction of the 1998 Act, there was confidence that the relevant rights (e.g. freedom of expression and freedom of association and assembly) were adequately addressed but some other matters also needed attention.

There was, for example, as issue as to whether a charity, particularly a government funded facility registered as a charity, would be a juridical entity and if so whether it would then be a "public body" for the purposes of accountability to Convention requirements? It was also abundantly clear that the interpretation of 'religion' would have to be sufficiently inclusive to accommodate ECtHR rulings regarding multi-theism and non-theism etc. and to safeguard against the possibility of discriminatory practice such as a Christian bias, or favouring the ancient religions to the detriment of the newly emerging evangelical and other faith groups.

---

[15] See, further, at: http://www.cofe.anglican.org/info/papers/info/papers/advancementofreligion.rtf.

[16] The Human Rights Act 1998, s 1(1), makes it unlawful for any public authority to act in a manner that breaches a Convention right or freedom as defined in Articles 2–12 of the Convention, Articles 1–3 of the First Protocol and Articles 1 and 2 of the Sixth Protocol as read with Articles 16–18 of the Convention.

6.2.5 *Political Incentives*

In the late twentieth century the developed world was experiencing the retraction of the State accompanied by a corresponding rolling forward of the nonprofit sector. This was partly the consequence of a political initiative aimed at broadening the established relationship between government and citizens, allowing the latter more participation and representation in the democratic process with the hope of thereby facilitating greater social cohesion. The only legal framework available to delineate the respective parameters of responsibility for government and the sector was that provided by the common law principles and the legislative provisions of charity law. It rapidly became apparent that this framework needed to be revised if it was to reflect the reality of contemporary rules of engagement between government and the sector and facilitate the further development of their social partnership. Promoting the growth of a vigorous and independent nonprofit sector was, in the developed nations, prompted by a pressing need to share the costs of public service provision. The burden of responsibility for future provision had to be shifted to some extent towards the nonprofit sector, where charities in particular had an entrenched involvement in health, education and social care services. This was also seen as, happily, serving the purpose of enhancing the capacity of democratic politics: encouraging the use of volunteers in public service provision being viewed by government as a means of promoting civic engagement and building social capital. However, the uncertain line to be drawn between the responsibilities of government and charity to provide services or utilities for the public benefit has long been governed by charity law. Any redistribution of responsibility would require that law to be revised.

6.2.6 *Reform Outcomes*

The reform processes proved to be long and challenging for government/sector relationships in all the jurisdictions concerned. Some reform processes collapsed as the domestic party political environment changed, in others the process has perhaps become stuck or petered out, but many achieved very significant changes.[17] In England the process started at the turn of the century and ended with the introduction of the Charities Act 2006 as subsequently incorporated into the Charities Act 2011. For present purposes, while a holistic legal or political comparative analysis of reform outcomes would be a distraction, it is necessary to examine not just those with a direct bearing on religion but some consideration must also be given to the changes in the context within which the reformed charitable purpose of religion will in future operate.

[17] Australia seemingly going furthest with its extension of reform provisions to the entire nonprofit sector.

6.2.7 Changes to the Regulatory Framework

The main outcomes achieved by the law reform processes were the statutory introduction of: a charity specific Commission-type regulator in all jurisdictions where one did not previously exist, the transfer of responsibility for determining charitable status from the Revenue to the Commission, a registration procedure and tighter audit and accountability mechanisms; and a new Charity Appeals Tribunal.

Until the recent law reform processes only a very few jurisdictions had in place a government body (or quasi government body), alongside but independent of the tax authority, vested not only with statutory duties requiring it to provide charities with support and supervision but also with statutory powers enabling it to play a developmental role in relation to charities and their purposes. The Charity Commission, alone among all such bodies, was statutorily equipped with such capacity and has been in a position to offset the revenue driven emphasis typical of the traditional regulatory approach to charities in all other common law jurisdictions. Its role and powers devolved from the *parens patriae* authority of the Crown, as subsequently exercised by the Chancellor and then by the Attorney General, to the Charity Commission when it was established by the 1601 statute. It maintains a national register of charities and monitors, supervises, supports and holds accountable, those registered. Initially its primary focus was on: protection for donors; prevention of deliberate abuse, careless inefficiency and misuse of status by charities; and providing for the removal of charitable status from bodies found by Commissioners to be in breach of stated standards. Over time its statutory terms of reference have grown though the addition of more extensive and sophisticated powers to include policing access to charitable status and the consequent entitlement to tax exemption. It is credited with broadening the interpretation of charitable purposes, particularly under the 4th *Pemsel* head, to permit a more elastic application of common law principles. Decisions of the Commission are subject to review by the courts but are binding, in particular on the Revenue.

The Charity Commission has developed to be an agency of central importance to the regulatory framework for charities in England & Wales[18] and its introduction in all other UK jurisdictions[19] and in Australia,[20] New Zealand[21] and Singapore[22] is a

[18] Introduced initially by the Statute of Charitable Uses 1601, revived by the Charitable Trusts Act 1858, its powers were considerably extended a century later by the Charities Act 1960, again by the 1993 Act, most recently by the Charities Act 2006 and are now to be found in the Charities Act 2011.

[19] See, the Office of the Scottish Charity Regulator established by the Charities and Trustee Investment (Scotland) Act 2005; and the Charity Commission for Northern Ireland, established by the Charities Act (Northern Ireland) 2008.

[20] See, the Australian Charities and Not-for-profits Commission (ACNC) established by the Australian Charities and Not-for-profits Commission Act 2012.

[21] See, the Charities Act 2005 which established a new Autonomous Crown Entity (ACE), the Charities Commission, but in May 2012 the Commission was disestablished, merged with the Department of Internal Affairs (DIA), and its registration and deregistration duties transferred to the Charities Registration Board.

[22] See, the office of the Commissioner of Charities, established by the Charities Act (cap. 37).

most important law reform outcome. Its pivotal role in balancing the government/ charity relationship has remained substantially unchanged by the reform process in this jurisdiction. However, in the post-reform era, its decisions on issues relating to the involvement of charities in matters of religion, human rights and trading are of growing significance for the Church of England and are therefore very relevant for this book (see, further, Chap. 7).

6.2.8 *Changes to the List of Charitable Purposes*

Of all the common law nations that, in recent years, have undertaken charity law reform, only a very few have introduced new charities legislation. Of these, fewer still have altered the existing charitable purposes by adding to the *Pemsel* list. Without exception, however, all nations have at least retained as charitable, if not added to, the purposes first identified and listed in the 1601 statute and as classified in *Pemsel*. Moreover, the core common law conceptual basis of charity was invariably grafted on to the statute law. So, throughout the common law jurisdictions for a charity to be recognized as such an entity must continue to: be confined exclusively to charitable purposes; be for the public benefit; be independent; be forbidden from distributing profits; and its purposes must not be illegal[23] nor be primarily political. There are some jurisdictional variations in the interpretation of these attributes, and donor intention can also be very relevant, but these have long been and will continue to be the legal hallmarks of charity. The bedrock of charity law in the future, throughout the common law world, will therefore remain firmly based on the *Pemsel* classification, the core concepts and on the accompanying vast body of case law principles and precedents.

For England & Wales – followed in due course by the remaining UK jurisdictions, Ireland and Australia – an important reform outcome was the statutory inclusion of a *Pemsel* plus list of charitable purposes, new definitions of core common law concepts including charitable purposes and the public benefit test.[24]

[23] It is worth noting that this requirement may present problems: Islamic and other religious organisations are registerable as charities but some of their beliefs (e.g. condoning or promote polygamy) are illegal in this jurisdiction.

[24] Under the Charities Act 2011, s.3(1):

A purpose falls within this subsection if it falls within any of the following descriptions of purposes –

(a) the prevention or relief of poverty;
(b) the advancement of education;
(c) the advancement of religion;
(d) the advancement of health or the saving of lives;
(e) the advancement of citizenship or community development;
(f) the advancement of the arts, culture, heritage or science;
(g) the advancement of amateur sport;
(h) the advancement of human rights, conflict resolution or reconciliation or the promotion of religious or racial harmony or equality and diversity;

The UK and Irish jurisdictions have now committed to much the same set of "*Pemsel* plus" charitable purposes. Their respective legislative provisions list, as separate purposes, a number of activities that have gained judicial recognition over time. These include the advancement of animal welfare, the advancement of environmental protection or improvement and the advancement of the arts, culture, heritage or science. However, they also and with remarkable consistency identify as additional charitable purposes certain specific matters of such central importance to government as:

- the advancement of human rights, conflict resolution or reconciliation, and promotion of multiculturalism etc.;
- the advancement of civil society;
- the advancement of health and related services; and
- promoting the welfare of specific socially disadvantaged groups.

This is a clear political statement of additional matters now statutorily defined within all the jurisdictions of these islands to be of contemporary public benefit and of such importance as to merit charitable status. The *Pemsel* plus list creates a new and more inclusive statutory platform that will facilitate the future contribution of charity to specific public benefit activity and clarify the terms of reference of government's intended partnership with the sector on related service provision issues. Of even greater significance is the fact that all charitable purposes are now placed on the statute book, thereby enabling any future government to swiftly and directly delete, adjust or add charitable purposes by simply amending the legislation.

6.2.9 Human Rights Compliant

The statutory encoding of core common law charity concepts is most important in the present context because it brings with it, for the first time in English law, something approximating a definition of 'religion'. The concern to address possible

(i) the advancement of environmental protection or improvement;
(j) the relief of those in need by reason of youth, age, ill-health, disability, financial hardship or other disadvantage;
(k) the advancement of animal welfare;
(l) the promotion of the efficiency of the armed forces of the Crown, or of the efficiency of the police, fire and rescue services or ambulance services;
(m) any other purposes –

    (i) that are not within paragraphs (a) to (l) but are recognised as charitable purposes by virtue of section 5 (recreational and similar trusts, etc.) or under the old law,
    (ii) that may reasonably be regarded as analogous to, or within the spirit of, any purposes falling within any of paragraphs (a) to (l) or sub-paragraph (i), or
    (iii) that may reasonably be regarded as analogous to, or within the spirit of, any purposes which have been recognised, under the law relating to charities in England and Wales, as falling within sub-paragraph (ii) or this sub-paragraph.

opportunities for discriminatory treatment resulted in that definition being so broad as to create uncertainty as to what the threshold might be for excluding belief or ethical systems. The introduction of a 'flat rate' public benefit test, equally applicable to religious purposes as to all others, was another strategy for eliminating discrimination but one that brought with it complications as to what exactly the test would be applied in the context of the mixed sacred and secular roles of religious organizations (see, further, Chap. 7).

6.2.10 Changes in Relation to the Public Benefit Test

As declared in what is now s.4 of the 2011 Act:

(3) In determining whether that requirement is satisfied in relation to any such purpose, it is not to be presumed that a purpose of a particular description is for the public benefit.

The public benefit test can only be satisfied by argument and proof in respect of all charitable purposes, even if any such purpose is listed in the Act as prima facie charitable. This is a very significant change both because it applies to the advancement of religion and also because the UK jurisdictions are alone in introducing it. For more than 400 years, since the Charitable Uses Act 1601, there has been a legal presumption that religion, religious organizations and gifts to them are for the public benefit and on that basis they are entitled to charitable status – which enabled very many religious entities across the common law world to acquire such status. That presumption is now removed in the UK. Consequently, while elsewhere those entities will maintain their status, in the UK their counterparts run the risk of losing it as they submit to the routine application of a test they were assumed to have satisfied when they initially registered as charities.

This change must be viewed in the light of the statement in s.4(3) of the 2011 Act that "any reference to the public benefit is a reference to the public benefit as that term is understood for the purposes of the law relating to charities in England and Wales". The term was duly subjected to considerable examination by the Upper Tribunal in *Independent Schools Council v. The Charity Commission*[25] which, in giving judgment declared that: "not only is there to be no presumption that religion is generally for the public benefit … but that there is no presumption at any more specific level and thus no presumption that Christianity or Islam are for the public benefit and no presumption that the Church of England is for the public benefit". The law must now be interpreted bearing in mind the guidance available from that judgment and in the light of new guidance issued by the Commission in September 2013.[26]

[25] [2011] UKUT 421 (TCC) (13 October 2011).

[26] The new guidance completely replaces the Commission's previous general public benefit guidance 'Charities and Public Benefit' and supplementary public benefit guidance on 'Public Benefit and Fee-charging' (the latter was removed from the Commission's website following the above

Also, although the 2011 Act does not expressly mention the concept of 'detriment' (introduced in equivalent Scottish legislation) the Charity Commission, when assessing the public benefit of a charity, including one for the advancement of religion, will "take detriment or harm into account where it is reasonable to expect that it will result from the individual organisation's purpose – this will be based on evidence …".[27] As Briggs J has explained "an organisation which proposes to fulfil a purpose for the public benefit will only qualify as a charity if, taking into account any dis-benefit arising from its modus operandi, its activities nonetheless yield a net public benefit".[28] Any such detriment must be proven by objective and informed evidence which in nature and degree can be less than needed to constitute illegal behaviour. The Charity Commission points out that the conduct of some religious groups might meet the definition of detriment, for example "the current charitable status of Christian Scientists and Jehovah's Witnesses might be … compromised by their absolute refusal to allow blood transfusions even for a child in a life-threatening situation".[29]

Again a rule not mentioned in the 2011 Act, but which can be safely assumed to be part of charity law is the 'activities test'. In this jurisdiction, the courts have long considered an activities test to be justifiable. For example, in *Inland Revenue Commissioners v. City of Glasgow Police Athletic Association*[30] it was explained that:

> … in order to ascertain what the purposes of an association are, the court is not limited to consideration of its rules or its constituent documents … I begin with the rules … But it will not do to stop there … The question is what are the purposes for which the association is established, as shown by the rules, its activities and its relation to the police force and the public.

In recent years, the Commission has come more firmly to the view that this additional test is necessary in circumstances where there is doubt regarding the alignment between a charity's purpose and its practice.[31]

---

ruling of the Upper Tribunal in 2011). – See more at: http://www.charitycommission.gov.uk/news/new-public-benefit-guidance/#sthash.kbL5nsJ6.dpuf.

[27] Ibid at 'Part Four: Detriment or Harm'.

[28] See, *Catholic Care (Diocese of Leeds) v. the Charity Commission for England and Wales and the Equality and Human Rights Commission* [2010] EWHC 520 (Ch), 17 March 2010, per Briggs J at para. 97.

[29] See, for example, *Re N (A Child: Religion: Jehovah's Witness)* [2011] EWHC B26 (Fam) where in relation to separated parents – the mother a Jehovah's Witness, the father an Anglican – exercising their parental responsibilities in respect of their 4-year-old child, the court ordered that in the event of any medical professional recommending a blood transfusion the mother should immediately inform the medical authorities of the father's contact details and of his ability to consent to such treatment.

[30] [1953] 1 All ER 747, per Lord Normand, at pp. 751–52.

[31] See, e.g., Charity Commission, RR2 Promotion of Urban and Rural Regeneration, (Version – March 1999), 'Tests for Charitable Status'. To be charitable, an organization will need to demonstrate that "the public benefit from its activities outweighs any private benefit" (at para. 4).

6.3 The Consequences of Reform for Religion and Religious Organisations

The Charities Act 2011 – which replaced most of the Charities Acts 1992, 1993 and 2006 and all of the Recreational Charities Act 1958 – came into effect on 14 March 2012. The law governing the relationship between charity and religion and, in that context, our understanding of the way in which religion contributes to public benefit in England then changed; with the other UK jurisdictions following suit. For religious organisations this has given rise to some uncertainty as to: their current legal standing in relation to the statutory meaning of 'religion'; how to determine 'religious belief'; the legal weighting to be given to the charitable purpose of 'advancing religion'; how to identify and weigh the 'benefit' quotient of religion; and the interpretation of activities which could be construed as constituting its 'advancement'. In reviewing the role traditionally played by religion and religious charities, governments in all the reforming jurisdictions have also been faced with some fundamental questions regarding secularism. In this jurisdiction the consequences are already being felt and as controversy increases so does the lobbying for Parliament to intervene to safeguard the position of the Church of England.

6.3.1 Religion and Religious Beliefs

The legal interpretation traditionally given to 'religion', 'religious organisations' and to 'the advancement of religion' will continue in the post-reform era and will be sufficient in all common law jurisdictions to determine charitable status (see, also, Chap. 1). It is the additions in the UK jurisdictions, the broader meaning now attached to some terms, and the exclusionary nature of some aspects of the law as statutorily stated, that give rise to difficulties. There is also the consequent difficulty that while problems can be anticipated for some UK religious bodies and gifts to them that seek to acquire or retain charitable status, they will also arise when equivalent bodies and gifts in other non-UK jurisdictions acquire or retain the status denied to those in England.

6.3.2 God/s

The Charities Act 2011, s.3(2), states that in charity law a religion "involves a belief in more than one god, and; a religion which does not involve a belief in a god". This stretches the previous common law requirement for a 'supreme being': removing the need for any theistic component; and accommodating polytheism and secularism. It is, however, an interpretation not far removed from that advanced in 1963 by John Robinson, a New Testament scholar and Anglican bishop, who suggested that a modern secular society required 'God' to be understood less in terms of a specific deity but more as "the ground of our being".[32]

6.3.3 Moral or Ethical Belief Systems

It is clear from the 2011 Act and Charity Commission guidance that moral or ethical belief systems may now fit within the 'advancement of religion' charitable purpose. An example of what this might mean in practice was provided by a ruling of the Commission which, in its consideration of spiritualism in a charity law context, took the view that promoting mediumship and communication with the spirit world was a legitimate aspect of the advancement of religion. The Commission then proceeded to confirm the charitable status of the Sacred Hands Spiritual Centre.[33] This decision is in keeping with the new statutory definition but seems to strip from the meaning of 'religion' any need for God, it removes the worship component and it accommodates a belief system that has at most only a remote link to religion as we have known it. The spectrum of belief systems that may constitute "religion" would seem to extend indefinitely, diluting and attenuating the original concept, which has given rise to concern. Acknowledging the problem, Weatherup J in *Christian Institute*[34] has suggested that some boundaries are now needed. In determining whether a system of belief would warrant charitable status he advised that[35]:

> The 'threshold requirements' are that the belief must be consistent with basic standards of human dignity or integrity, it must possess an adequate degree of seriousness and importance and it must be intelligible and capable of being understood …

This is interesting. Weatherup J pointedly stresses that a 'believer' is not necessarily a person whose beliefs are as set down in a doctrine to which he or she subscribes and which brings with it membership obligations to behave in a prescribed manner. Since then a number of cases have further explored the range of beliefs that may now qualify for charitable status alongside the traditional religious bodies. In *Grainger v. Nicholson,*[36] for example, the Employment Appeal Tribunal considered whether the appellant Mr Nicholson's allegedly strongly held philosophical belief about climate change and the alleged resulting moral imperatives (that carbon emissions must be urgently cut to avoid catastrophic climate change) were capable of constituting a philosophical belief within the meaning of paragraph 2(1) of the 2003 Regulations which

---

[32] See, Robinson, J. 1963. *Honest to god*. Norwich: SCM Press (new edition May 2009).

[33] See, Charity Commission, "Decision to register Sacred hands Spiritual Centre as a Charity". This was a review of the decision on July 24, 2001 which had then rejected an application for registration.

[34] *Christian Institute and Others v. Office of First Minister and Deputy First Minister* Neutral Citation no. [2007] NIQB 66.

[35] Ibid, at para 48.

[36] [2009] UKEAT 0219 09 0311 (EAT).

states that "*belief* means any religious or philosophical belief".[37] The Tribunal found that "the claimant has settled views about climate change, and acts upon those views in the way in which he leads his life … his belief goes beyond mere opinion".[38] Within a year other tribunals had applied this test to extend recognition to a range of belief systems, such as anti-fox hunting[39] to a belief in the higher purpose of public service broadcasting.[40] However, a limit of sorts was reached when a Employment Tribunal rejected a claim that wearing a poppy in commemoration of the sacrifices made by the British armed forces military personnel constitutes a philosophical belief deserving protection under the Equality Act 2010.[41] The Tribunal took the view that "the belief that one should wear a poppy to show respect to servicemen, however admirable … seems to lack the characteristics of cogency, cohesion and importance".

The Charity Commission also broadened its approach, as became evident when it recognised the Druid Network as charitable.[42] The Commission decided that the combination of Druid belief in a supreme being, its rationale for connecting with 'sacred nature', its emphasis on the importance of ancestors, cultural heritage and the natural environment, and its common elements of worship and their integration into an ethical and moral system were a sufficient demonstration of an 'identifiable positive, beneficial, moral or ethical framework' to qualify for charitable status. Then, in October 2011, the Commission registered the British Humanist Association as a charity, thereby recognising as charitable the Association's aim to pursue the "advancement of humanism, namely a non-religious ethical life stance, the essential elements of which are a commitment to human wellbeing and a reliance on reason, experience and a naturalistic view of the world".[43] A spokeswoman for the Commission explained that: "both religious organisations and non-religious organisations promoting the moral and spiritual improvement of the community may have purposes that are potentially recognisable as charitable. The requirement of public benefit for both kinds of purpose is considered by the Commission to be the same." This decision to register as a charity an organisation which has non-religious beliefs and which campaigns for a secular society is something of a milestone in the post-reform era. It may be anticipated that many non-religious belief systems previously registered under the 4th *Pemsel* head, where they were required to demonstrate public benefit, will now be registerable under the broader interpretation of 'religion' available in the post-reform era.

---

[37] This wording resulted from an amendment inserted in April 2007 by the Equality Act 2006, s.77(1). Prior to the amendment, the word "similar" appeared before the words "philosophical belief" but to be defined as 'similar' to religion was viewed by some as offensive to humanists and atheists.

[38] *Grainger v. Nicholson*, *op cit*, at para 13.

[39] See, *Hashman v. Milton Park (Dorset) Ltd (t/a Orchard Park)* ET/3105555/09.

[40] See, *Maistry v. BBC* ET/1313142/10.

[41] See, *Lisk v. Shield Guardian Co Ltd*, ET/3300873/11.

[42] See, *The Druid Network* [2010] Ch Comm Decision (21 September 2010). The Druid Network explains that it exists for "Informing, Inspiring and Facilitating Druidry as a Religion".

[43] See, further, at: http://www.charity-commission.gov.uk/.

Most recently, the Supreme Court in *R (on the application of Hodkin and another) v. Registrar General of Births, Deaths and Marriages*[44] gave further consideration to religion and belief systems when it ruled that a Scientologist chapel is 'a place of meeting for religious worship' for the purposes of s.2 of the Places of Worship Registration Act 1855. Although this ruling stops short of re-defining Scientology as a religion, still less as a charity, it does greatly increase the probability that the Commission will now have to grant such status to this organization. Of particular note is the following comment offered by Toulson LJ:[45]

> I would describe religion in summary as a spiritual or non-secular belief system, held by a group of adherents, which claims to explain mankind's place in the universe and relationship with the infinite, and to teach its adherents how they are to live their lives in conformity with the spiritual understanding associated with the belief system. By spiritual or non-secular I mean a belief system which goes beyond that which can be perceived by the senses or ascertained by the application of science. I prefer not to use the word 'supernatural' to express this element because it is a loaded word which can carry a variety of connotations. Such a belief system may or may not involve belief in a supreme being, but it does involve a belief that there is more to be understood about mankind's nature and relationship to the universe than can be gained from the senses or from science.

For present purposes, however, it is the conjunction of the Toulson LJ comment together with the finding that the s.2 phrase "has to be interpreted in accordance with a contemporary understanding of religion and not by reference to the culture of 1855"[46] which is interesting. The fact that the highest court in the land is now clearly stating that the meaning given to 'religion', 'belief' and associated concepts must (or may) be translated rather than transplanted – to fit within contemporary culture rather than reflect the meaning ascribed by the culture of origin – carries significant implications for the approach to be adopted in future by court, Commission and, indeed, by government.

6.3.4 Doctrine, Tenets, Worship etc.

The traditional reliance, in charity law terms, on a body of doctrine, liturgical and ecclesiastical teachings, modes of worship etc. to verify the substantive nature of a religion, would seem not to have survived the reform process. Again, while this traditional component will still be regarded by courts and regulators as helpful, it is no longer viewed as essential. As Toulson LJ reminded the court in *Hodkin*, to come within the definition of religion and for adherents to enjoy the freedom to worship, "should not depend upon fine theological or liturgical niceties".[47] Neither court nor

[44] [2013] UKSC 77.

[45] Ibid at para 57.

[46] Ibid, per Toulson LJ at para 34. Citing in support the judgment of Adams CJ in *Malnak v. Yogi* 592 F.2d 197 (1979) and *Church of the New Faith v. Comr of Pay-Roll Tax (Victoria)* (1983) 154 CLR.

[47] *R (on the application of Hodkin and another) v. Registrar General of Births, Deaths and Marriages, op cit,* at para 63.

Commission will involve itself in matters of doctrine except where the outworking of particular doctrinal beliefs impacts upon the public benefit of the organisation. In practice this requires an assessment of the extent to which any such manifestation of religious beliefs through secular activity does, or may, constitute a benefit to the public as well as to its adherents. Certainly the opportunity was not taken to include any reference to doctrines etc. in the 2011 Act.

However, as was demonstrated in the post-reform case of *Gallagher v. Church of Jesus Christ of Latter-Day Saints,*[48] the established rule that places of worship must allow for public access if they are to qualify for charitable status continues in effect. In this case the House of Lords considered whether the Temple of the Mormon Church in the Borough of Chorley in Lancashire was a hereditament that could be defined as a 'place of public religious worship' such as to qualify for charitable exemption from rates under the Local Government Finance Act 1988. The premises were not open to the public, and not even open to all Mormons, as a right of entry was reserved to those members who had acquired a "recommend" from their bishop. The court considered itself bound by an earlier decision of the House[49] when it held that the Mormon Temple at Godstone was not exempt from rates as a "place of public religious worship" as the term could not apply to such places from which the public was excluded. It also considered and dismissed a claim that to deny exemption would be to discriminate against the Church on the grounds of religion (see, further, Chap. 7). Nor could a claim be sustained that the Temple was entitled to exemption on the ground that its use was ancillary to the use of other buildings which were so entitled because, as Lord Denning MR had said 40 years earlier[50]:

> The short answer is that this temple is not a church hall, chapel hall nor a similar building. It is not in the least on the same footing as a church hall or chapel hall. It is a very sacred sanctuary, quite different from a building of that category.

6.3.5 Subjective Understanding

A significant aspect of the *Grainger* case, repeated in such other post-reform cases as *Williamson*[51] and *Begum*[52] (see, further, Chap. 8) is the judicial insistence that it is the subjective experience of religious belief that is all-important. As Elias P explained in *Eweida*[53]: "it is not necessary for a belief to be shared by others in

---

[48] *Gallagher v. Church of Jesus Christ of Latter-Day Saints* [2008] 1 WLR 1852, 1867 [51].

[49] *Gallagher v. Church of Jesus Christ of Latter-Day Saints* [2008] 1 WLR 1852, 1867 [51].

[50] *Henning (Valuation Officer) v. Church of Jesus Christ of Latter-Day Saints* [1962] 1 WLR 1091 at p. 1099.

[51] *R (Williamson) v. Secretary of State for Education and Employment* [2005] 2 AC 246.

[52] *R (On the application of Begum (by her litigation friend, Rahman) v. Headteacher and Governors of Denbigh High School* [2006] UKHL 15 (HL).

[53] *Eweida v. British Airways PLC* [2008] UKEAT 0123 08_2011 (20 November 2008) at para 29.

order for it to be a religious belief, nor need a specific belief be a mandatory requirement of an established religion for it to qualify as a religious belief". This relates to the point made by Weatherup J. Although religious belief, or the lack of it, is clearly a deeply personal matter, the pre-reform understanding of belonging to a religion seemed to imply that in so 'belonging' the individual had chosen one faith in preference to others – presumably on the basis of one set of objectively specified beliefs being preferred to any alternative – and had joined with fellow adherents in a collective membership that would uniformly conduct itself in accordance with those beliefs. This interpretation would seem to be exemplified by the directive in the Second Epistle of Peter that "no prophecy of the Scripture is of any private interpretation".

Such a frame of reference at least had the merit of clear ground rules: it was relatively straightforward to judge from the specification of beliefs whether or not the entity could be construed as religious and, similarly, whether beliefs and conduct of an individual sufficiently corresponded with that specification to warrant the conclusion that he or she was an adherent of that religion; the law then became a matter of administration. The post-reform era would seem to have opened a Pandora's box. Providing admission for idiosyncratic beliefs into the world of settled religions, the creeds and rituals of which have been venerated for millennia, is to invite a dilution of the latter's established theological and social significance. It also requires the law to be adjudicative rather than administrative and the resulting uncertainty leaves room for inconsistency in the treatment of those seeking recognition from regulator or court of their claim to have religious beliefs, which in turn is likely to generate claims of discrimination.

6.3.6 The Advancement of Religion

The law relating to the definition of this charitable purpose remains as pre-reform. For a religious body to be charitable it must still demonstrate that it is advancing religion: meaning that it is promoting, maintaining or practicing it, thereby increasing belief and adherents; and is doing so through means and methods that have become well recognised in charity law. However, and unlike anywhere else in the common law world, in the UK jurisdictions this charitable purpose is now subject to the mandatory application of the public benefit test[54]; for the first time this requires the submission of evidence of benefit to the public before charitable status can be acquired or retained (see, also, Chap. 1).

[54] The presumption in English law that gifts for the advancement of religion satisfy the public benefit test probably dates from the decision in *Morice v. The Bishop of Durham* (1804) 9 Ves 405 when Lord Eldon made a finding which in effect over-ruled the decision of Thurlow LJ in *Brown v. Yeall* 7 Ves 59 which rejected as charitable trusts providing for the distribution of religious books.

6.3.7 Religion and Post-reform Public Benefit

The reversal of the public benefit presumption as a determinant of the charitable status of religious organisations has been and continues to be contentious. Many have questioned what seems to be a reductionist approach whereby religion is to be viewed purely in secular terms: its social worth treated the same as any other charitable purpose and measured against the common benchmark of public benefit; thereby elevating the significance of public benefit relative to a corresponding diminution in the weighting given to religious values. Where is there recognition for the intrinsic value of belief in the transcendent, the spiritual? How should its public benefit be calibrated?

Proof of benefit to the public – hard evidence of measurable improvement to a sufficient number of people – was clearly always going to be more difficult in relation to this particular charitable purpose. The post-reform guidance offered by the Charity Commission has not greatly helped. It states that[55]:

> … to be recognised as charitable, all organisations advancing religion must be able to show that there is a moral or ethical framework which is promoted by the religion. In charity law, it is the existence of an identifiable, positive, beneficial moral or ethical framework that is promoted by a religion which demonstrates that the religion is capable of impacting on society in a beneficial way.

It adds that:

> In respect of charities whose aims include advancing religion, public benefit might be satisfied where the religious beliefs and practices, reflected in the doctrines and codes of the particular religion, encourage its followers or adherents to conduct themselves in a socially responsible way in the wider community. The wider public benefits when the values held and expressed by the religion are put into practice in a way that leads to the moral or spiritual welfare or improvement of society.

It is worthy of note that the Commissions' reference to the possibility of the test being satisfied by doctrines that include a statement of aims and objectives encouraging adherents to engage in socially responsible activities is prefaced by 'might'. This is a cursory acknowledgement of an overriding truth – the activities test will be applied to ascertain whether stated objectives are borne out by actual practice. The Commission advises that in determining public benefit it will be guided by certain principles which it regards as equally applicable to all charitable purposes. The first principle being that there must be an identifiable benefit or benefits: it must be clear what the benefits are; the benefits must be related to the aims; and the benefits must be balanced against any detriment or harm. The second principle is that the benefit must be to the public, or a section of the public: the beneficiaries must be appropriate to the aims; where benefit is to a section of the public, the opportunity to benefit

---

55 See, Charity Commission for England and Wales, *The Advancement of Religion for the Public Benefit* (Version December 2008, as amended December 2011, and again in September 2013), at para D2. Now see, further, at: http://www.charitycommission.gov.uk/detailed-guidance/charitable-purposes-and-public-benefit/

must not be unreasonably restricted by ability to pay any fees charged and people in poverty must not be excluded from the opportunity to benefit; and any private benefit must be incidental.

6.3.8 Public Benefit and the Activities Test

Given the decidedly more onerous burden of proof now resting on such organisations it is hard to envisage the courts taking an approach any less rigorous than that adopted by Donovan J in the pre-reform case of *United Grand Lodge of Free and Accepted Masons of England and Wales v. Holborn Borough Council*,[56] when he considered whether the activities of freemasons could be said to advance religion. Although freemasonry required its members to have faith in God and a belief in good works Donovan J found that as "there is no religious instruction, no programme for the persuasion of unbelievers, no religious supervision to see that its members remain active and constant in the various religions they profess, no holding of religious services, no pastoral or missionary work of any kind" it did not advance or promote any particular religious beliefs and therefore could not itself be a religious charity.

The difficulties in establishing a link between specific religious purposes and public benefit were illustrated by the Charity Commission's post-reform assessment of three applicants. The first, from the Church Mission Society (CMS), concerned a missionary organisation established in 1799 by William Wilberforce and John Newton among others, that proclaims the Christian gospel through 'missionary and outreach activities'.[57] On the facts it upheld the Society's application for charitable status. In the second, the Charity Commission rejected an application from the Gnostic Centre for charitable status.[58] Conceding that gnosticism possessed some of the legal qualities of a religion, such as belief in a supreme being, the Commission held that it nevertheless failed the public benefit test as gnosticism did not promote "a positive, beneficial, moral or ethical framework" because it focused too narrowly on the spiritual welfare of individuals. The Commission found no evidence of "shared morals or ethics" among the movement's followers and said the centre needed to provide hard evidence that as people's spiritual awareness increased, they "exhibited positive behaviours for the benefit of society" i.e. belief was not enough, good works must ensue.

The third post-reform case concerned an application by the Preston Down Trust[59] to be registered as a charity. The Plymouth Brethren, to which the Trust belonged,

[56] [1957] 1 W.L.R. 1080; 121 J.P. 595; 101 S.J. 851; [1957] 3 All E.R. 281.

[57] Charity Commission for England and Wales, *Church Mission Society – A public benefit assessment report*, July 2009 2.

[58] See, Charity Commission for England and Wales, the Gnostic Centre decision made on 16 December 2009, reviewed and confirmed on 11.01.2010.

[59] *Preston Down Trust (Exclusive Plymouth Brethren) v. Charity Commission for England & Wales*, June 2012.

is a religious group, established in 1828 which had been a registered charity for 50 years, with about 16,000 adherents. Far from being a closed sect, this organisation welcomes public participation in its activities. These are said to include support for families, care for young people, disaster relief, visits to prisons, hospitals, donations of substantial funds to many charities, including the British Heart Foundation, Royal National Lifeboat Institution, Macmillan nurses, and many others. In what was the first post-reform instance of charitable status being refused to an established religious group, the Charity Commission expressed its doubts as to the extent of public access to the Trust's services and rested its case on the rather weak grounds that that "the evidence in relation to any beneficial impact on the wider public is perhaps marginal and insufficient to satisfy us as to the benefit of the community." The suggestion that the Trust was in breach of the 'public' arm of the public benefit test by not being more proactive in inviting a public presence (if not participation) in its worship, sacraments, its teaching on the scriptures may have implications for the Church of England, other Christian churches and religious groups. It certainly highlighted the consequences that result from removing the presumption of public benefit and placed the Commission at odds with its regulatory counterpart in Australia where the effect of the presumption was to enable an equivalent Brethren organisation to retain its charitable status. The prospect of the Trust lodging an expensive appeal to the Tribunal was forestalled when, in January 2014, the Commission announced that it would accept an application for charitable status as the Trust had agreed certain changes to its governing documents. In truth, the Commission had little option following the intervening Supreme Court decision in *Hodkin*[60] when, overturning *Segerdal*[61] the court unanimously decided that a Scientologist chapel is 'a place of meeting for religious worship'. The court found that to recognise Scientology as a religion but to then deny its chapel registration as a place of worship would be "illogical, discriminatory and unjust"[62].

6.3.9 The Church of England and Post-reform Public Benefit

One direct consequence of the *Preston Down Trust* case was the prompt introduction in parliament of a well supported private members bill – the Charities Act 2011 (Amendment) Bill 2012–13 intended to re-instate the public benefit presumption traditionally enjoyed by religious organisations – because otherwise "is Judaism, the Catholic Church or even the Church of England itself going to come under pressure to prove their public benefit?"[63] The Bill to amend the

[60] *R (on the application of Hodkin and another) v. Registrar General of Births, Deaths and Marriages* [2013] UKSC 77.

[61] *R v. Registrar General, ex p Segerdal* [1970] 2 QB 697.

[62] *Hodkin*, op cit, per Toulson LJ, at para 64.

[63] See, the speech of Tory MP Mr Bones when introducing the Bill to he House of Commons (18 December 2012). See further at: http://www.telegraph.co.uk/news/politics/9756187/Treat-all-churches-as-charities-MPs-say.html.

Charities Act 2011 failed to complete its passage through Parliament before the end of the session. In June 2013 Mr Bone sponsored a similar private members' bill – the Charitable Status for Religious Institutions Bill 2013–14 – which is due for a second reading in November 2013. Also, and not coincidentally, in June 2013, the House of Commons Select Committee published its report '*The Role of the Charity Commission and "public benefit"*.[64] The Committee accepted the Commission's admission that there is a "lack of certainty as to the law relating to the public benefit requirement for the advancement of religion" and noted its statement that "it is not to be presumed that a purpose of a particular description is for the public benefit".[65] It took the view that "it is for Parliament to resolve the issues of the criteria for charitable status and public benefit, not the Charity Commission" but "we are far from happy with the manner in which the Charity Commission has conducted policy concerning public benefit".[66] The Committee went on state that: the Charities Act 2006 is critically flawed on the question of public benefit ... we recommend that the removal of the presumption of public benefit in the Charities Act 2006 be repealed, along with the Charity Commission's statutory public benefit objective"[67]; adding, for the avoidance of any doubt, that "Parliament must legislate to clarify the flawed legislation on charities and public benefit".[68] Counter-intuitively, perhaps, the Committee also took note of the Commission's submission that it had registered "1,000 new Christian or Christian- related charities in the last year, and 400 new charities of other faiths".[69] So, while uncertainty as to the public benefit test has not hampered the registration of emerging religious charities, the issue of whether they should enjoy exemption from it has not yet been laid to rest and will continue until the matter is revisited by Parliament.

Applying the reformed public benefit test may also become problematic when applied to the traditional religious activities of proselytism and evangelising in a modern human rights context. For example, any benefit to the public inherent in the 1980s activities of the present Archbishop of Canterbury (smuggling bibles into eastern Europe on behalf of the charity Eastern European Mission)[70] may be more difficult to establish following the removal of the charity law presumption and in the face of a counter human rights presumption favouring equality among religions and between those with and those without religious belief. Possibly, if there is a difficulty, it is one that lies primarily with the charity: being based in the U.S. its

[64] See, the House of Commons Select Committee report *The Role of the Charity Commission and "public benefit": Post-legislative scrutiny of the Charities Act 2006* (Third Report of Session 2013–14), London, the Stationery Office Ltd, 2013.

[65] Ibid, citing Ev 152, Charities Act 2006, s.3.

[66] Ibid, at paras 86–87.

[67] Ibid, at paras 91–92.

[68] Ibid at para 163.

[69] Ibid, at para 82.

[70] See, further, Eastern European Mission website where its charitable objects are stated as 'the religious and spiritual instruction of Eastern Europeans', at: http://www.eem.org.

activities, as generated from that jurisdiction, remain unaffected by UK charity law reform (though perhaps open to challenge on human rights grounds from groups representative of non-Christian or secular concerns in eastern Europe); but as it is also registered in the UK, it may well have difficulty in identifying the benefit accruing to the public, and demonstrating that this outweighs any possible detriment, resulting from partisan religious activities in unstable societies.

6.3.10 Public Benefit and Private Piety

However, it can be argued that the persons and other entities engaged in furthering this charitable purpose do not lend themselves to measurement by any standardised public benefit calibration. Applying the Commission's principles may not capture the innate benefits derived from being so engaged: religion per se does not require a social utility function; the effects of intercessory prayer are not measurable. A process designed for the salvation of the soul or souls in the next life is not readily amenable to a quality audit in this one. Where there is a tangible socially beneficial product it may well be wholly extraneous to the core nature of this charitable purpose, if that purpose is essentially concerned with the spiritual welfare of the individual. An alternative way forward specific to this charitable purpose, might lie in recognising its inherent distinctive characteristics and construing the public benefit in terms of the extent to which prayerful activity improves the civic conduct of adherents and the lives of others who may be inspired to self-improvement due to the example set by those adherents: evidence of socially responsible conduct being necessary; without any evidence of accompanying detrimental effects.

Arguably, the courts indicated the appropriateness of such an approach some 50 years ago in the case of *Neville Estates Ltd v. Madden*[71] when Cross J was prepared to confirm the charitable status of a Jewish synagogue that was not open to members of the general public, on the basis that "some benefit accrues to the public from the attendance at places of worship of persons who live in this world and mix with their fellow citizens".[72] This approach allows a religious organisation to simultaneously restrict its activities to its own adherents and to satisfy the test by claiming that the wider public will thereby benefit from both the fact that religious beliefs are being practiced and by the edification which may flow from that practice into the wider community (unlike the practice of such beliefs by a closed order) and thereby teach people to behave better.

---

[71] [1962] 1 Ch 832.

[72] Ibid 853 (Cross J). See further, Iwobi, A. 2009. Out with the old, in with the new: religion, charitable status and the Charities Act 2006. 29 *Legal Studies*: 619, 635–636 citing Haddock, T. 2001. Charitable trusts for the advancement of religion: Judicial rejection of metaphysical benefits and the emergence of public interaction. 7 *Charity Law and Practice Review*: 152.

6.3.11 *Religion and Other Charitable Purposes*

The customary use of other charitable purposes, together with the subliminal nature of religion, has always facilitated the utilisation of schools, hospitals and social care by religious organisation as vehicles for pursuing a blend of spiritual and secular activity. The *Pemsel* plus statutory extension of purposes invites a further diffusion of such activity into newly specified areas.

6.3.12 *The* Pemsel *Plus Charitable Purposes*

For England & Wales the new and extended statutory specification of charitable purposes with possible relevance for religious organizations are to be found in s.3(1) of the 2011 Act: subsections (d) the advancement of health or the saving of lives; (e) the advancement of citizenship or community development; and (j) the relief of those in need by reason of youth, age, ill-health, disability, financial hardship or other disadvantage. Religious charities might be expected to develop a role in relation to all these new statutorily encoded charitable purposes, if they have not already done so. In addition, the inclusion of the advancement of human rights among the new charitable purposes, under s.2 of the Charities Act, could be confidently anticipated to raise issues for religious charities (see, further, Chap. 7).

6.4 Reform Implications for the Church of England

From a post-reform charity law perspective, religion no longer requires a god nor is religion itself, as legally understood, necessarily a 'good thing'. These fundamental changes have set England (and the rest of the UK) apart from other common law jurisdictions and apart from its own developmental history. For all religions and religious organizations seeking charitable status in England the new statutory requirement – to demonstrate how they are adding to the quotient of public benefit and how that contribution outweighs any possible detraction from it – is a challenge. It is one that faces not only all religious entities seeking charitable status in the future, but also all that have already acquired that status, and may well provide an incentive for subsidiaries of English religious charities to transfer their operations to other jurisdictions. The corollary being that any foreign registered religious charity seeking to operate in England may have difficulty in acquiring parity of charitable status. Arguably, for the Church of England the challenge is all the greater because its locus standi as the established Church raises the public benefit bar. In addition, there is some potential for difficulties to arise as a consequence of a lack of reform in certain areas, perhaps most obviously in relation to trading activities which could prove problematic in terms of charitable status.

6.4.1 Religion, Belief Systems and the Church of England

Christianity, as one of the earliest religions, and Protestantism, as embodied in the Church of England, will continue to be assured of recognition as such within the terms of reformed charity law. Indeed, in some post-reform decisions the Charity Commission has made the finding that the beliefs and practices of the Christian religion are capable of advancing religion for the purposes of charity law, while promoting the morals and ethics of the Christian faith is deemed in law to be capable of impacting upon the public in a beneficial way.[73]

For many generations the Church has been treated as an 'excepted' charity meaning that is has been excepted from the obligation to register with the Charity Commission as there is another umbrella organization with supervisory responsibilities in respect of it.[74] However, as with other religions and religious organizations, it will no longer be so defined as among the reforms introduced was the requirement that any such church with an annual income over £100,000 must now register with the Commission and their legal status will change from 'excepted' to 'registered' charity – although the phasing in of this duty has been continually extended.[75]

6.4.2 Traditional Religious Beliefs

As a component part of one of civilisation's most ancient religions, the Church of England and its beliefs, doctrines and liturgy that have continued virtually intact the since the Reformation will remain untroubled by the reformed charity law. As before – its monotheism, the Thirty Nine Articles, the Book of Common Prayer the Ordinal, the liturgy together with the body of doctrines, cannons and all else that has for it, over the centuries, come to constitute 'religion' – will continue to satisfy the requirements necessary to meet the legal definition of that term.

---

[73] See, for example, Church Mission Society, a public benefit assessment report by the Charity Commission, (July 2009) at: http://www.charitycommission.gov.uk/Charity_requirements_guidance/Charity_essentials/Public_benefit/assesschurch.aspx.

[74] Others currently excepted under Statutory Instrument (SI) 2007/2655 include: the Baptist Union; Church in Wales; Congregational Federation; Evangelical of Congregational Churches; Fellowship of Independent Evangelical Churches (FIEC); Grace Baptist Trust Corporation; Methodist Conference; Presbyterian Church in Wales (also known as Calvinistic Methodist Church); Religious Society of Friends; Strict and Particular Baptists; and the United Reformed Church. The Parochial Church Council (PCC) is the registerable entity for the Church of England. Statutory Instrument 2012/1734 issued in July 2012 extended the Regulations until 31 March 2014.

[75] Note that s.23 of 2011 Act permits the Minister to make order in relation to the exempt status of – a Measure of the Church Assembly, or of the General Synod of the Church of England.

6.4.3 *The Public Benefit Test and the Church of England*

As the Chief Legal Advisor for the Charity Commission has recently advised, "there is no presumption that religion generally, or at any more specific level, is for the public benefit, even in the case of Christianity or the Church of England".[76]

Legally, for all UK religions and associated organizations and gifts to them, that statement is accurate. Since the post-reform legislation took effect, the Church of England must prove the fact and nature of its benefit to society – if it wishes to continue its registration as a charity; a status which, for several centuries, the presumption assisted it to retain. However, it is unlikely that the Charity Commission's new approach to public benefit presents any serious threat to the Church's charitable status. Indeed, there is an argument that from a constitutional perspective the fact that the Church is the 'established' religion, chosen above all others to act in partnership with the State, amounts in itself to a clear declaration that it is for the public benefit; it would be strange if was found not to be.

More generally, for this purpose, a distinction is usually drawn between 'religion' as an institution with its body of theology, Churches, ministers etc. and the purely secular role that a religious organization may have in the community. This suggests that the latter dimension is the one to which the public benefit test should be applied to quantify the socially beneficial output of the Church of England. The following might serve as indicators of such benefit.

6.4.4 *The Institutional Presence of the Established Church*

At its most basic, the social benefit of this institution may be construed to lie in its physical presence and in its exercise of ecclesiastic authority which, woven into the landscape, the law and culture of Britain and that of the commonwealth nations, over countless generations, have made an inestimable contribution to the evolution of our present civilization. If it should be considered that past performance is an insufficient indicator of current public benefit then, while the body of acquired theological and legal knowledge may need to be set aside, there is still the mosaic of churches, cathedrals etc. which adorn all corners of the land and provide ongoing visual benefit and a source of solace to many. Similarly, the Book of Common Prayer of 1547 and 1549 as revised in 1662, and the King James Bible of 1611, are among the most enduring of English cultural artefacts and continue to inspire. There is also the function of the Church at christenings, weddings and funerals for the benefit of a large proportion of citizens and in officiating at all ceremonies of State its role as the established Church. To the extent that public benefit may be gauged by the prospective loss of a commonplace social asset, then the removal or denial of access to the Church's many examples of what is best in the English architectural heritage would constitute a serious reduction in the quantum of public benefit currently available.

---

[76] [2011] UKUT 421 (TCC) (13 October 2011) at para 85.

6.4.5 Moral Leadership

Leaving aside its past theological contribution to broadening our understanding of life and its meaning, the Church of England continues to stand as the social institution that in particular embodies civilized standards and values and offers moral leadership on emerging social issues. It may satisfy the public benefit test solely on the grounds that as the national Church it physically represents pastoral care and signifies a refuge or somewhere to turn for those in need. Notwithstanding its superior purpose to prepare those of faith for a supernatural existence: its beliefs embody mankind's highest aspirations; its values as modelled by adherents contribute to making contemporary society a better place; and, anyway, for some millennia, civilisation has accorded religion a special status. Christian principles – as epitomized by the Church – of good and evil, justice and mercy, continue to inform and set boundaries for acceptable social relationships. The Church has gifted civilization a considerable heritage of values centered on generosity, altruism, philanthropy and care for the poor and needy – generated by its doctrines, teachings and practice – which has done much to counterbalance other social pressures. The fact that as a 'pillar of society' it continues to uphold and represent virtuous and decent behaviour serves as a continuing reminder to citizens that 'good works' are needed if society is to be a better place.

6.4.6 Social Utility

The *raison d'etre* of religion does not require it to have any measurable social utility. Quite apart from any socially binding or divisive side effects, the contribution of religion to public benefit rests on the solace, strength and equanimity it may instil in individuals that in this life – their beliefs, and the activities undertaken in giving effect to those beliefs – will be rewarded in the next. Those so comforted may then be motivated to do good for others. While this has been referred to, perhaps unfairly as the resulting 'placebo effect of religion', it may also serve to instil an acceptance of personal deficits, cultivate a more responsible civic polity, generate a greater awareness of community need and the altruism necessary to do something about it. In short, applying the public benefit test so as to ascertain and measure the social utility of religion may be inappropriate, unfair and entirely beside the point.

6.4.7 Public Benefit Test, Trading and the Church of England

Charity law reform left untouched the customary constraints on trading by charities. When considered alongside the bearing of the public benefit test this could result in future difficulties for the Church of England.

6.4.8 Trading and the 'Established' Factor

Here, perhaps, there is an issue of proportionality. Its 'established' status inevitably gives the Church of England greater leverage than that available to any other religion or religious organisation within the jurisdiction (see, further, Chaps. 2, 4 and 7). In the context of the dealings religious charities have with government bodies in relation to service provision contracts, the Church may expect and be expected to have a greater commitment to such provision than any of its counterparts. For example, the Church has for many generations had a very substantial investment in education and is currently poised to seek academy status for several hundred schools. It can be anticipated that other charities, not all religious, are likely to challenge the Church on the grounds of exercising undue influence and market dominance.

Another aspect of the 'established' factor is whether the Church is, for some purposes, acting as a 'public body'. Classification as such is not dependent upon any single factor, but is based on the totality of an organization's relationship with government. If government can be shown to be acting conjointly with the Church then the legal relationship could in fact be one of principal and agent, with the Church being in effect a public body when it is so acting. Relative to all other organizations, religious or not, the constitutionally underpinned close relationship between government and the Church is one which is likely to raise this question. The role of the Church in provision of education services is particularly vulnerable to such a challenge (see, further, Chap. 7).

6.4.9 Direct Service Provision

It can be argued that religious organisations will do what they do with or without charitable status: piety requires good works; such organizations are impelled by their beliefs to engage in public benefit service provision; they need neither charitable status nor tax exemption privileges to continue an established social role that is integral to religious belief. On that basis, the Church and all ancillary religious organisations (i.e. those with a community role) would be ineligible for charitable status as there is no true altruism in doing what you have a duty to do.

However, as economic recession in the UK forces cutbacks in public benefit provision, there is a growing likelihood that government will look to the wealthy institutional structure of the established Church for assistance in making good the public services shortfall. Should the Church of England further develop direct social service provision this could well become the default for identifying and measuring the public benefit contribution necessary for continuation of its charitable status. Consequently, issues may arise as to how stringently secular that contribution should be: would benefit be measured solely on utility or would the religious component be acknowledged as added value; or, alternatively, would the secular function need to be wholly insulated from any possible religious 'contagion'?

Currently, in refutation of its supposed 'congregationalist' approach, the Church of England has a huge investment in education, through many hundreds of schools, and it also provides poverty relief services with food banks, soup kitchens and other services to the socially disadvantaged.

6.4.10 Fees

The Church is in a powerful position in relation to the possibility of raising funds through fees: it is the custodian of a large proportion of the country's architectural and cultural heritage; it provides education through many hundreds of its schools; and in these and other areas it can charge admission fees. The issue for such a fee-charging charity is the effect that charging fees has on those who have the opportunity to benefit from its services or facilities and, where relevant, whether there is sufficient opportunity to benefit for people who cannot afford to pay the full fees charged. High fees may shrink the 'public' input to the point where the public benefit test cannot be satisfied. This is likely to be an issue where the service or facility for which there is a charge forms a significant part of the charity's aims, or the way it carries out those aims, and/or when the fees being charged for that service or facility are high. The higher the level of fees, the greater the number of people who will be denied access to the service and, therefore, the more the charity will have to do to provide those people with sufficient opportunity to also derive some benefit; that benefit must be one that in nature is meaningfully related to the charity's aims, and in quantity is reasonable in proportion to the service (both would most obviously be achieved by providing access on a free, subsidized, or concessional basis to those who cannot afford the fees). If the charity cannot demonstrate that it is addressing that correlation, then it will be in breach of the public benefit test. The imposition of unreasonable admission fees could threaten the charitable status of the buildings concerned, although a requirement that benefit is not unreasonably restricted by ability to pay fees was removed and is currently being revised following a decision by the Upper Tribunal regarding the Commission's guidance on public benefit and fee-charging in relation to educational charities.[77]

6.5 Conclusion

Charity law reform in England (and in the other UK jurisdictions) went much further than other countries in reworking some basic common law precepts. Most other reforming countries settled for altering the regulatory regime: changing the lead

[77] See, Charity Commission for England and Wales, *The Advancement of Religion for the Public Benefit* (Version December 2008, as amended December 2011, and still under review in November 2013), at para E3. See, further at: http://www.charitycommission.gov.uk/RSS/News/pr_public_benefit_fee_charging.aspx.

regulator and tightening supervision and accountability systems; but otherwise they simply encoded the existing common law into statutory provisions. The scale of change to the law in this jurisdiction is extensive with implications for all charities but none will be more radically affected than those dedicated to the advancement of religion – unless Parliament revisits the reform measures and readjusts the provisions relating to public benefit.

The Church of England is now in the curious position of remaining 'established' while at the same time being no longer regarded by the State as necessarily a force for good. Along with all other religions, big and small, ancient and modern, the Church will be required to prove that it is for the public benefit if it is to retain the charitable status it has enjoyed for centuries; and will no longer be shielded from regulatory intrusion by its former 'excepted' privilege. In asserting its claim to be advancing religion, the Church may need to find new ways of calibrating the public benefit of its institutional and civic presence and/or of its social care services and it way well be that weighting will need to be given to the added value that religion can bring to secular activities. On the separate matter of affirming its substantive position as a 'religion' the position of the Church remains unchanged. It is, however, chastening to realise that although the Church will be able, as before, to submit its record of centuries of Christian leadership, of reverence and worship of god – aided by a body of material that includes canon law, ordinals, the Thirty Nine Articles and the Book of Common Prayer – this will not place it in any stronger a position than a newly emerged group with a belief system that does not include a belief in god. The Church's impressive and venerable weight of evidence is wholly predicated on and oriented towards theistic worship which is no longer an essential or even necessary component for substantiating the status of 'religion' for the purposes of reformed charity law. In this post-reform era, the centuries old relatively unchallenged theological standing of the Church of England together with its status as 'established', the presumption of it serving the public good, and the terms upon which it acquires government funding and service contracts are all open to question.

Chapter 7
The Impact of Human Rights

7.1 Introduction

> It seems difficult, if not impossible, to conceive of an official 'State religion' that in practice does not have adverse effects on religious minorities, thus discriminating against their members.[1]

This warning, given by the United Nations Special Rapporteur Heiner Bielefeldt, at a recent session of the UN Human Rights Council, was blunt but timely. Due to its 'established' status, the Church of England is already in a preferential position relative to all other religions and, as it enjoys a closer relationship with government than any other social institution, it is able to speak to it on matters of law and policy in ways that the others cannot. However, the Church must now function in an ever-more enveloping human rights environment. Some of the policies it has recently adopted in relation to its functioning as a religious organisation – designating certain posts to be held on a gender specific or sexuality specific basis – will bring the Church into direct conflict with at least the ethos, and possibly also with the law, governing equity, equality, and discrimination. Other aspects of its secular role as a large corporate employer and service provider will expose it to much the same flux of human rights issues as any other corporate organisation might expect to encounter in today's marketplace. As torch-bearer for the nation on matters of morality and social justice, the Church is of course very aware of and sensitive to its human rights environment. Nonetheless, some of the challenges it faces are quite pressing.

This chapter begins by outlining the legal framework that gives effect to human rights and provides the constraint parameters within which Church of England must now operate. Naturally, this centres on Articles 9 and 14 of the European Convention. It then considers the range of human rights case law with a bearing on religion and the activities of religious charities in order to appreciate the circumstances in which

[1] See, Report of the Special Rapporteur on freedom of religion or belief, Heiner Bielefeldt, (A/HRC/19/60), Geneva (6th March 2012) at: http://reliefweb.int/report/world/report-special-rapporteur-freedom-religion-or-belief-heiner-bielefeldt-ahrc1960.

K. O'Halloran, *The Church of England - Charity Law and Human Rights*, Ius Gentium: Comparative Perspectives on Law and Justice 36, DOI 10.1007/978-3-319-04319-7_7,

the Church may become vulnerable to allegations of inequitable or discriminatory practice. This leads into a concluding section focusing on those contemporary issues with a human rights dimension that the Church will inevitably have to address.

7.2 Human Rights: The Legal Framework

Human rights law, with a bearing on religion and religious organisations, including the Church of England, is to be found in the provisions of both domestic and Convention legislation. Of the former, the most notable are the Human Rights Act 1998 and the Equality Act 2010; the Employment Tribunals Act 1996 (as amended), the Employment Equality (Religion or Belief) Regulations 2003 and the Employment Appeal Tribunal Rules 1993 (as amended) are also relevant. Of the latter, the United Nations Declaration of Human Rights is largely of academic interest while the European Convention is of practical importance, particularly: Article 14 and the right not to suffer discrimination on grounds such as religion; Article 9 and the right to freedom of thought, conscience and religion; Article 11 and the right to freedom of association; Art 18 of the International Covenant on Civil and Political Rights; and the Article 2 of Protocol 1. Also relevant is the Employment Framework Council Directive 2000/78/EC, issued by the Council of the European Union, which provides that 'persons who have been subject to discrimination based on religion or belief, disability, age or sexual orientation should have adequate means of legal protection.' Certain governing principles applied by the European Court of Human Rights (ECtHR) must also be borne in mind.

The twin European institutions applying this law are: the Council of Europe, which includes 47 States, and is responsible for the ECtHR which in turn enforces the 1950 European Convention on Human Rights, as well as other treaties on specific human rights issues; and the European Union, that includes 27 States and has responsibility for the European Court of Justice, which enforces the Charter of Fundamental Rights that is binding on all EU institutions, as well as member States when they are implementing EU law.

The constraints imposed by this legal framework, on the Church and more generally upon religious beliefs, can be gauged from the broad application of the resulting case law. The complexities for regulators and judiciary are formidable as they strive to resolve issues of discrimination by cross-referencing the provisions of charity law, equality law and the growing body of European Convention jurisprudence.

7.2.1 Human Rights

Since the Human Rights Act 1998 came into effect on 2 October 2000, all UK legislation, including any provisions granting exemption to charities such as the Church, have been subject to s.3 whereby, as has been rightly pointed out, "it is incumbent on domestic courts to construe domestic laws compatibly with Convention rights, and therefore the same (or at least no less favourable) approach must be adopted to the concept of religion and belief …"[2] While the Act specifically requires public authorities to act in accordance with such rights,[3] it has remained controversial as to whether or to what extent organizations such as religious charities, which undertake functions as agents of public authorities, are also subject to the same requirement. Such a charity may avoid compliance requirements if it can show that it is not acting as a 'public body' or that its activities are statutorily exempt.

7.2.2 The United Nations Declaration of Human Rights

Article 18 declares that the freedom to manifest religion or belief in worship, observance, practice, and teaching may be exercised in public or in private, individually or in community with others.

7.2.3 The European Convention and Discrimination

For present purposes the important Convention provisions are Articles 9 and 14. The first, fully incorporated into UK domestic law by Article 9 of the Human Rights Act 1998,[4] provides for the right to freedom of thought, conscience and religion. The second broadly prohibits discrimination "on any ground", specifically including discrimination on religious grounds. It can only be used in conjunction with another Convention provision and has similarly been incorporated into UK domestic law by Article 14 of the 1998 Act. Although not specifically referred to, sexual orientation discrimination is plainly within the ambit of Article 14.[5]

---

[2] See, *Eweida v. British Airways plc* [2009] ICR 303, per Elias P, at para 27.

[3] See, the Human Rights Act 1998, s.6(1): 'it is unlawful for a public authority to act in a way which is incompatible with a Convention right, unless the public authority in question is required so to act by legislation'; and the Human Rights Act 1998, s.3. See, also, Office for Democratic Institutions and Human Rights, Organization for Security and Co-operation in Europe and European Commission for Democracy through Law, 'Guidelines for Review of Legislation Pertaining to Religion Or Belief', Venice, 2004.

[4] Together with the associated ECtHR case law, including: *Buscarini and Others v. San Marino* (application No. 24645/94), 1998; *Kokkinakis v. Greece* (application No. 14307/88), 1993; *Leyla Sahin v. Turkey*, 2004; *Pichon and Sajous v. France*; *Leela Forderkeis E.V. and Others v. Germany* (application No. 58911/00), 2008; *Universelles Leben E.V. v. Germany* (application No. 29745/96), 1996; and *Lautsi v. Italy*, 2011.

[5] As noted in *Catholic Care (Diocese of Leeds) v. the Charity Commission for England and Wales and the Equality and Human Rights Commission* [2010] EWHC 520 (Ch), per Briggs J at para 57, citing *Salgueiro Da Silva Mouta v. Portugal* (2001) 31 EHRR 47.

7.2.4 Convention Principles of General Application

Convention principles include 'necessity', 'proportionality' and 'equality of arms' against which the relevant national legislative provisions and decision-making processes of all democratic signatory States can be tested.

The ECtHR in *Olson v. Sweden (No 1)*[6] explained that to be justifiable, State interference in family life must be "relevant and sufficient; it must meet a pressing social need; and it must be proportionate to the need". The principle requires that a measure chosen to realise a legitimate aim must be both suitable in general, and necessary in the circumstances.[7] Frequently the ECtHR can be seen applying the test – is this form of State intervention necessary in a democratic society?

The ECtHR looks at the interference complained of in the light of the case as a whole to determine whether it was "proportionate to the legitimate aim pursued" and whether the reasons adduced by the national authorities to justify it are "relevant and sufficient". For example, an application of the proportionality test to the third of the four *Pemsel* heads, the advancement of religion, might conclude that it would be breached by any narrow common law interpretation of what constitutes a 'religion' (e.g. by the exclusion of non-theistic religions such as Buddhism[8]).

The principle that the State should ensure that those presenting or defending a case are not disadvantaged, relative to the opposing party, by inadequate resources, is also clearly of considerable importance.[9]

Additionally, as with other Convention provisions, the State enjoys a margin of appreciation in assessing what constitutes 'discrimination' and the extent to which differences in otherwise similar situations may justify a difference in treatment. However, as the ECtHR has stressed, "if a restriction on fundamental rights applies to a particularly vulnerable group in society that has suffered considerable discrimination in the past, then the State's margin of appreciation is substantially narrower and it must have very weighty reasons for the restrictions in question".[10] The court had previously drawn attention to the narrowness of that margin in relation to the justification of differential treatment on grounds of sexual orientation.

7.2.5 The Equality Act 2010: Exemption, Protected Grounds and Public Bodies

The 2010 Act, which mostly came into effect in October of that year, revoked a cluster of different discrimination statutes (including the Equal Pay Act 1970, the Sex Discrimination Act 1975, the Race Relations Act 1976 and the Disability

[6] (1988) 11 EHRR 299.

[7] See *Kozak v. Poland* [2010] ECHR 280, at para 92.

[8] *R v. Registrar General ex p. Segerdal* [1970] 2 QB 697.

[9] See, for example, *Steel and Morris v. the United Kingdom*, (application no. 68416/01) (2005).

[10] *Kiyutin v. Russia*, (application no. 2700/10), March 2011.

Discrimination Act 1995) while also updating the public sector equality duty (requiring public bodies to consider and apply fairness and equality, especially in making decisions or policies). It covers the same groups that were previously protected under that range of legislation – age, disability, gender reassignment, race, religion or belief, sex, sexual orientation, marriage and civil partnership and pregnancy and maternity – it extends protection to some of the groups not previously covered, and also strengthens particular aspects of equality law. It now provides, along with, *inter alia*, the Human Rights Act 1998, a consolidated statutory anti-discrimination framework for the United Kingdom which: prohibits unfair treatment on any of nine 'protected grounds'; whether occurring in the workplace, when providing goods, facilities and services, when exercising public functions, in the disposal and management of premises, or in education and by associations (such as private clubs); and whether the discrimination takes the form of direct, indirect, harassment or victimisation. It is important to note that the Employment Equality (Religion or Belief) Regulations 2003 have since been extended to cover philosophical beliefs, whether or not they are similar to religious beliefs.

7.2.6 *The Statutory Exemptions*

Specific exceptions for charities – previously to be found in Regulation 18[11] – are now more restricted than formerly and consigned to s.193 of the Equality Act 2010. These allow a charity to limit its benefits to people who share a 'protected' characteristic where either: the restriction is justified as a means of furthering the charity's aim to tackle a particular disadvantage borne by people with such a characteristic; or the charity is seeking to achieve some other legitimate aim in a fair, balanced and reasonable ('proportionate') way. Section 193 also exempts any charity which, prior to 18 May 2005, made acceptance of a particular religion or belief a condition of membership with an entitlement to the benefit, service or facility provided by that charity, and has since continued to impose that condition, from being in contravention of the Act. Certain schools and associations also benefit from exemptions. In addition to this charities' exception, the 'positive action' provisions enable charities to target their resources on what would ordinarily be considered a discriminatory basis where this is either a proportionate means to achieve a legitimate aim or for the purpose of preventing or compensating for disadvantage. This accords with Convention principles which hold that equality is not synonymous with equal treatment: differentiation, or affirmative action, may be required in order to diminish or eliminate conditions which perpetuate discrimination.[12]

---

[11] The Sexual Orientation Regulations 2007, Regulation 18, issued under powers provided by the Equality Act 2006.

[12] See, *Thlimmenos v. Greece* (2001) 31 EHRR 411 and the Human Rights Committee statement in Comment No. 18.

7.2.7 The 'Protected Grounds'

The nine grounds which permit a charity to discriminate in its activities are the established six (sex, race, disability, sexual orientation, religion or belief and age) together with an additional three (marriage and civil partnership, gender reassignment and pregnancy and maternity) transferred from the Sex Discrimination Act. Despite the new legislation, the law is substantially unchanged: the definitions of direct and indirect discrimination now appear in ss.13(1) and 19; the statement regarding the immaterial differences between marriage and civil partnership is to be found in s.23(3); the prohibition of discrimination in providing services is located in s.29; while other carried-over provisions are in the Schedules. Essentially, the same set of principles is now applied uniformly, including to all charities – religious or otherwise – along with the Church, unless relieved by a statutory exemption.

7.2.8 A Public Body and the Agency Relationship

While it is certain that a local authority is among those that come within the definition of 'public body' for Convention purposes, it has been a matter of some debate as to whether, or in what circumstances, a charity may be so defined. The principal/agency relationship is relevant in this context.

The common law principle of "agency" found early expression in the Latin maxim *qui facit per alium, facit* per se (the one who acts through another, acts in his or her own interests). It has been defined as "the relationship between a principal and an agent whereby the principal, expressly or impliedly, authorizes the agent to work under his control and on his behalf."[13] Public bodies, for the purposes of human rights law, will include non-government organizations – such as the Church or other religious charity – functioning in an agency capacity on behalf of a government body. Determining whether or not an agency relationship exists is an imperfect science which turns on the facts in each case: not all delegated authority necessarily constitutes agency; the span of control exercised is crucial.

Charities, in particular, have always been required to demonstrate a sufficient, if uncertain, degree of independence from government. As Brody and Tyler have pointed out, "foundations and other charities are not inherently public bodies and their assets are not public money".[14] Lately there have been increasing indications of a judicial willingness to explore the circumstances in which a contract between government and charity might denote the existence of a de facto agency relationship and, in that case, to assess the implications that may then arise for the parties

[13] See, Markesinis, B.S., and R.J.C. Munday. 1998. *An outline of the law of agency*, 4th ed. London: LexisNexis.

[14] See Brody, E., and J. Tyler. 2009. *How public is private philanthropy? Separating reality from myth*, 63. Washington, DC: The Philanthropy Roundtable.

concerned. It is now reasonably clear that there are circumstances in which a charity may lose its statutory exemption privileges because it has surrendered all freedom of decision-making to a government body. It will then be treated as a 'public body' (see, further, below).

7.2.9 The Racial and Religious Hatred Act 2006

Additional protection continues to be available in the provisions of the Racial and Religious Hatred Act 2006 (amending the Public Order Act 1986), of which s.29B(i) provides that 'a person who uses threatening words or behaviour, or displays any written material which is threatening, is guilty of an offence if he intends thereby to stir up religious hatred'.

7.2.10 Proportionality

The following caveat, embedded in the statute reveals the legislative intent to achieve proportionality when licensing intervention in the right of an individual to manifest his or her religious beliefs:

> s.29 J. Nothing in this Part shall be read or given effect in a way which prohibits or restricts discussion, criticism or expressions of antipathy, dislike, ridicule, insult or abuse of particular religions or the beliefs or practices of their adherents, or of any other belief system or the beliefs or practices of its adherents, or proselytising or urging adherents of a different religion or belief system to cease practising their religion or belief system.

This serves as a reminder that freedom of speech is an important right that must not be lightly interfered with.

7.3 Freedom of Religion and Discrimination

Article 9 of the European Convention includes the freedom to: change religion or belief; exercise religion or belief publicly or privately, alone or with others; and to exercise religion or belief in worship, teaching, practice and observance. It also provides for the right to have no religion and to have non-religious beliefs protected. As the ECtHR has pointed out[15]:

> [as] enshrined in Article 9, freedom of thought, conscience and religion is one of the foundations of a "democratic society" within the meaning of the Convention. It is, in its religious dimension, one of the most vital elements that go to make up the identity of believers and their conception of life, but it is also a precious asset for atheists, agnostics, sceptics and the unconcerned.

[15] See, *Kokkinakis v. Greece* A 260-A (1993), 17 EHRR 397 at para 31.

Article 14 of the same Convention provides for the right not to suffer discrimination which the ECtHR has defined as "treating differently, without an objective and reasonable justification, persons in analogous, or relevantly similar, situations".[16] For the purposes of Article 14, no 'objective and reasonable justification' is to be understood as meaning "that it does not pursue a *legitimate aim*" or that there is no "reasonable proportionality between the means employed and the aim sought to be realised".[17] The Equality Act 2010 prohibits discrimination against an individual on the basis of a protected characteristic, in relation to several areas including employment and the provision of goods and services, while also providing exemptions for religious charities in certain circumstances.

Article 18 of the United Nations Universal Declaration of Human Rights states that everyone has the right to freedom of thought, conscience and religion; this right includes freedom to change his religion or belief, and freedom, either alone or in community with others and in public or private, to manifest his religion or belief in teaching, practice, worship and observance.

7.3.1 Article 9 and Interference with the Manifestation of Religious Belief

Article 9 is a qualified right and as such the freedom to manifest a religion or belief can be limited, or subject to 'interference', so long as that limitation: is prescribed by law; is necessary and proportionate; and pursues a legitimate aim (viz. the interests of public safety, the protection of public order, health or morals or the protection of the rights and freedoms of others). This allows the provision of services or 'benefits' to a certain section of society if such actions are a proportionate means of achieving a legitimate aim, such as improving health or the protection of children. It is also important to bear in mind that Article 9 is not restricted to protecting the rights of the religious, it provides protection for those with no beliefs and for those with non-religious beliefs. As Nicholls LJ pointed out in *Williamson*[18]:

> Article 9 embraces freedom of thought, conscience and religion. The atheist, the agnostic, and the sceptic are as much entitled to freedom to hold and manifest their beliefs as the theist. These beliefs are placed on an equal footing for the purpose of this guaranteed freedom.

However, given the preferential status of the Church as 'established', together with the cultural weighting of the Judeo-Christian tradition in this jurisdiction, there are issues regarding the extent to which equal recognition and protection can be afforded to those with no beliefs, with beliefs that are not Christian or with beliefs that are not religious (see, further, Chap. 1).

---

[16] See, *Kiyutin v. Russia*, (application no. 2700/10), March 2011.

[17] See, *EB v. France* (2008) 47 EHRR 21, at para 91.

[18] *Ex parte Williamson* [2005] UKHL 15, [2005] 2 AC 246 (HL), at para 24.

7.3.2 *Interference*

Weatherup J. in *Christian Institute*[19] provided the following useful appraisal of what constitutes 'interference' in this context[20]:

> It is not every impact on the manifestation of religious belief that constitutes 'interference' for the purposes of Article 9. To constitute sufficient interference for the purposes of Article 9 it must be shown that (it) interfere(s) 'materially, that is, to an extent which was significant in practice, with the claimant's freedom to manifest their beliefs in this way'[21] ... The position in which persons seeking to manifest religious belief have placed themselves may bear on whether the matter to which they object constitutes interference[22] ... There will be instances where the impact on the individual does not amount to an interference with the right to manifest religious belief.

Subsequently, additional authority for this approach was provided by the ruling of the House of Lords in *Gallagher v. Church of Jesus Christ of Latter-Day Saints*,[23] when it considered the argument that s.3 of the Human Rights Act 1998 required the ratings legislation (the 1988 Act) to be "read and given effect" in a manner compatible with Convention rights: whether restricting a rating exemption to places of 'public religious worship' contravened the Art 9 rights of a group (the Mormon Church) which excluded the public from some of its worship spaces. This argument rested on the assertion that the exclusion of the public from the Temple (their place of worship) was a manifestation by the Mormons of their religion and, therefore, to deny them rates exemption would be to discriminate against them on the grounds of religion, contrary to Articles 9 and 14 of the Convention: in effect that the legislation discriminated between religious groups on the basis of whether or not they allowed for public religious worship. The eventual decision to deny rates exemption rested

[19] Neutral Citation no. [2007] NIQB 66.

[20] Ibid, at paras 66 and 68.

[21] Ibid, citing *R (Williamson) v. Secretary of State for Education and Employment* [2005] 2 AC 246, per Lord Nicholls. A case where the Secretary of State contended that the interference complained of (regulations prohibiting corporal punishment) did not interfere materially with the claimant parents manifestation of their beliefs, as it left open to the parents several adequate alternative courses of action, but the House of Lords did not accept that the suggested alternatives would be adequate and held that there had been interference with the belief.

[22] Ibid, at para 68, citing *Kalac v. Turkey* [1997] EHRR 552 where the applicant was protesting against his compulsory retirement from the military, due to his alleged involvement with a fundamental Muslim sect contrary to the secular nature of the Turkish State, but the court found that in choosing a military career the applicant had accepted a military system that placed limitations on individuals that would not be imposed on civilians.

[23] *Gallagher v. Church of Jesus Christ of Latter-Day Saints* [2008] 1 WLR 1852, 1867. Note this matter has since been referred to the ECtHR: *The Church of Jesus Christ of Latter-day Saints v. United Kingdom* (application no. 7552/09). The applicant complains under ECHR Article 9, alone and in conjunction with Article 14, of discrimination as regards its failure to receive statutory tax exemption for one of its places of worship. There is a further complaint under Article 1 of Protocol 1 alone and in connection with Article 14 that denial of the statutory exemption is disproportionate discrimination on the grounds of religion. Finally, the applicant complains under Article 13 of failure by the British House of Lords to adequately apply the Convention.

on the grounds that the "the loss of the opportunity to gain a financial advantage was too remote from interference with the right [to manifest religion] in question".[24]

7.3.3 *The Manifestation of Religious Belief*

As Nicholls LJ pointed out in *Williamson* "everyone is entitled to hold whatever beliefs he wishes".[25] Problems only arise when action is taken to manifest that belief. Under Article 9, any such manifestation must be directly related to the belief[26]: the existence of such a firm nexus has been required since this principle was first established in *Arrowsmith v. United Kingdom.*[27] The 'Arrowsmith test' has been employed as a filter to narrow the possible scope of 'manifestation' and, as it has generally only been applied in cases relating to mainstream forms of religious belief, has arguably served to artificially confine the range of acceptable manifestations.

Weatherup J, in his determination of *Christian Institute and Others v. Office of First Minister and Deputy First Minister,*[28] gave some preliminary consideration to what in law might constitute a 'manifestation of belief'. This case concerned an application from a coalition of Christian organizations protesting against a perceived inequality of treatment in the Equality Act (Sexual Orientation) Regulations (Northern Ireland) 2006 between anti-discrimination measures on the grounds of sexual orientation and orthodox religious beliefs. In an analysis of the legal requirements for a properly constituted 'religious belief', which owed much to Nicholls LJ's earlier pronouncement, Weatherup J advised that[29]:

> … issues as to the manifestation of a belief must satisfy certain modest objective minimum requirements. The 'threshold requirements' are that the belief must be consistent with basic standards of human dignity or integrity, it must possess an adequate degree of seriousness and importance and it must be intelligible and capable of being understood … the conduct that constitutes the manifestation of a belief must be intimately connected to the belief. In deciding whether the conduct constitutes manifesting a belief in practice it is first necessary to identify the nature and scope of the belief. If the belief takes the form of a perceived obligation to act in a specific way then the act will be intimately linked to the belief and will be a manifestation of that belief. However a perceived obligation is not a prerequisite to manifestation of a belief in practice.

---

[24] Ibid 1857–8. Lord Scott agreed that Art 9 was not infringed, but went on to consider the application of Art 14 in the context of the Art 9 right.

[25] *Ex parte Williamson* [2005] UKHL 15, [2005] 2 AC 246 (HL), at para 23.

[26] See, Taylor, P.M. 2005. *Freedom of religion: UN and European human rights law and practice*, 347. Cambridge: Cambridge University Press.

[27] Application No. 7050/75, Comm. Report para 71 D.R. 19. The Commission then stated the principle that "the term 'practice' as employed in Article 9(1) does not cover each act which is motivated or influenced by a religion or a belief".

[28] Neutral Citation no. [2007] NIQB 66.

[29] Ibid, at para 48.

Possibly Briggs J had this in mind when, in *Smith v. Trafford Housing Trust*,[30] he considered whether the charity concerned was entitled to discipline an employee, a Christian manager, for posting on Facebook his view that holding civil partnership ceremonies in churches was "an equality too far". Expressing his opinion that the posting was not "viewed objectively, judgmental, disrespectful or liable to cause upset or offence," Briggs J accepted that the complainant could have considered this as homophobic and have been offended but "her interpretation was not in my view objectively reasonable".[31] The judge advised that[32]:

> The frank but lawful expression of religious or political views may frequently cause a degree of upset, and even offence, to those with deeply held contrary views, even where none is intended by the speaker. This is a necessary price to be paid for freedom of speech.

This approach, centred on the principle of proportionality and the extent of any intrusion upon the rights of others, is evident in many of the cases where plaintiffs allege interference with a manifestation of beliefs: while much turns on evidence of the importance attached by the individual concerned, to the action taken as a significant demonstration of the sincerity of their beliefs, this cannot be determinative because as Laws LJ pointed out in *McFarlane v. Relate Avon Ltd*[33]:

> in the eye of everyone save the believer religious faith is necessarily subjective, being incommunicable by any kind of proof or evidence. It may of course be true; but the ascertainment of such a truth lies beyond the means by which laws are made in a reasonable society. Therefore it lies only in the heart of the believer, who is alone bound by it.

An insistence, for example, that the wearing of a chastity ring[34] was an appropriate manifestation of Christian belief was judged to be facile while a wish for open air cremation was accepted as appropriate in relation to Hindu religious beliefs.[35]

7.3.4 Proselytism as a Manifestation of Religious Belief

In itself a time honoured religious and charitable activity, proselytism has become somewhat suspect as a means of advancing public benefit as western societies grow more pluralistic and as elsewhere religious differences become more volatile.

---

[30] [2012] EWHC 3221.

[31] Ibid at para 85.

[32] Ibid at para 82.

[33] [2010] EWCA Civ B1 (29 April 2010).

[34] See, *Playfoot (a minor), R (on the application of v. Millais School* [2007] EWHC 1698 where a schoolgirl challenged the decision of her school to prohibit her wearing a 'purity ring' as a symbol of her Christian commitment to celibacy before marriage.

[35] See, *Ghai, R (on the application of) v. Newcastle City Council & Ors* [2010] EWCA Civ 59 which concerned a request from Ghai, a Hindu, that the Council make available some land outside the city precincts to allow the practice of open-air cremation as his religion required that cremation take place by traditional fire, in direct sunlight and away from man made structures.

The ECtHR had the opportunity to consider the contemporary significance of proselytism in *Kokkinakis v. Greece*,[36] which concerned attempts to forbid the proselytising activities of a Jehovah's Witness. The court confirmed that a democratic society has a plurality of beliefs. It held that freedom to manifest one's religion includes in principle the right to try to convince one's neighbour. The court did however maintain that:

> … a distinction has to be made between bearing Christian witness and improper proselytism. The former corresponds to true evangelism, which a report drawn up in 1956 under the auspices of the World Council of Churches describes as an essential mission and a responsibility of every Christian and every Church. The latter represents a corruption or deformation of it. It may, according to the same report, take the form of activities offering material or social advantages with a view to gaining new members for a Church or exerting improper pressure on people in distress or in need; it may even entail the use of violence or brainwashing; more generally, it is not compatible with respect for the freedom of thought, conscience and religion of others.

Moreover, as Pettiti J. then stated, "religion is one of the foundations of a democratic society within the meaning of the Convention and the pluralism that cannot be disassociated from a democratic society depends on religious freedom". Essentially, proselytism can no longer be assumed to be an inherently appropriate manifestation of religious belief (less so than formerly, as far as the Church is concerned, since the removal of the public benefit presumption).

The decision in *Kokkinakis*, like the earlier one in *Gottesmann v. Switzerland*,[37] has been criticized for "not heeding the principle that it is not the State's concern if somebody attempts to induce another to change one's religion".[38] The court gave insufficient attention to the right to change religion and the freedom of others to bring their non-coercive influence to that decision.

7.3.5 *Article 14 and Discrimination*

The right under Article 14 not to be discriminated against is violated when States treat differently persons in analogous situations without providing an objective and reasonable justification. However, *Thlimmenos v. Greece*[39] provides authority for the view that Convention requirements for discrimination will also be breached when States, without objective and reasonable justification, fail to make appropriate differentiation in certain cases: the right not to be discriminated against is violated when States fail to treat differently persons whose situations are significantly different.

---

[36] A 260-A (1993), 17 EHRR 397. Also, see, *Larissis and Others v. Greece* (Ser. A) No 65 ECtHR (1998 – V) 363.

[37] App. No. 101616/83 (1984) 40 D&R 284.

[38] See, Taylor, P.M. 2005. *Freedom of religion: UN and European human rights law and practice*, 341. Cambridge: Cambridge University Press.

[39] (2001) 31 EHRR 411 at para 44.

Article 14 needs to be considered in conjunction with Protocol 2 which, unlike the article, is not dependent upon other rights provided by the Convention. It states that[40]:

> 1. The enjoyment of any right set forth by law shall be secured without discrimination on any ground such as sex, race, colour, language, religion, political or other opinion, national or social origin, association with a national minority, property, birth or other status.
> 2. No one shall be discriminated against by any public authority on any ground such as those mentioned in paragraph 1

Although this Protocol still awaits UK ratification, it is significant as it highlights the liability of a public authority and thereby indicates the anticipated problems for government. However, the principles established in the case law leading up to the Equality Act 2010, retain their currency and continue to benchmark the rulings of judiciary and regulators in the post-2010 era.

7.3.6 Principles

The principles of 'legitimate aim' and 'proportionality' are important in this context.

According to the Charity Commission, a legitimate aim is one that: has a reasonable social policy objective (e.g. health improvement or the protection of children); is consistent with the lawful carrying out of the charity's stated purpose for the public benefit, though not necessarily identical with that purpose (e.g. a purpose of relieving poverty and sickness could be a legitimate aim and a subsidiary aim of helping children out of poverty could also be a legitimate aim); and it is not itself discriminatory.[41]

In assessing what constitutes 'proportionality' Mummery LJ in *Elias*[42] adopted a three-stage approach:

> First, is the objective sufficiently important to justify limiting a fundamental right? Secondly, is the measure rationally connected to the objective? Thirdly, are the means chosen no more than is necessary to accomplish the objective?

Shortly afterwards the House of Lords in *Huang v. Secretary of State for the Home Department*[43] explained the principle of proportionality as "… the need to balance the interests of society with those of individuals and groups". While at

[40] Protocol No. 12 to the Convention for the Protection of Human Rights and Fundamental Freedoms (ETS No. 177) is an anti-discrimination treaty of the Council of Europe. It was adopted on November 4, 2000, in Rome and entered into force on April 1, 2005, but has yet to be ratified by the UK.

[41] See, Charity Commission, 'Equality Act guidance for charities: Restricting who can benefit from charities', 2012, at para C4.

[42] *R (Elias) v. Secretary of State for Defence* [2006] EWCA Civ 1293.

[43] [2007] UKHL 11. See, also: *De Freitas v. Permanent Secretary of the Ministry of Agriculture Fisheries, Lands and Housing* [1999] 1 AC 69, per the Privy Council; and *R v. Oakes* [1986] 1 SCR 103, per Dickson CJ.

much the same time Weatherup J in *Christian Institute*[44] suggested that the approach to proportionality required consideration of:

> ... the overarching need to balance the interests of society with those of individuals and groups; recognition of the latitude that must be accorded to legislative and executive choices in relation to the balance of public and private interests; the legislative objective being sufficiently important to justify limiting the fundamental right; the measures designed to meet the legislative objective being rationally connected to it, that is, the measures must not be arbitrary, unfair or based on irrational considerations; the need for proportionate means being used so as to impair the right or freedom no more than necessary to accomplish the objective, that is, that the measures are the least intrusive, in light of both the legislative objective and the infringed right ... the Court should consider whether the measures fall within a range of reasonable alternatives, rather than seeking to ascertain whether a lesser degree of interference is a possibility; and the need for proportionate effect in relation to the detrimental effects and the advantageous effects of the measures and the importance of the objective.

7.3.7 Religious Discrimination in Practice

The Equality Act 2010 identifies four types of religious discrimination: direct, indirect, harassment or victimisation. The first takes the form of unequal treatment whereby some are directly treated less favourably than others because of their religious beliefs. The second incidentally disadvantages a certain religious group as when a service provider's provision, criterion or practice imposes restrictions that affect their ability to access services available to others. The third results from 'whistleblower' circumstances involving a complaint about religious discrimination while the fourth is behaviour that may range from physical attack, verbal abuse, to causing discomfort because of a religious or racial difference.

7.3.8 Unequal but Not Discriminatory

The Church of England is perfectly entitled to provide services and benefits, such as schooling, only to Anglicans; this in itself does not constitute discrimination. The Equality Act 2010, s.193, provides exceptions for charities such as the Church: unequal treatment is permissible in respect of persons who share one or more of the protected characteristics; but any charity that wishes to limit benefits to such people, even if this conforms wholly to the aims set out in its governing documents, must now also justify that restriction. The justification can be provided by satisfying one of two tests outlined by the Charity Commission[45]: where the governing document

---

[44] *Christian Institute and Others v. Office of First Minister and Deputy First Minister,* Neutral Citation no. [2007] NIQB 66.

[45] See, Charity Commission, 'Equality Act guidance for charities: Restricting who can benefit from charities', 2012 at para C.

restricts benefits to people with a shared protected characteristic and are provided in order to tackle a particular disadvantage or need linked to that protected characteristic; and, otherwise, where the governing document restricts benefits to people with a shared protected characteristic and the restriction can be justified as being a fair, balanced and reasonably necessary way of carrying out a legitimate aim, taking into account the discrimination involved. The Commission adds that[46]: in deference to a person's religion or belief or their sexual orientation, religious or belief based charities can impose restrictions on membership, participation in their activities, the services they provide or the use of their premises; and in doing so are exempted from the justification tests. A restriction can only be made: on the grounds of religion or belief, where necessary because of the organisation's purpose, or to avoid causing offence to followers of the religion or belief on which the organisation is founded; and in relation to sexual orientation, if this is necessary to comply with the organisation's doctrine or to avoid conflict with the religious or belief-based convictions of many followers of the religion or belief on which the organisation is founded. Further, if an organisation contracts with a public body to carry out an activity, such as the provision of services, then it cannot discriminate because of sexual orientation in relation to that activity. Given its extensive programme of contracted service provision on behalf of various government departments, the Church of England will need to exercise caution in imposing filtering restrictions on those who may access those services.[47]

7.3.9 Unequal but Not Discriminatory: Contractual Obligations

There have been a number of cases concerning allegations of discriminatory treatment by employers for failure to respect the religious beliefs of staff which will have clear implications for the Church of England in its role as employer. *McClintock v. Department of Constitutional Affairs*,[48] for example, concerned the request of a JP member of a statutory panel that he be excused from officiating in cases where he might have to decide whether same sex partners should adopt children. He considered there was insufficient evidence that such a placement was in a child's best interests and felt that children were being treated as guinea pigs in a social experiment. When his request was refused he resigned from the Family Panel and commenced proceedings alleging that he had been subject to direct and indirect discrimination and harassment on the grounds of religion and belief. The Employment Appeal Tribunal found that McClintock had not been disadvantaged because of any religious belief he held and, even if he had been, such discrimination would have been justified.

[46] Ibid, at para F5.

[47] See, for example, *R (Begum) v. Head Teacher and Governors of Denbeigh High School* [2006] 2 All ER 487.

[48] [2008] IRLR 29.

A year later, in *Ladele v. London Borough of Islington,*[49] the Court of Appeal considered the dismissal of Ms Ladele, a Christian marriage registrar, who refused to be involved in registering same-sex "civil partnerships" in accordance with newly introduced statutory procedures.

The Court took the view that the registration process was a public service, that it had significant human rights implications for the community and that administering the process formed part of Ms Ladele's contractual duties. It noted that "the effect on Ms Ladele of implementing the policy did not impinge on her religious beliefs: she remained free to hold those beliefs, and free to worship as she wished." Again, in *Eweida v. British Airways PLC,*[50] Ms Eweida, a committed Christian working for British Airways ("BA") in a customer service area, wanted to display a small cross around her neck contrary to BA policy that no jewellery was to be visible. She claimed that BA's refusal to allow this was indirect discrimination, but the EAT ruling that there had been no indirect discrimination, because she had been unable to demonstrate that there were any other Christians who wanted to wear a visible cross but had been prevented from doing so, was upheld by the Court of Appeal. Similarly, in *McFarlane v. Relate Avon Ltd,*[51] which concerned a charity that provided relationship support including counselling for couples, families, young people and individuals, sex therapy, mediation and training courses. Mr M, a relationship counsellor, had been dismissed when he indicated to his employer that he did not approve of same sex relationships on biblical grounds and did not wish to be involved in counselling such couples. The court, following the approach it had earlier adopted in *Ladele,*[52] ruled that Mr M had not suffered religious discrimination.

These cases were appealed to the ECtHR which eventually issued its ruling in January 2013. Only the *Eweida* case succeeded with the court determining that British Airways had breached Ms Eweida's human rights, in particular her right to freedom of thought, conscience and religion, when it banned her from wearing a crucifix while at work. The court took the view that her desire to wear a cross openly was a sincere manifestation of her religious beliefs and there was no evidence that in so doing she was encroaching on the rights of others. In the *Ladele* and *McFarlane* cases, however, where the appellants argued that their Christian beliefs concerning homosexuality were in conflict with the duties of their jobs, which required them to perform services for gay couples, the court was not convinced and both appeals failed. The significance of these rulings for the Church of England, as for other organisations, lies in the judicial recognition given to the onerous responsibility resting on an employer to balance their obligation to make reasonable accommodation for staff to manifest their religious beliefs in the workplace against their obligation to

---

[49] [2009] EWCA (Civ) 1357 (15 December 2009).

[50] [2010] EWCA Civ80 (12 Feb 2010). OUP, 2012, at p. 14. This case followed on from the Kirklees Metropolitan Borough Council case in April 2007 before the EAT concerning a Muslim teacher, Mrs Azmi, who refused to remove her veil during lessons when male colleagues were present. She lost her claims for direct and indirect discrimination and harassment.

[51] [2010] EWCA Civ B1 (29 April 2010). Also, see, *R (Johns) v. Derb City Council* [2011] EWHC 375 (Admin); [2011] 1 FLR 2094.

[52] [2009] EWCA Civ 1357, [2010] IRLR 211.

ensure that this does not intrude upon the rights of other staff. The rulings also provide authority for an employer's right to require staff to perform the tasks they knowingly committed to undertaking when they signed their employment contract.

7.3.10 Unequal and Discriminatory: Restricting Employment Opportunities

Religious charities, such as Church of England schools, are permitted to give preference to employing staff that share its religious ethos where to do so enables the charity to give effect to its purpose,[53] but this privilege must be exercised reasonably. For example, in *Reaney v. Hereford Diocesan Board of Finance,*[54] the employment tribunal held that where a homosexual was committed to working for the Church of England, he could expect to discuss the perceptions of homosexuality within the Church during a job interview and, as the questions put to the job applicant (about his sexuality and future intentions about relationships) had been reasonable and had been expected by him, he had not been subjected to harassment. The tribunal found the requirement (that the applicant declare either that he had made a positive choice of celibacy for the future or that he would abstain from sexual behaviour) was both for compliance with the doctrines of the Church of England and to avoid conflict with the strongly held religious convictions of a significant number of the religion's followers. However, as he had been the preferred candidate after competitive interview, the failure to offer him the job was an act of direct sexual orientation discrimination. The defence of a genuine occupational requirement was not available to the Church. Again, in *Board of Governors of St Matthias Church of England School v. Crizzle*[55] the complaint of an unsuccessful Asian applicant for the post of headteacher that the criterion of being 'a committed communicant Christian' constituted discrimination was treated as indirect discrimination on the grounds of race and therefore justifiable. In both cases the Church had been justified in taking the measures it did, in the legitimate aim of seeking to protect the religious ethos of the school, but in the first it had gone a step too far by directly discriminating against an applicant who had successfully completed the Church's selection process.

This exception to the discrimination prohibition is directly linked to the religious functions of the charity and is not to be interpreted as carte blanche for operating a 'closed shop' employment policy exclusively favouring persons of a designated religion or belief as was clearly illustrated in *Hinder & Sheridan v. Prospects for People with Learning Disabilities*[56] which concerned Prospects, a Christian charity,

[53] See, the School Standards Framework Act 1998, s.60, which provides that foundation or voluntary schools with a religious character can give preference in employment, remuneration and promotion to teachers whose beliefs are in accordance with the tenets of that religion.

[54] 1602844/2006, (April 2007).

[55] [1995] ICR 401.

[56] *Hender & Sheridan v. Prospects for People with Learning Disabilities* [2008] Employment Tribunal (nos. 2902090/2006 & 2901366) (2008).

that provided housing and day-care for people with learning disabilities. Prospects introduced a policy based on its Christian ethos whereby it would recruit only practicing Christians for the vast majority of roles (except cooking, cleaning, gardening, maintenance), as those in post might have to lead prayers or give spiritual guidance,[57] and told existing non-Christian employees that they were no longer eligible for promotion. The Tribunal found that it was insufficient to assume that, as a matter of principle, every job in a Christian organisation should be done by Christians. In a decision that sent a clear message to faith-based organisations regarding blanket policies which discriminate on this protected characteristic, the Tribunal held that the charity had unlawfully discriminated against one of its managers by requiring him to only employ Christians and not to promote its existing non-Christian employees.

These decisions accord with the ruling of the ECtHR in *Schüth v. Germany*[58] which concerned Schüth a church organist who separated from his wife in 1994 and started a relationship with another woman in 1995 with whom he had a child. In 1998 he was fired by his Catholic Church employers because, as the latter stated, an extramarital relationship violated basic Catholic teaching. Schüth claimed that his employment rights were ignored and successfully appealed to the ECtHR relying on the Article 8 protection afforded to family and private life. The court found that Schüth's employment with the Church did not give that body control over his private life and specifically that "his signature on the (employment) contract could not be interpreted as an unequivocal undertaking to live a life of abstinence in the event of separation or divorce." Interestingly, however, on the same day the ECtHR in *Obst v. Germany*[59] ruled in favor of a German Mormon Church that fired Michael Obst, a public relations director, over an affair. In that case, the court said the prominence of his position left Church officials with few options. The court said Obst should have known that his enhanced position carried greater responsibilities, and risks. Obst's dismissal was proper under his employment contract under which he owed "increased duties of loyalty" to the Church. It is possible that among the factors playing their part in the courts' rigorous balancing exercise in both cases and perhaps contributing towards the difference in outcome, was the relative locus standi of the two Churches: the ECtHR may have concluded that the institutional presence of the Catholic Church in Germany for many centuries placed a greater onus upon it, than upon the more recent and culturally marginalised Mormon Church, to safeguard the secular rights of employees when these are found to be in conflict with the Church's religious beliefs; the proportionality principle may again have been in play. If, as seems likely, such a principle was in play then the decision in *Schüth* carries clear implications for the 'established' Church of England in regard to the manner in which it balances morality and religious belief in the context of making available appointment opportunities for its clergy.

---

[57] Thereby ostensibly complying with the 'genuine occupational requirement' of the Employment Equality (Religion or Belief) Regulations 2003.

[58] (Application no. 1620/03), 23 September 2010.

[59] (Application no. 425/03), 23 September 2010.

The provisions in the 2010 Act that frame employment related exceptions to the prohibition against discrimination have further narrowed the scope of permissible restrictions and present a challenge to the established policies and practices of some religious charities.

7.3.11 Unequal and Discriminatory: Restricting Access to Services

Article 2 of the First Protocol to the European Convention on Human Rights states that:

> In the exercise of any functions which it assumes in relation to education and to teaching, the State shall respect the right of parents to ensure such education and teaching in conformity with their own religious and philosophical convictions.

This recognizes a right to educate children in the religious beliefs of their parents and provides the rationale for exempting faith schools[60] from the prohibition on religious discrimination. In exercising this right a school may discriminate in its admissions policy in favour of pupils who share their own faith but it does not stretch to refusing admissions to children of other faiths if there are vacant places. The content of education programmes and religious practice within the school are entitled to reflect its particular faith orientation even if this disadvantages those of other or no religion. This provision extends recognition and protection for the role of the Church of England in its role as the largest education service provider for nation's children.

The ECtHR has, on occasion, explored the parameters of this right. In *Folgerø & Others v. Norway,*[61] for example, it examined an objection to the compulsory teaching in State schools of religious knowledge that concentrated on Christianity to the detriment of other religions. Finding that such an institutional representation of a nation's majority religion did not in itself contravene Article 2 of Protocol No. 1 the Grand Chamber ruled that: "in view of the place occupied by Christianity in the national history and tradition of the respondent State, this must be regarded as falling within the respondent State's margin of appreciation in planning and setting the curriculum." More recently, in *Lautsi v. Italy,*[62] the Grand Chamber affirmed the approach adopted in previous cases and emphasized that Article 2 of Protocol No. 1 did not prohibit a State from including any matters touching on religion in the schools' curriculum; rather, the aim of the provision was to safeguard pluralism in education and to prevent indoctrination by the State.[63] It emphasized that the State's

[60] Where a faith school is a voluntary aided school, as JFS is, and so maintained by public funding, its religious character has to be designated by the Secretary of State (School Standards and Framework Act 1998, s.69).

[61] App. No. 15472/02 (Eur. Ct. H.R. [GC] June 29, 2007).

[62] App. No. 30814/06 (Eur. Ct. H.R. Mar. 18, 2011).

[63] Ibid at para 66.

duty to respect parents' religious and philosophical convictions was also relevant to the organization of the school environment. While both rulings serve to confirm the rationale for faith based service provision they also hint that this should be weighed against the pattern of needs in the prevailing social context: where that context is social pluralism then the State may need to have particular regard for the proportionality principle when contracting with the 'established' Church for the provision of education services.

In *R (on the application of E) v. Governing Body of JFS and the Admissions Appeal Panel of JFS*[64] the applicant challenged the rules of admission to a Jewish school that had, for 52 years, required a child to have a mother who was born Jewish. The issue for the court was whether the school could claim an exemption against a charge of racial discrimination on the grounds of their religious commitments? The High Court ruled that a school that accepts State funding must not discriminate in its admission policy on the basis of ethnicity. Subsequently, the UK Supreme Court, in a majority ruling, held that such a matrilineal religious condition was direct racial discrimination. It found that what in the High Court had been characterised as religious grounds were in fact racial grounds, notwithstanding their theological motivation, and no faith school could be excused from the prohibition on race discrimination. This ruling has clear implications for the Church of England as for all publicly funded schools that set faith-based selection procedures to filter access.

Allegations of a discriminatory restriction on access to services also formed the basis for recent rulings by judicial and regulatory authorities in relation to the policy of a Catholic adoption agency to confine adoption services to heterosexual couples.[65] Catholic Care, a charity based in Leeds and one of 11 UK Catholic adoption agencies, with strong connections to the Roman Catholic Church which provided much of its funding, sought exemption from the 2007 Sexual Orientation Regulations.[66] These required it to consider gay and lesbian couples as prospective parents. The agency took the position that it was outside the tenets of the Roman Catholic Church to provide adoption services to same-sex cohabiting couples or civil partners and, in fact, provided adoption services only to married couples. The Commission noted that other such agencies, for example those under the auspices of the Church of England, had found a way of accommodating the prohibition on sexual orientation discrimination within their continued activities, without breaking their ties with that

---

[64] *R(E) v. Governing Body of JFS* [2010] IRLR 136; [2009] UKSC 15 on appeal from [2009] EWCA Civ 626. See, also, *Mandla (Sewa Singh) and another v. Dowell Lee and others* [1983] 2 AC 548.

[65] A decision in keeping with the policy statement made by Tony Blair, the then Prime Minister, on announcing the preparation of the Sexual Orientation Regulations 2007:

> there is no place in our society for discrimination. That is why I support the right of gay couples to apply to adopt like any other couple. And that is why there can be no exemptions for faith-based adoption agencies offering publicly-funded services from regulations which prevent discrimination.

[66] See, the Equality Act 2006, s.81, together with the Equality Act (Sexual Orientation) Regulations 2007. A main effect of the Regulations was, subject to important exceptions, to make it unlawful for a person to discriminate on grounds of sexual orientation in the provision of goods, facilities or services to the public or a section of the public.

Church. Ultimately, the First-tier Tribunal (Charity)[67] held that the charity had failed to meet the statutory test imposed by s.193 of the Equality Act 2010 which required it to demonstrate that the less favourable treatment it proposed to offer same sex couples would constitute a proportionate means of achieving its legitimate aim of providing suitable adoptive parents for a significant number of 'hard to place' children.[68] Because adoption is a public service, funded (in part) by local authorities, Catholic Care could not avail of the protection afforded by the exemptions under the 2010 Act. Again, this decision is one with clear implications for the Church of England in its role as a government contracted service provider: it must exercise due diligence to ensure that its religious beliefs do not translate, as they did with Catholic Care, into policies that discriminate against and exclude from government funded services those of different or no beliefs.

7.3.12 Unequal but 'Positive Action'

The general positive action provisions, in the Equality Act 2010, replicate provisions in earlier legislation and allow employers to target measures such as training towards groups such as ethnic minorities, which are under-represented or disadvantaged in the workplace, or to in other ways address their particular needs. Other positive action provisions, relating specifically to recruitment and promotion in employment, protect people from being treated less favourably because they have a particular protected characteristic but the 2010 Act explicitly requires charities to justify any restriction, based on a protected characteristic, on who can benefit from the charity. Positive action gives effect to a policy which recognises that more needs to be done to bridge the gap between those social groups that are not burdened by discrimination but have yet to achieve equality with others.

7.4 Human Rights, and the Church of England: Some Pressing Issues

The Church would seem to be set on a trajectory that can only bring it into conflict with the human rights framework. Certain issues of a theological nature, on which the Church has made a resolute and in that context an entirely credible stand,

[67] *Catholic Care (Diocese of Leeds) v. The Charity Commission for England and Wales* [2011] EqLR 597.

[68] In closing remarks the Tribunal noted that the Public Sector Equality duty imposed by s.149(1) of the Equality Act 2010 requires public bodies to pay due regard to the need to eliminate unlawful discrimination and to promote equality of opportunity. It appeared to the Tribunal that, even if the charity were permitted to discriminate in reliance upon s.193 of the 2010 Act, the Public Sector Equality duty would be likely in due course to impact upon the willingness of local authorities to work with a charity which discriminated on.

may in due course present before the courts more mundanely as issues of equal opportunity or in relation to the terms and conditions of employment and may then not appear so credible. To be found to have been acting in breach of human rights could have strategic consequences for its status as 'established' and for its leadership of the Anglican Communion.

7.4.1 Facilitating Pluralism

The community cohesion and sense of civic solidarity that religion and its institutions can generate when members conspicuously belong to the same faith, is now reversed to some degree as population movement has required England, in common with western society generally, to absorb a broad range of cultures and religions. The dilution in population homogeneity has been accompanied by a general decline in the role of religion and the traditional powerful position of the Church: fewer people now have religious convictions, belong to any church or, most tellingly, attend religious services; while respect for religious organisations has been greatly damaged by evidence of their role in promoting mass sectarian violence, involvement in genocide and by revelations of systemic child abuse. In addition, the struggle to accommodate the rapidly expanding variants of Christianity and New Age religions, together with the rising social profile of non-Christian religions, particularly Islam, has become steadily more pronounced in the aftermath of 9/11. While some adherents strive to accentuate religious distinctiveness by resorting to fundamentalist activity, others stimulate public controversy regarding sites for worship, religious dress and ornaments. Such conduct gives rise to doubt as to the future capacity of religion to promote equity, equality and pluralism, to deliver public benefit rather than advance member benefit and to promote social cohesion rather than social divisions.

The capacity of the Church of England to provide the leadership necessary to overcome these difficulties and actively facilitate the growth of a healthy pluralistic society is handicapped not just by particular practices, as detailed below, but also by its status as the 'established' Church.

7.4.2 Convention Case Law, the Church and Pluralism

In *Metropolitan Church of Bessarabia and others v. Moldova*[69] the ECtHR was concerned with the Moldovan authorities' refusal to recognise the applicant (Orthodox Christian) church. The applicants alleged that under the relevant domestic legislation a religious denomination could not be active inside Moldovan territory

[69] (2002) 35 EHRR 306. See, also, *Moscow Branch of the Salvation Army v. Russia*, (2007) 44 EHRR 46, paras 58–9.

unless it had first been recognised by the authorities. The latter responded with an assertion that the applicant's claim for recognition threatened the destabilisation not just of the Orthodox Church but of the whole of Moldovan society. In upholding the application, the Court warned that:

> in its relations with the various religions, denominations and beliefs, the State has a duty to remain neutral and impartial.[70] What is at stake here is the preservation of pluralism and the proper functioning of democracy, one of the principle characteristics of which is the possibility it offers of resolving a country's problems through dialogue, without recourse to violence, even when they are irksome.[71] Accordingly, the role of the authorities in such circumstances is not to remove the cause of tension by eliminating pluralism, but to ensure that the competing groups tolerate each other.[72]

For present purposes, the significance of this decision lies in the unavoidable conclusion that in England the State cannot, as emphasised by the Court, give effect to its "duty to remain neutral and impartial". The status of 'established' clearly places the Church in a complicit relationship with the State and constrains the ability of the latter to treat the interests of the Church and all other religions equally. The State cannot function in a neutral and impartial role in relation to religion when that State retains an 'established' Church, thereby giving rise to the possibilities of entanglement if not preferment (e.g. in terms of funding for schools, service contracts, public ceremonies etc.) which flow from that unique relationship. To that extent, in England the capacity of both Church and State to facilitate pluralism must remain impaired.

7.4.3 Unequal and Discriminatory: Service Restrictions

There are different ways of imposing constraints on service provision, some will be in breach of Convention law governing discrimination, others may be within the law but not the spirit of Convention provisions.

7.4.4 Discriminatory Policy

The Catholic Care case[73] (see, above) concerned an independent religious organisation with charitable status which was in receipt of public funds and provided a public statutorily governed service and which could not, therefore, avail of the protection

[70] Citing *Hasan & Chaush v. Bulgaria* (2002) 34(6) EHRR 1339.

[71] Citing *United Communist Party of Turkey and Others v. Turkey*, judgment of 30 January 1998, *Reports* 1998-I, at p. 27.

[72] Citing *Serif v. Greece*, no. 38178/79, § 53, ECHR 1999-IX.

[73] *Catholic Care (Diocese of Leeds) v. The Charity Commission for England and Wales* [2011] EqLR 597.

afforded by the exemptions under the 2010 Act.[74] The decision that it could not claim charitable exemption from its obligation to make its services available on a non-discriminatory basis, is one which may have created an awkward precedent for the Church of England. The latter's policy of not blessing same-sex partnerships and its equivocal approach to allowing women priests to conduct Church services may leave it open to a charge of sexual and gender discrimination as regards the basis on which it makes its services available. As it prepares to allow lesbian and gay relationships to be blessed in church, following a civil partnership, (though without the use of authorised liturgy), questions will then of course arise as to why a same sex wedding should be denied similar treatment.

There may also be implications arising from the Church's decision to transfer 70 % (3,360) of its 4,800 state schools from local authority control to academy status by 2016. Should this proceed as planned then a large proportion of the nation's children will be educated in an environment freed of impartial local authority administration and instead be more exposed than formerly to the direct religious influence of the Church. This may give rise to challenges from those parents who live within a school's catchment, have no alternative school available, and object to the Church's influence on their child's education. Indeed, there is something inherently suspect about a situation where State anti-discrimination laws allow exemptions for religious charities that are then availed of, by a State funded and State 'established' organization, free to deliver a nationwide service in a discriminatory manner. Arguably, there is an issue here about the authenticity of religious freedom when access to such a fundamental human right as childhood education is subject to the duality of Church/State control: an imbalance between individual choice and institutional power.

As has occurred in other countries, such as Canada, where same sex marriages are legal, it may also be anticipated that similar 'downstream' difficulties will arise in this jurisdiction and legal challenges will be levelled against Anglicans and other Christians who refuse on principle to endorse that status. Teachers, chaplains, registrars and boarding house proprietors will be among those seeking legal redress to defend their refusal to provide services that treat homosexual and heterosexual marriages equally.

7.4.5 Fees

Access to many of the nation's most valued social facilities is controlled by the Church of England. As the owners of exceptional buildings (e.g. the cathedrals of Canterbury and Durham) and of exceptional private schools (e.g. Westminster School and King's School Canterbury) the Church is clearly entitled to impose admittance fees. These

[74] The Tribunal noted that the Public Sector Equality duty imposed by s.149(1) of the Equality Act 2010 required public bodies to pay due regard to the need to eliminate unlawful discrimination and to promote equality of opportunity.

are already quite expensive. Should they be raised to the point where they prohibit access of the poor, there could be allegations of discriminatory treatment.

7.4.6 Gay Marriage

The recently passed Marriage (Same Sex Couples) Act 2013 is inevitably going to raise human rights issues: some of which will impact upon the Church of England; not least because the canons clearly restrict marriage to heterosexual relationships.[75]

Although the Convention does not specifically address the issue, there is no doubt that government is entitled to redefine marriage to include same sex relationships. Article 12 of the European Convention simply provides that "men and women of marriageable age" have the "right to marry and to found a family, according to the national laws governing the exercise of this right." While Article 9 of the Charter of Fundamental Rights of the European Union[76] adjusts the wording of Article 12, by removing the reference to men and women, to declare that: "the right to marry and the right to found a family shall be guaranteed in accordance with the national laws governing the exercise of these rights."

This neutral stance was reinforced by the ruling of the ECtHR, in *Schalk and Kopf v. Austria,*[77] to the effect that it would not force States to make marriage available for same-sex couples. The court then noted that the right to marry is granted to "men and women", and it includes the right to found a family. Whilst this could be interpreted as granting the right to two men or two women, the court observed that all other Convention rights are granted to "everyone". The court did, however, state that it would no longer consider that the right to marry enshrined in Article 12 must in all circumstances be limited to marriage between two persons of the opposite sex and consequently, it could not be said that Article 12 is inapplicable.[78] It took the view that same-sex couples were just as capable as different-sex couples of entering into stable committed relationships and, consequently, were in a relevantly similar situation to a different-sex couple as regards their need for legal recognition and protection of their relationship.[79]

It was further noted that currently there was no European consensus regarding same-sex marriage: it was permitted in no more than 6 out of 47 Convention States.

---

[75] In July 2002, the General Synod resolved: that this Synod

a) Affirm in accordance with the doctrine of the Church of England as set out in Canon B 30, that marriage should always be undertaken as a "solemn, public and life-long covenant between a man and a woman".

[76] The Charter of Fundamental Rights was signed on 7 December 2000 and became binding in December 2009.

[77] Application no. 30141/04, Council of Europe: European Court of Human Rights, 24 June 2010.

[78] Ibid, at para 61.

[79] Ibid at para 99.

In effect the court held that the issue fell to be determined by each individual State in accordance with the 'margin of appreciation' doctrine.

The fact that under the proposed new legislation, accompanied by amendments to the Equalities Act 2010, the Church is to be relieved of any duty to conduct gay marriages is also going to be problematic.[80] This will compromise the Church's status as 'established': as such it is legally obliged to provide the full range of services required by the nation e.g. baptism, communion, last rites, burial and marriage; but is now statutorily relieved from providing the latter service if it involves a same sex couple. It is thereby statutorily handicapped relative to other religions, its functional capacity diminished by the State. Moreover, it will also compromise the equality principle. This law will force many Anglican same gender couples who would prefer to avail of a service that is available exclusively to heterosexual couples, to settle for something less (marriage in a registry office). This will inevitably give rise to a charge that the law operates in a discriminatory fashion to the clear detriment of Anglican same gender couples. There can be no right without a reciprocal duty. Once the law recognizes a right to same sex marriage it cannot be Convention compliant to then relieve one specific organisation, explicitly on religious grounds, of an obligation imposed on other similar organisations to respond to an exercise of that right by permitting a church wedding.

There is, of course, also the fact that the permission not to officiate at same sex marriages is restricted exclusively to the Church: all other religious institutions, wishing for similar exemption, may well protest that this provision discriminates against them.

7.4.7 *Unequal and Discriminatory: Restricting Employment Opportunities*

The ECtHR in *Christine Goodwin v. The United Kingdom*[81] stated that: "the very essence of the Convention is respect for human dignity and human freedom. Under Article 8 of the Convention in particular, where the notion of personal autonomy is an important principle underlying the interpretation of its guarantees, protection is given to the personal sphere of each individual ..." It is difficult to reconcile some of the Church's recent policy decisions with this principle.

---

[80] The Church of England, as the established Church, will be able of its own accord, under the Church of England Assembly (Powers) Act 1919, to bring legislation before Parliament to enable it to 'opt in'.

[81] 28957/95 [2002] ECHR 588 (11 July 2002), at para 90: citing *Pretty v. the United Kingdom*, no. 2346/02, judgment of 29 April 2002, at p. 62, and *Mikulić v. Croatia*, no. 53176/99, judgment of 7 February 2002, at p. 53.

7.4.8 Gender and Sexual Inequality

The Civil Partnership Act 2004 amended the Sex Discrimination Act 1975 to give civil partners the right not to be discriminated against on the grounds of their civil partnership. This right does not square with the exemption from the Employment Equality (Sexual Orientations) Regulations 2003/1661 which enables the Church to discriminate in the context of employment against people on the grounds of sexual orientation 'where it is necessary to comply with the doctrines of the religion or to avoid conflicting with the strongly held religious convictions of a significant number of the religion's followers'. Arguably, however, when the Church in *Issues in Human Sexuality* stated that sexual orientation is no bar to office provided that celibacy is practiced, it thereby waived its exemption privileges in respect of the employability of LGBT persons as clergy.

Restricting opportunities for ordination to the office of bishop to those of one gender is clearly prejudicial to all possible candidates of the other gender and to transsexuals.[82] It is indefensible in terms of the principles underpinning equality legislation. Similarly, restricting the ordination of gay priests to those who undertake to remain celibate and the consecration of gay bishops to those who are not sexually active, cannot be human rights compliant. This, in fact, was the determination in *Reaney v. Hereford Diocesan Board of Finance*[83] which concerned an applicant for the position of Youth Officer for the Diocese of Hereford who, although selected unanimously by the interview panel, was subsequently not appointed following a meeting with the Bishop due to the latter's expressed concern that the appointee would be unable to make a promise not to have a future homosexual relationship. The Tribunal unanimously held that the claim of direct discrimination succeeded. In fact, in the above *Schalk and Kopf v. Austria* ruling, the court took the opportunity to pointedly reject the reasoning of earlier decisions and to state its acceptance of the view that a same-sex couple can enjoy "family life" within the meaning of Article 8 of the European Convention (the right to private and family life). Previously, in the eyes of the court same-sex couples had been restricted to being able to enjoy private but not family life. This finding is important as it places gay clergy in the

[82] Note that the ordination of women bishops is expressly prohibited by Canon C2 *Of the consecration of bishops*:

> 5. Nothing in this Canon shall make it lawful for a woman to be consecrated to the office of bishop.

[83] 1602844/2006, (April 2007). The Tribunal in this case found it to be an agreed fact that the teaching of the Church of England with regard to homosexuality is to be found in the following documents:

(a) a resolution of the General Synod dated 14 July 1997;
(b) a resolution of the General Synod dated 11 November 1987;
(c) resolution 1.10 of the Lambeth Conference 1998;
(d) Issues in Human Sexuality, a statement by the House of Bishops of the General Synod of the Church of England, dated December 1991;
(e) Some Issues in Human Sexuality, a guide to the debate (2003); and
(f) A Companion to Some Issues in Human Sexuality 2003.

position of claiming that the Church's policy of celibacy is denying them the enjoyment of a right now recognized by the Convention.

7.4.9 Agency/Principal Relationship with Government

An agent acting within the scope of authority conferred by the principal binds the principal in respect of any obligations created against third parties; the authority may be expressly conferred by the principal or may arise by implication. For the Church, issues associated with such an agency/principal dynamic may arise, as a consequence of its current relationship with government, in two ways: firstly, in the context of its 'established' status'; and secondly, due to service provision contracts. The existence of an agency/principal relationship matters for several reasons: such a lack of independence at least threatens the agent's eligibility for charitable status; the agent will be unable to claim the statutory exemption available to a charity from human rights requirements; the government will be accountable to the parents of school attenders for any service deficiencies/anomalies etc. (e.g. if schools are used for improper proselytism); other religions and religious institutions have good cause to feel relatively disadvantaged; and, ultimately, such an arrangement is open to the charge of being undemocratic.

7.4.10 The Established Church

Indisputably, the special status of 'established' places the Church in a different relationship to government, relative to all other religions and religious institutions. This must inevitably compound, if not strengthen, the assumption that the Church is in certain circumstances acting in an agency capacity. The probability of the latter is disclosed, for example, in some of the distinguishing characteristics of the Church/State relationship: government appointment of all senior clergy; religious representation in the House of Lords restricted exclusively to Anglicans; and all State ceremonies conducted exclusively by the Church etc.

The issue is perhaps particularly evident in relation to the Church being the major provider of the State's education programme to the nation's children. Given the special ties that bind Church and State, it is difficult to envisage circumstances in which the government would bypass the Church when making decisions regarding the delivery of education services and equally difficult to see how the Church could retain any independent capacity to determine the educational content of the service it then delivers. Indeed, although it will acquire more independence in respect of those schools with academy status, this may in practice free the Church to enable its schools to become more overtly

Anglican. Both Church and State are committed to furthering a common cultural agenda, which may indeed be in the best interests of the nation, but it does necessarily constitute an unfair imposition on other cultures that are not assured of equal representation when choices are made regarding services governed by an agency/principal relationship.

7.4.11 Church as Government Contracted Service Provider

Like any other contractor delivering services on behalf of a government department, the Church may find that the terms of the contract are such that it has in effect ceded all control regarding service provision. Where the evidence points to the contractor performing a function that is wholly government controlled then, when so doing, the contractor will be held to be acting as a public body. In which case it will be subject to the public sector equality duty (s.149 of the Act) that came into force on 5th April 2011. The Equality Duty applies to public bodies and others carrying out public functions.

An example of a service delivery contract, performed by a charity for a government body, being subsequently judicially defined as falling into an agency/principal relationship, can be seen in *Weaver v. London and Quadrant Housing Trust.*[84] The Court of Appeal then upheld the Divisional Court's decision that the management and allocation of housing stock by a registered social landlord (the trust was an industrial and provident society with charitable status) was a function of a public nature. It held by a majority that there were several reasons for concluding that the trust was operating as a public body, including: a "substantial public subsidy which enables it to meet its objectives"; a statutory duty to co-operate with local authorities and help the authority to achieve its objectives; and the provision of subsidized housing, which is a function that can be described as governmental. In addition, it found that the trust "makes a valuable contribution to the government's objectives of providing subsidised housing," and that the regulation applying to associations is not simply about ensuring better performance, but "regulations over such matters as rent and eviction are designed, at least in part, to ensure that the objectives of

[84] See, *R (Weaver) v. London & Quadrant Housing Trust* [2009] EWCA Civ 587; [2008] EWHC 1377 (Admin); [2008] WLR (D) 207. In November 2009 the Supreme Court rejected the appeal application of London & Quadrant Housing Trust to the House of Lords. See, also *Poplar Housing and Regeneration Community Association Ltd v. Donoghue* [2001] EWCA Civ 595, [2002] QB 48, where the decision that the Association was exercising "functions of a public nature" was largely attributable to the fact that the local council was heavily represented on the Association's board and controlled its tenancy arrangements; and *Bath Festivals Trust Ltd v. Revenue and Customs* [2008] UKVA V20840, where it was held that when the activities of a trust, which had taken over the provision of services previously the responsibility of the local authority, fell within the scope of the council's strategy relating to the promotion or improvement of the social wellbeing, the trust was acting as a public authority.

government policy … are achieved." Moreover, it found that the termination of a tenancy was "so bound up with the idea and principles of social housing that such acts must be seen as public functions."

Another interesting and relevant case in point is that of *National Union of Teachers v. Governing Body of St Mary's Church of England (Aided) Junior School*,[85] where the Court of Appeal found that the Church of England school was in the State system, the governors were a body charged by the State with the running of the school and were exercising their functions with a view to securing provision by the school of the national curriculum. The local education authority and the Secretary of State had extensive powers to control the actions of the governors and duties were imposed on them by general legislation and statutory instrument. In these circumstances the governors were to be regarded as an emanation of the State for the purposes of the doctrine of direct effect. As the ECJ stated in *Calì & Figli*, an entity acts a public body when it is performing "a task in the public interest which forms part of the essential functions of the State and where the activity is connected by its nature, its aims and rules to which it is subject with the exercise of powers … which are typically those of a public authority."[86]

A charity, such as the Church, may well lose its statutory exemption privileges and find itself fully bound by the compliance requirements of the Equality Act 2010 if the evidence shows that the nature of its relationship with government is such that it is acting as a 'public body'. Arguably, the Church's provision of education services places it in a position analogous to that of the above London and Quadrant Housing Trust as regards its relationship to government.

7.5 Conclusion

The freedom of manoeuvre available to the Church of England is clearly becoming steadily more constrained by human rights. Religious belief and equality provisions have been in conflict over a number of issues but, perhaps most notably, the Church's concession to gay clergy subject to the caveat that they are and remain chaste, has been particularly unsatisfactorily. Should it manage to bridge the deep differences that now divide both its congregations and the provinces that constitute the Anglican Communion, and do so in a manner that is wholly Convention compliant, the Church by virtue of being 'established' will still remain compromised in equality terms. The fact that this status places it in a preferential position relative to all other religions, and binds it closer to government and monarchy than any other institution, gives the Church a continuing and arguably an inordinate leverage in a contemporary pluralistic, and increasingly secular, society.

[85] [1997] 3 CMLR 630.

[86] *Cali & Figli SrL v. SEPG* [1997] ECR I-1547, [1997] 5 CMLR 484 at para 23.

Chapter 8
Moral Jeopardy: The Challenges for the Church and for Religion Internationally

8.1 Introduction

> We can expect to see a continued increase in liberal attitudes towards a range of issues such as abortion, homosexuality, same-sex marriage, and euthanasia, as the influence of considerations grounded in religion declines.[1]

From 1983 to 2011, according to the British Social Attitudes Survey, religious affiliation dropped from 68 to 53 % of the population. Consequently, it advises, we can expect the already hotly disputed agenda of social issues, which includes the items it lists above, to become more prominent and more vociferously contested. The corollary, of course, being an expectation of matching antipathy from the resolutely religious towards the same agenda of issues, leading to increased recourse to the courts. The growing confrontation between religious beliefs and human rights in this jurisdiction would seem set to become more strident.

This agenda is inescapably one that encapsulates some of the more significant moral dilemmas of our age. It could be readily extended to accommodate many other items similarly freighted with moral jeopardy, such as: birth control; the death sentence; stem-cell research; and genetic modification. It is an agenda that can only spread to other nations and grow; and with it will grow an expectation that religion can, as it has in the past, engage with the challenge, offer guidance and exercise leadership. To do so religion in general, and the Church of England most pressingly, must itself first demonstrate a moral coherence that is now somewhat lacking.

The concern of this concluding chapter is – How did we get to this point? What is it about these issues that makes them so loaded, generates such powerful confrontational attitudes, and has led to the current polarised, deeply divisive cold war standoff between large sections of our society; each of which claims to represent the high moral ground? What exactly is the link with religion? Is there a cause

[1] See, the National Centre for Social Research, annual publications of BSAS results since 1983; further at http://www.secularism.org.uk/british-social-attitudes-survey.html.

K. O'Halloran, *The Church of England - Charity Law and Human Rights*, Ius Gentium: Comparative Perspectives on Law and Justice 36, DOI 10.1007/978-3-319-04319-7_8,

and effect dynamic at work which results in these issues becoming more contested as the irreligious proportion of the population grows? Given that we are where we are, what are the implications for the Church and for the Anglican Communion? Are there any indications from contemporary case law that suggest a way forward?

This chapter begins by looking to the history of canon law and to the Scriptures for the origins of the present impasse. It considers the Church's record in relation to sexuality and draws, from its stand on nonmarital sex-as-a-sin paradigm, a link with the present agenda of 'moral imperatives'. It then examines that agenda, assessing the respective positions of those with and those without religious beliefs in relation to it. The chapter explores the speculative assertion that the Church's present crisis arises at least in part as a consequence of a conflict of laws. It concludes with some contemporary judicial observations that suggest a different approach to interpreting religious belief may offer the beginnings of a way out of the present impasse.

8.2 Canon Law, the Scriptures and Sexuality

Canon law has always been at the heart of the Church of England: for the first 350 years or so this took the form of the 1603 Code; since the 1960s, a revised Code has been in force. While the stringent processes set out in the earlier version were themselves quite punitive in their pursuit of a 'name and shame' policy with regard to those suspected of immoral conduct, both versions are indissolubly tied to the Scriptures. The teachings of the latter, often harsh and inflexible in relation to matters of morality, provide fixed reference points for the canons. To understand the current significance of sexuality for the Church, it is necessary to appreciate its importance in the past: firstly, how reliant Church doctrine is upon the Scriptures, as underpinned by canons and for centuries enforced in the courts; and secondly the priority given, throughout that time, to the teachings of the Scriptures in relation to sexual conduct.

8.2.1 *The Canons*

The present Code was promulgated by the Convocations of Canterbury and York in 1964 and 1969 replacing the whole of the Code of 1603 (excepting the proviso to Canon 113), subject to some amendments and revocations made by the General Synod since 1969.[2] While this modernized promulgation removed much archaic material, the Church ensured that the canons would continue to be read alongside and subject to the Scriptures. The Church continues to retain considerable control of the content of canon law through Measures, created by the Church of

[2] See, Church House Publishing, *Canons of the Church of England* (7th ed.), March 2012, at: www.churchofengland.org.

England Assembly (Powers) Act 1919, which enable it to make amendments and create new provisions.[3]

8.2.2 *The Canons of 1603*

This original body of ecclesiastical law was very largely inherited from the Catholic Church at the time of the Reformation.[4] It then formed part of the common law and as such was binding upon both clergy and laity but thereafter the jurisdiction was limited to the clergy. When, towards the end of the sixteenth century, statutory law was introduced to address immoral conduct[5] it applied to the laity but functioned in harmony with canon law and often explicitly focused on canon law issues (see, further, Chap. 3). Then as now, the Church was concerned with what in canon 113 is referred to as 'the licentiousness of these times' and, in canon 109, it identifies such 'notorious crimes and scandals' as 'adultery, whoredom, incest or drunkenness'. Church and State may have had separate jurisdictions but they were both united in their intent to police immorality as defined by the Scriptures.

8.2.3 *The Scriptures*

The fact that Church doctrine is deeply rooted in the Scriptures is frequently asserted in the canons: canon A.5 states that 'the doctrine of the Church of England is grounded in the Holy Scriptures'; while Canon C.15 declares that the Church of England 'professes the faith uniquely revealed in the Holy Scriptures'. This is evident also in the Thirty-nine Articles: article 6 of which makes plain the fundamental importance of the Scriptures to the Church, it simply states that 'Scripture contains all things necessary to salvation'[6]; while articles 20 and 21 add that there is no right to interpret Scripture, nor to decree anything contrary to Scripture, or to

[3] Canon law relies on Royal Assent and License: Measures must be submitted to the Ecclesiastical Committee of Parliament and are ultimately subject to Parliamentary scrutiny and approval.

[4] See, *The Constitutions and Canons Ecclesiastical*, Society for Promoting Christian Knowledge, London, 1900, further, at: http://archive.org/stream/constitutionscan00lond#page/n3/mode/2up.

[5] For example: buggery (5 Eliz. I, c.17.) 1563, bastardy (18 Eliz. 1, c 3.) 1576, and bigamy (1 Jac. 1, c.11) 1603.

[6] Archbishop Cranmer explains the meaning of this statement in his homily 'A Fruitful Exhortation to the Reading of Holy Scripture' in the *First Book of Homilies* where he writes that in Scripture: 'is fully contained what we ought to do, and what to eschew; what to believe, what to love, and what to look for at God's hands at length. In these Books we shall find the Father from whom, the Son by whom, and the Holy Ghost, in whom all things have their being and keeping up, and these three persons to be but one God, and one substance. In these books we may learn to know ourselves, how vile and miserable we be, and also to know God, how good he is of himself, and how he maketh us and all creatures partakers of his goodness.'

teach that anything additional to Scripture is necessary for salvation. Moreover, their importance for Anglicanism at home and abroad has been repeatedly emphasized in the resolutions of the Lambeth conferences.[7]

8.2.4 Scriptures and Sexuality

For the Church, sexuality is a theological and doctrinal matter and any issues arising can and should be resolved by recourse to the Scriptures. Indeed, there is no shortage of teachings in the Scriptures regarding what does and does not constitute Christian sexual morality and none either of evidence of the Church's consistent strivings to adhere to such teachings. Essentially, sexual activity is to be confined within a marital relationship where it is understood, at least implicitly, to be for the purposes of procreation: anything else was held to be both illegal and sinful; and continued to be so until some were decriminalized. Instances of what is Scripturally defined as illicit sexuality are legion and include: fornication, adultery, incest, bigamy, buggery, prostitution, bestiality and homosexuality. The long and strong historical record of both Church and State in prosecuting the perpetrators of such activities has prepared the ground for current policies regarding marriage and homosexuality.[8]

8.2.5 Marriage

The traditional characteristics of marriage, as outlined in the Scriptures and adhered to by Church and State (at least until the introduction of divorce), have always been understood to be monogamy, heterosexuality, and lifelong duration.[9] Until the Marriage Act 1754, the policing of matrimonial matters lay with the Church and the rules it had applied to resolve related issues were thereafter very largely continued by the civil courts (see, further, Chap. 1). In the most recent edition of the Code, canon B30 provides the following definition of marriage:

> The Church of England affirms, according to our Lord's teaching, that marriage is in its nature a union, permanent and lifelong, for better for worse, till death them do part, of one man with one woman, to the exclusion of all others on either side.

---

[7] See, for example: Resolution 11 of 1888; Resolution 9 (vi) of 1920; Resolution 3 of 1930; and Resolutions 1 and 3 of 1958.

[8] See, Brundage, J.A. 1 *Law, sex, and Christian society in medieval Europe*. University of Chicago, Press Chicago,1990.

[9] Jesus is held to have taught that marriage is for life. See, for example: Mk 10:9; Jn 8:11; Mt 5:28; and Mk 7:21–23.

This is endorsed in the government's consultation document which explicitly states that[10]:

> ...marriages solemnized through a religious ceremony and on religious premises would still only be legally possible between a man and a woman. The Government is not seeking to change how religious organisations define religious marriage...

The Book of Common Prayer is often cited as authority for procreation as the purpose of marriage: the preface to the 1662 edition does give this as the first of three reasons for marriage; the revised 1928 edition substitutes, in a slightly different form of words, the reason as being for the increase of mankind according to the will of God, and that children might be brought up in the fear and nurture of the Lord. It would seem that procreation had come to be viewed as less important than formerly. This may reflect an acceptance in the Church that procreation could be: precluded for many by factors such as age, infertility or contraception; or substituted for by adoption, artificial insemination and surrogate parenthood. It may also more simply be a form of acknowledgement that the link between sex and procreation was broken sometime ago with the introduction of contraception and IVF, developments which provided a bypass for the age-old religious equation of sex = sin unless occurring for the purposes of marital procreation.

8.2.6 *Homosexuality*

Church and State traditionally viewed homosexuality as a deviant form of sexual activity, not only sinful and illegal, but singled out for particular opprobrium that continued even after its de-criminalisation in 1967. It is condemned in the Scripture as sinful regardless of the context and there are several references in both the Old and the New Testaments to a homosexual lifestyle being expressly forbidden.[11] As an ancillary point, it is also rejected by the Church on the grounds that it defines sexuality in purely hedonistic terms, as it cannot fulfill the procreative purpose assigned to sexuality within a marital relationship.

8.2.7 *The Church and Its Present Stand on Sexuality Issues*

At the turn of the century, faced with ongoing rumbling protests regarding issues of gender and sexual inequality, the Church together with the wider Anglican Communion seemed to take a firm Scriptural stand in defence of traditional Protestant values.

---

[10] See, *Equal Marriage: a Consultation*, 2012, further at: https://www.gov.uk/government/consultations/equal-marriage-consultation.

This accords with the Matrimonial Causes Act 1973, s.11(c), which states that "a marriage shall be void on the ground that the parties are not respectively male and female".

[11] See, for example: Leviticus (18:22 and 20:13); Romans (1:26–32); and Corinthians (6:9).

8.2.8 Lambeth 1.10 etc.

With resolution 1.10 of the 1998 Lambeth conference,[12] the Church and the wider Anglican Communion drew a line in the sand: there would be no compromise on the definition and role of 'marriage' and 'homosexuality' as understood in the Scriptures. While this resolution has come to represent the present theological position of the Church it was neither the first nor the last such step in that direction.

The first probably came in 1991with the House of Bishops publication *Issues in Human Sexuality*.[13] This document set out a variety of views on homosexuality, bisexuality and transsexualism and sought to promote informed reflection without suggesting any changes to Church policy. It was followed in 1994 by *Issues in Human Sexuality: A Statement by the House of Bishops* and in 2003 by a further document in this series entitled *Some Issues in Human Sexuality: A Guide to the Debate*. As is stated in the Foreword to the latter, 'it works within the parameters of the House's 1991 Statement *Issues in Human Sexuality* and does not seek to change the position of the House of Bishops from the one expressed there'.[14] It was a study guide, designed to complement *Issues* rather than to make specific policy statements or recommendations. A further phase in the series came in 2011 when the House of Bishops launched a 'Human Sexuality Review'.[15]

However, Resolution 1.10, passed by an overwhelming majority at the 1998 Lambeth conference, was a landmark for the Church because of the clear stand taken on the main issues by so many Anglicans. In the resolution: marriage is defined as "between a man and a woman in a lifelong union"; sexual abstinence is required for those who are not called to marriage; homosexual practice is held to be "incompatible with Scripture"; it avows that there must be a rejection of any "legitimising or blessing of same sex unions" and of the ordination of "those involved in same gender unions"; and there must be a recognition of the need to "minister pastorally and sensitively" to all, including those who practice homosexuality. In retrospect, coming at the close of the twentieth century, this appears as a remarkable benchmark for almost five centuries of consistency in the Church regarding its stand on morality, marriage and sexual relationships. It is all the more remarkable for having received endorsement across the Anglican Communion.

In 2004, the *Windsor Report*[16] was published which renounced the initiatives taken by dioceses in the U.S. and Canada in support of gay clergy. While it stopped short of offering comment on homosexuality per se, the report nevertheless

[12] See, Lambeth Conference 1998, Resolution 1.10 *Human Sexuality*, at: http://www.anglicancommunion.org/windsor2004/appendix/p3.6.cfm.

[13] See, *Issues in Human Sexuality, a Statement by the House of Bishops*, Church House Publishing, December 1994.

[14] See, *Some Issues in Human Sexuality: A Guide to the Debate*, Church House Publishing, 2003.

[15] See, further, at: http://www.anglicancommunion.org/search/index.cfm.

[16] See, Eames, R. 2004. Archbishop of Armagh, Lambeth Commission on Communion, the *Windsor Report 2004*, the Anglican Communion Office, London, at: http://www.anglicancommunion.org/windsor2004/appendix/p3.6.cfm.

recommended a moratorium on any further consecrations of actively homosexual bishops and of any public blessings of same-sex unions. Then in November 2013 the Church published the results of the above-mentioned further stage in its study on *Human Sexuality* conducted by a review group established by the House of Bishops under the chairmanship of Sir Joseph Pilling.[17] The 200 page Pilling Report, like others in this series, clearly states that its status is not that of a policy document: thereby leaving intact Church policy as stated in Lambeth resolution 1.10. While it recognizes the importance of the issues facing the Church it offers little more than suggestions for "facilitated conversations" and "pastoral accommodation" which leaves the process open for continuing study and further defers any formal change to existing policy. More internal debate may be anticipated in the future as the Church attempts to circle its remaining wagons around Resolution 1.10 in the hope that Scripturally compliant beliefs that have prevailed for centuries will withstand the sustained attacks from human rights compliant policies.

8.3 'Moral Imperatives' and the Politics of Secularism

There is an argument that religious beliefs are separable from moral and ethical concepts. The latter may be seen as independent variables that can lend themselves to being used to further the purposes of either: those of religious belief who wish to assimilate such key concepts into their religion, to ground theistic and spiritual beliefs on a balanced sense of fairness and social justice; or those secularists who wish to apply them to achieve a civil society with an infrastructure of impartial social institutions the functionality of which is impervious to religious influence. Either way, they are important with potentially crucial political leverage. A capacity to respond meaningfully to the current agenda of 'moral imperatives' is essential for the credibility and coherence of the Church of England and the wider Anglican Communion. These matters are by their nature deeply moral and present a test bed for the credibility of those who aspire to lead a religious life, whatever their beliefs. They reveal more about the meaning of religion in contemporary society – than, for example, the practices of usury and banking etc – and require the Church to provide careful, balanced, religious interpretation and leadership if it is unify its adherents, engage secularists and contribute to pluralism rather than polarisation.

8.3.1 The 'Moral Imperatives'

Given the circumstances in which Church, State and charity established their symbiotic relationship at the turn of the sixteenth century, it is unsurprising that from

[17] The Report of the *House of Bishops Working Group on Human Sexuality* (the Pilling Report), published by Church House Publishing, at: http://www.churchofengland.org/media/1891063/pilling_report_gs_1929_web.pdf.

such beginnings it was the principles of Christianity that thereafter identified the moral imperatives that came to inform the law. This was demonstrated in relation to a succession of social issues that constituted the moral battleground of their day including: temperance; slavery; suffrage; contraception; and divorce. Contemporary moral issues – most notably between abortion and pro-life groups, between LGBT libertarians and advocates for traditional family units – that have come to feature so prominently in the 'culture wars' of the US, are derived from the core moral values instilled by Christianity and headlined in the Scriptures. The Christian influence, always most obvious in relation to the family, now provides the grounds for those of traditional religious beliefs to challenge the changes being driven by equality and human rights legislation.[18]

8.4 Family Oriented Moral Imperatives: The Christian Legacy

As Lord Finlay LC commented in *Bowman v. Secular Society Ltd.*, when reflecting on previous centuries of case law[19]:

> It has been repeatedly laid down by the Courts that Christianity is part of the law of the land, and it is the fact that our civil polity is to a large extent based upon the Christian religion. This is notably so with regard to the law of marriage and the law affecting the family.[20]

He was quite clear that up until then the courts would have considered themselves bound by such principles when called upon to interpret 'religion' in a charity law context.[21] The distinctively Christian dimension to those principles then included: monogamous, heterosexual marriage for life; the sanctity of marriage to the exclusion of non-marital sex, any children thereof, and unmarried partnerships; the criminalisation of homosexuality and repudiation of all other forms of non-marital sex; and the rejection of a Darwinian approach to the meaning of 'life'. This was in keeping with many centuries of Christian religious doctrine, underpinned by statute and common law, which prohibited any infringement of Church approved marital family relationships (e.g. bigamy, incest, abortion, sodomy, etc.). Christian

[18] Laws LJ acknowledged as much in *McFarlane v. Relate Avon Ltd.*, [2010] IRLR 872; 29 BHRC 249 when he observed that "the Judaeo-Christian tradition, stretching over many centuries, has no doubt exerted a profound influence upon the judgment of lawmakers as to the objective merits of this or that social policy" at para 23. Also, see, Taylor, C. 2007. *A secular age*. Cambridge, MA: Belknap Press/Harvard University.

[19] [1917] AC 406 (H.L.). Also, see, *R* v. *Dibdin* [1910] P 57, CA.

[20] Ibid, citing: *Briggs v. Hartley* (1850) 19 L. J. (Ch.) 416; *Cowan v. Milbourn* (1867) L. R. 2 Ex. 230; *De Costa v. De Paz* (1754) 2 Swanst, 487; and *In re Bedford Charity* (1819) 2 Swanst. 470, 527.

[21] A long catalogue of cases beginning with *De Costa v. De Paz* (1754) 2 Swans 487, Chancery, including *Lawrence v. Smith, Murray v. Benbow* (1822) The Times 2 Feb. 1822, *Briggs v. Hartley* (1850) 19 L. J. (Ch.) 416, and ending with *Pare v. Clegg* (1861) 29 Beav 589, 54 ER 756, established that "the Courts will not help in the promotion of objects contrary to the Christian religion".

dogma associated with the 'Nazarene family' model, allowed Church and State to staunchly maintain that any form of sexual relationship outside the marital family unit was prohibited and punishable by God and the courts: these were moral imperatives, any transgression of which was both a sin and a crime. Not only would the judiciary assiduously uphold Christian principles, but they would not countenance any alternative: there could be no equality of religions; neither would the views of atheists or agnostics be allowed to undermine the Christian law of the State. The principles were firmly rooted in a Christian and Protestant culture.

8.4.1 Family Oriented Moral Imperatives: The Contemporary Agenda

The latter part of the twentieth century, in a rehearsal of issues that would later emerge in a human rights context, saw State and Church begin to disentangle their hitherto joint stand on such family matters as 'illegitimacy', the indissolubility of marriage; and abortion: where the State led, in terms of legalising divorce and contraception etc., the Church eventually followed. On certain core issues, however, seemingly ring-fenced by the Scriptures – such as the conditions regulating abortion and the status of homosexual relationships- the Church as defender of Protestantism could not give way. The list of morally charged social issues with potential to challenge the Church has in recent decades been extended beyond matters relating to the nuclear marital family unit and now includes, among other subjects: the death penalty; adoption by same gender couples; female genital mutilation and circumcision; genetic screening, programming and cloning; the use of human tissue, research involving human embryos and stem cell research; and the use of medical intervention to aid human reproduction and death. This agenda of moral imperatives promises to be further extended in keeping with the ebb and flow of advances in science, collapse of confidence in social institutions and retreat into conservative values.

8.4.2 Polarisation

Past experience of theocratic rule in England is in many respects not unlike that of present practice in some Islamic states: both featuring a religiously homogeneous population within a religiously legitimated State; public and private interests co-existing under the umbrella of State supported religion; non-State religion being suppressed; and the moral imperatives of religious belief enforced by the harsh punishments of Church/State law. The contemporary tendency towards 'fundamentalism' – apparent in Islam, Judaism and Christianity – increasingly practiced by minorities in the developed nations of the West, if not as lethally as in parts of Africa and the Middle East, is serving as intended to accentuate religious differences. Currently, the irreconcilability of traditional religious beliefs with the values and lifestyle choices of modern civil society would seem to be driving a wave of didactic moralism: polarizing views and politicizing the role of religion within many developed nations and between them and other, largely Islamic, nations; while reducing the likelihood of negotiable change. The consequent hardening of interfaces, domestically and internationally, is a challenge and an opportunity for the Church of England to demonstrate moral leadership – but to do so it will first need to achieve and demonstrate a new and more nuanced appreciation of the balance to be struck between beliefs and equality: as represented by the Scriptures and human rights.

8.4.3 Religious Pluralism

In addition to the trend towards a narrowing of religion – a retreat into fundamentalism and polarisation – another trend, often overlapping with it, is becoming steadily more conspicuous. Emerging from the U.S. in the latter decades of the twentieth century, and now making inroads in the UK, there has been an explosion of some innovative and many derivative religious groupings, that cumulatively have broadened the spectrum of what could be construed as a 'religious belief' well beyond the imaginings of early traditionalists. It's not just a profusion of Christian related religions (though evangelicism in its many forms, is itself a phenomenon) such as Christian Science, or wholly original ones such as Scientology, there are also a host of African/American churches and a stream of 'New Age' religions and semi-philosophical or mystical belief systems, some of which may touch upon Gaia or other 'mother earth' ideologies. Almost all of these are concerned not with honouring and perpetuating inherited beliefs but in relating to immediate environmental and lifestyle issues, and may do so through engaging in communal forms of celebratory ceremonies rather than priest led ritualised worship. The multiple variants of belief systems fit into social context of fluid marital and parenting arrangements where mobile nuclear family units are accustomed to needs led, user driven choices in which most attachments are negotiable. The modern 'supermarket' environment can apply to religious beliefs with new products advertising their USPs, competing with traditional religions and tempting the unfulfilled with better offers. It is becoming not uncommon in some areas for consumers to trade-in their religious commitment as they would their brand loyalty to car, school or supermarket as part of a new lifestyle package; or to 'mix-and-match' by maintaining their adherence to a traditional religion but with add-ons from membership of a new one. For the 'me' generation that characterises some aspects of life in contemporary western society, religious belief can mean no more than an optional affiliation: part of a personal growth experience that may pass through different phases encompassing, for example, sequential adherence to a birth religion, Zen Buddhism (or some such meditative and instructive religious discipline), then a form of evangelism before returning to their birth religion or perhaps choosing atheism.

The proliferation of new forms of religion, together with the increased rate of transference between them, reveals that for the growing numbers of those concerned the theological roots and doctrines of religion are of less importance than its capacity to address immediate social issues and pressures: the transcendental dimension must relate to the contemporary context. The challenge of religious pluralism may turn out to be as threatening for the traditional religions as both the lapse into fundamentalism and the growth in secularism.[22]

8.4.4 The Politics of Secularism

In England, as in many other countries, the need for rules of engagement between those with and those without religious belief to facilitate negotiation on their common agenda of issues, largely associated with Christian moral imperatives, would seem quite pressing.[23]

8.4.5 The Secularists

In the UK the proportion of the population without religious beliefs is steadily growing. In keeping with their increasing numerical strength is the added weight this gives to the argument that an established Church does not and cannot represent their interests. To which they might add that as such it cannot ensure equality between religions, nor between the religious and the non-religious, and furthermore that the Church also patently institutionalises inequality within itself by perpetuating the enforced celibacy of homosexual clergy but not that of heterosexual clergy and denying women an equal opportunity to be ordained as bishops.

The essential secularist position is well expressed by Jurgen Habermas who argues that "every citizen must know and accept that only secular reasons count beyond the institutional threshold that divides the informal public sphere from parliaments, courts, ministries and administrations."[24] He explains[25]:

> The principle of separation of church and state demands that the institution of the state operate with strict impartiality vis-a-vis religious communities; parliaments, courts, and the administration must not violate the prescription not to privilege one side at the cost of another.

[22] See, further, Berger, P.L. 2001. *Reflections on the sociology of religion today*. 62 Sociology of Religion: 443–444.

[23] See, further, for example, Lerner, N. 2012. *Religion, secular beliefs and human rights*, 2nd ed. The Hague: Martinus Nijhoff.

[24] Ibid, at p. 9.

[25] Ibid, at p. 6.

The principle of secularism broadly suggests that matters of government should be wholly insulated from any religious influence. This can be interpreted as licensing the State to assume responsibility for all decision-making, facilities, administrative systems and processes associated with matters in the public interest, without any concessions to a religion or religions nor of any input from religious organisations. While the term clearly would not accommodate an established Church, or any State preferencing of religion, there is doubt as to whether it extends to suggesting that religion per se, or religions, or religious values should not be recognised and respected by the State. Interestingly, Habermas has no such doubts but instead urges that the State "must not discourage religious persons and communities from also expressing themselves politically as such …".[26] In fact, in an observation that applies domestically and internationally, he sees the problem as one requiring a change of perspective on the part of secularists[27]:

> As long as secular citizens are convinced that religious traditions and religious communities are to a certain extent archaic relics of pre-modern societies that continue to exist in the present, they will understand freedom of religion as the cultural version of the conservation of a species in danger of becoming extinct … The insight by secular citizens that they live in a post-secular society that is epistemically adjusted to the continued existence of religious communities first requires a change in mentality that is no less cognitively exacting than the adaptation of religious awareness to the challenges of an ever more secularized environment.

Arguably, however, secularism poses a dichotomy: the public arena is either an open market in which all religions are equally free to proclaim and manifest their beliefs, compete for adherents and be assured of equal respect and engagement from State authorities; or, alternatively, the public arena is one in which all religions are equally prohibited from exercising any presence, that space is reserved entirely for secular entities and their activities, and all religions can be assured that they will be equally ignored by the State authorities. In either case, however the State would remain impartial.

8.4.6 *The Religious*

Individually, religious adherents are seen as looking to their particular set of beliefs as to a rule book and energy source for tackling everyday problems: discretionary judgment being displaced by, or confined within, doctrinal principles. Collectively, they are seen as required to stand by the doctrines of their religion, asserting the beliefs subscribed to, in any circumstance (religious, social or political) where these may be challenged. In either instance they are held to be left with no room for compromise: the point of religious doctrine being to assure members that the one

---

[26] Habermas, J. 2006. Religion in the public sphere. *European Journal of Philosophy* 14(1): 1–25, at p. 10.

[27] Ibid at p. 15.

true way is as ordained in their set of beliefs and require them to demonstrate this and seek to convince others. As has been said[28]:

> It belongs to the religious convictions of a good many religious people in our society that they ought to base their decisions concerning fundamental issues of justice on their religious convictions. They do not view it as an option whether or not to do it. It is their conviction that they ought to strive for wholeness, integrity, integration in their lives: that they ought to allow the Word of God, the teachings of the Torah, the command and example of Jesus, or whatever, to shape their existence as a whole, including, then, their social and political existence. Their religion is not, for them, about something other than their social and political existence.

This conviction that for 'believers' all conduct must conform to their beliefs is a very potent force which, as has been argued by Jurgen Habermas and others, is capable of divisive social and political consequences.[29] He notes that this imposes an unreasonable burden on such 'believers' as they are not free to take any action or advance any views which may compromise their beliefs. He suggests that "the liberal state must not transform the requisite institutional separation of religion and politics into an undue mental and psychological burden for those of its citizens who follow a faith".[30] The challenge is to find a way of engaging with those of religious belief to ensure that their interests find proportionate representation in the institutions and public policy that give effect to contemporary politics; subject to the caveat that the body politic must not in that process allow itself to become hostage to a possible religious veto. This requires religious adherents and organisations to acquire a sense of permission to represent, articulate and be accountable for their particular perception of how their beliefs apply to current issues.

8.5 Conflict of Laws: Canon Law, Charity Law and Equality Law

It was inevitable that the twenty-first century would see a clash between the Scripture led theology of the Church (with its social policy application) and the equality led provisions of the European Convention on Human Rights. For the Church it is singularly unfortunate that this should coincide with the introduction of new domestic legislation following the radical reform of laws governing charity and equality: these significant bodies of law, each heavily laden with moral and ethical considerations, necessarily impact upon Church theology and policies. Working through the implications of overlapping sets of legislative provisions, while taking into account ongoing human rights case law developments, is a process that will take time. The

---

[28] Woltersorrf, N. 1997. The role of religion in decision and discussion of political issues. In *Religion in the public square: The place of religious convictions in political debate,* ed. R. Audi, and N. Woltersorrf. New York: Rowan & Littlefield.

[29] Habermas, J. 2006. Religion in the public sphere. *European Journal of Philosophy* 14(1): 1–25.

[30] Ibid at p. 9.

outcomes – in terms of the Church's status as 'established', retention of theological coherence, the continuation of the Anglican Communion and the future leadership of that body – are impossible to predict.

8.5.1 Canon Law

In theory all law must relate to its cultural context. Canon law, however, – concerned with preserving and passing on a body of immutable religious beliefs, expressed in tenets, doctrines, and the timeless rites of worship – is, to a large extent, an exception.

8.5.2 Areas of Conflict

The canons of the Church of England define marriage, in accordance with the Scriptures, as being between a man and a woman. Since canon law and the prayer book have long been on the statute books there will now be a clash between the provisions of canon law and same-sex marriage legislation. The fact that the Church has the legal/constitutional status of being 'established' compounds this difficulty: being legally joined at the hip, Church and State can only act as one on a statutorily defined matter; though they remain free to express different views. Should the government enact provisions that flatly contradict core tenets of canon law, then Church and State become constitutionally separable and dis-establishment would seem inevitable, leaving only the politically interesting question as to which party would instigate such a divorce.

Other areas of difficulty arise in relation to the Church's discriminatory policies regarding gender and sexuality as preconditions for appointment to certain posts. While the latter is linked to the canon law renunciation of non-marital sexuality, this compromise is clearly unsatisfactory as, apart from being unverifiable, it is morally untenable, and legally inequitable. It would seem to be in conflict with at least Article 8 of the Convention.[31] Again the Church's 'established' status restricts its freedom to act contrary to the State's legislative provisions.

It is also salutary to reflect that canon law was seen as the unifying thread, giving the many different constituent cultures of the Anglican Communion their collective identity, and which could provide the common ground for reunification following the debacle over the ordination of homosexual clergy. The significance attached to the principles of canon law would be difficult to overestimate: for adherents their case rests ultimately on the argument that homosexuality is condemned in the Scriptures, a renunciation that the Anglican Communion in Resolution 1.10 and

[31] See, *Schalk and Kopf v. Austria*, Application no. 30141/04, Council of Europe: European Court of Human Rights, 24 June 2010.

elsewhere has overwhelmingly endorsed; therefore anyone believing differently cannot be an Anglican. Consequently those North American dioceses that have chosen to take an opposing stand on this issue can no longer be Anglicans and should be expelled.[32] The dissenters, on the other hand, were not so wedded to the absolutism of this particular aspect of canon law; human rights principles had also to be weighed in the balance.

The Covenant initiative, as first proposed in the Windsor Report, was set firmly in the context of canon law and in the belief that this could itself be a unifying force in Anglicanism. The Covenant set out to transfer the idea of 'covenantal affection' into political reality. That it failed utterly was due to the gathering strength of opposing human rights principles. Far from being the banner around which the provinces could rally, putting aside their differences to affirm their solidarity in support of a greater cause, the Covenant plea for recognition of the importance of a shared canon law heritage seemed to provoke further dissension: it largely served to exacerbate existing culturally based differences between the two camps.

8.5.3 *Charity Law*

The recent reform of charity law is the most radical in its 400 year history. The changes introduced, including a redefinition of religion and alterations to the relationship between charity and religion, will inevitably impact upon the Church.

8.5.4 *Areas of Conflict*

The definition of 'religion' in charity law, although now a great deal broader than in canon law, does not in itself present any direct challenge to the latter. The problems that may arise are in the changes made to certain key charity law concepts and their application to the Church.

The reversal of the public benefit presumption requires the Church to identify the contribution it is making to benefit the public, in addition to any member benefit. Again, for reasons outlined earlier, this should not present any direct threat (see, further, Chap. 7) but there are some indirect potential difficulties in relation to the Church's role as a religious institution and in respect of its secular activities.

In relation to the former, the Church must demonstrate both its actual public benefit contribution and that this outweighs any possible disbenefit: in the light of the numerous official reports confirming systemic child abuse by religious organisations, together with evidence from Northern Ireland of the capacity of religious leaders to incite violence, the latter caveat no longer seems unreasonable.

[32] Note that the U.S. census showed 646,000 same-sex-couple households in 2010.

Given the increasingly volatile religious interface in this country, there is an equally increasing expectation that the Church will contribute to maintaining social harmony in local communities: many churches are very active in this cause with outreach services and social events tailored to welcome different ethnic groups; others may, however, contribute to raising local social tensions by retreating into a more fundamentalist or socially intrusive evangelicism. Clearly this civic space will now be much more competitive as other organisations and 'moral or ethical belief systems' acquire charitable status under the advancement of religion head, which they were previously denied, and make their own public benefit contribution (or not) by modelling ethical conduct and generating a sense of shared morality and social responsibility to develop more caring communities. Also relevant is the fact that the new charity legislation has enacted[33] the advancement of human rights as a charitable purpose which might be expected to bring more equality related charities into this field. Arguably, it would be more beneficial than otherwise if the Church could now show that it was helping to cultivate civic society values by embracing equity and equality in the opportunities provided for the ordination of its clergy.

In relation to its secular activities, as mentioned earlier the Church could find itself compromised by the duality of its role as 'established' and as contracted service provider on behalf of government. In this context it is also worth noting that the 'exclusivity' condition (requiring activity to be exclusively for the advancement a charitable purpose) has been continued by the new charity legislation. This could impinge upon the charitable status of some Church facilities, to which expensive fees restrict access, by implying that they are oriented towards income generation and so serve a purpose that may not be exclusively charitable.

8.5.5 *Human Rights and Equality Law*

Human rights provisions, as set out in the European Convention and given effect by the Human Rights Act 1998, make an over-arching constitutional contribution to domestic law. As such they must have a more particular bearing upon the established Church than on any other religious organisation: the obligation to act in compliance with the spirit and requirements of human rights must be that much greater.

In marked contrast to canon law, human rights law is constantly evolving in response to ever-changing fluctuations in a matrix of varied cultural contexts. In this jurisdiction, the compression of many statutes into the Equality Act 2010 constituted a major reform and simplification of the law relating to discrimination. However, it is the ongoing ECtHR case law developments that are likely to present most challenges for the Church.

[33] See, the Charities Act 2011, s.3(1)(h).

8.5.6 Areas of Conflict

The secularists, in keeping with those of religious belief, can look to Articles 9 and 14 of the Convention for support from discrimination. This avenue has yet to be fully explored but there are some indications that future secularist initiatives may impact upon the Church.

Article 9, for example, was considered in *Kokkinakis v. Greece*,[34] a case which concerned proselytism. As the court then pointed out, although the right guarantees freedom of religion or belief it is not limited to a freedom to believe: it includes the freedom to reject belief. Article 9 was held to be also "a precious asset for atheists, sceptics and the unconcerned."[35] Similarly, Article 14 is not limited to providing for the freedom to hold or reject beliefs, it also provides protection from discrimination based on religion or belief. This interpretation may have implications for the Church's current rejection of the principle of equality in its application of gender and sexuality criteria to the ordination of clergy. While it may be granted legal exemption on the grounds of being a religious charity, in the eyes of the general public the Church will have greater difficulty in avoiding moral culpability. The refusal to extend to women, the same opportunities afforded to men, is clearly indefensible, contrary to Convention principles and is particularly contrary to the Convention on the Elimination of all Forms of Discrimination Against Women (CEDAW*)* in which discrimination is defined as[36]:

> ...any distinction, exclusion or restriction made on the basis of sex which has the effect or purpose of impairing or nullifying the recognition, enjoyment or exercise by women, irrespective of their marital status, on a basis of equality of men and women, of human rights and fundamental freedoms in the political, economic, social, cultural, civil or any other field.

Regarding discrimination on the grounds of sexuality, this also is non-compliant with Convention principles. As emerging case law gives cautious incremental recognition to a right to 'family life' that extends beyond the traditional Nazarene model, it seems inevitable that there will come a point some time in the future when the Church will have to follow the ECtHR and accept that homosexual clergy are as entitled as their heterosexual colleagues to a family life with a sexual dimension.

The broader Convention principles – 'proportionality', and 'in keeping with a democratic society' – may well have a bearing upon the undoubted right of the Church to manage the intake, staffing and curriculum of its many thousands of schools in accordance with its doctrines. This right is one which will have to be

---

[34] (1994) 17 EHRR 397.

[35] Ibid at para 31. See, also, *R (Williamson) v. Secretary of State for Education and Employment* [2005] 2 AC 246: "the atheist, the agnostic, and the sceptic are as much entitled to freedom to hold and manifest their beliefs as the theist", per Nicholls LJ.

[36] Adopted in 1979 by the UN General Assembly, it is often described as an international bill of rights for women. Its Optional Protocol came into effect in this jurisdiction in 2005 followed in 2007 by the Gender Equality Duty in 2007 which was subsequently absorbed into the Equality Act 2010.

exercised in a manner that is not oppressive, or reasonably perceived as such, by any pupils, staff and parents that do not share those beliefs. An analysis strengthened by the fact that Church schools are almost wholly funded by government which together with the 'establishment' factor may give rise to a query that these (unlike any other faith schools) could be construed as an 'emanation of the State'.[37]

Then there is what has become, for the Church, the moral minefield of same sex marriages with its many accompanying legal issues. The Marriage (Same Sex Couples) Act 2013 contains, for example, provisions for a so-called 'quadruple lock' that are intended to protect those faith groups not wishing to solemnize same-sex marriages. This is likely to present difficulties.[38] The 'lock' comprises: (1) the explicit statement that no religious organization, or individual minister, can be compelled to marry same-sex couples or to permit this to happen on their premises; (2) provision for an "opt-in" system for religious organizations that wish to conduct marriages for same-sex couples; (3) amendments to the Equality Act 2010 exempting religious organizations and individual ministers from claims alleging discrimination, should they refuse to either marry a same-sex couple or to allow their premises to be used for that purpose; and (4) an assurance that the legislation will not affect the canon law of the Church, though opting in would require it to instigate a change to primary legislation and a change to canon law. It is hard to avoid concluding that this lock is essentially discriminatory: designed to protect the Church and canon law; it ascribes a different *locus standi* to the Church relative to all other religions; it has no relevance for some religions, such as the Religious Society of Friends, that welcome the opportunity to officiate at gay weddings; and before the Church or any of its clergy can opt in a further legislative step is required (i.e. the Church is placed at a disadvantage relative to all other religious organisations), without which any such initiative by clergy must be construed as illegal.

Moreover, there is a definite culture of sympathetic understanding towards LGBT issues among many clergy, as corroborated by the stand of some anti-Covenanters. This makes it highly unlikely that all will uniformly and indefinitely hold the line by refusing to officiate at gay weddings. It would be a safe prediction that within a short time some will break ranks with Church policy and offer to officiate at gay weddings held on Church premises.[39] Any clergy who, in breach of (4) above, thereby seek to unilaterally exercise the Church's right to 'opt in' will place themselves and the Church in a difficult position: such a breach of canon law will, as it has done in the U.S. and Canada, trigger local diocesan schisms. However, and unlike the position in North America, such dissension here will also raise the establishment issue: it does not seem constitutionally possible for the Church not to act in conformity with the State on a matter specifically prescribed by statute; if there is division in the Church on such a matter, then schism and disestablishment of all or part of the Church must surely follow.

---

[37] As in *National Union of Teachers v. Governing Body of St Mary's Church of England (Aided) Junior School*, [1997] 3 CMLR 630.

[38] See, further, at: http://www.bbc.co.uk/news/uk-politics-20680924.

[39] See, further, *Spetz v. Sweden*, no 20402/92 (1994).

8.6 Religion and Other Belief Systems: Some Contemporary Judicial Guidance

There have been some interesting developments in the judicial approach to the difficult business of how best to treat contentious matters relating to religion, other forms of belief and their adherents. This, in part, has been necessitated by the extraordinary proliferation of religions and belief systems in recent decades. The need to assess religious status often presents before a court or regulator because such an organisation is seeking registration as a charity together with the accompanying entitlement to tax exemption. Also, there are instances when a member of such a group comes before court or regulator as plaintiff or defendant in relation to an alleged interference with a purported rightful manifestation of belief. A determination then needs to be made as to whether the believer and/or the relevant religion/belief system and the action complained of, sufficiently satisfy the appropriate legal definitions to justify recognition and the remedies available under discrimination law. In the processing of such cases, some novel judicial initiatives have been taken which may have a possible bearing on the present impasse.

8.6.1 Religious Belief

While the traditional Christian, Islamic and other religions continue to numerically dominate, they have themselves generated subsidiaries and have been joined by a great many new religions, belief systems and cults, some of temporary duration, and quite a number of which have no theistic component. This New Age world with its myriad of often transient organisations, each with its own system of beliefs, offers little scope for using the approach customarily applied in respect of traditional religions. The judicial task of evaluating and weighing the credentials of yet another sect of 'believers' – which often have no body of doctrine, no liturgy nor any set form of worship–is becoming progressively more challenging. Accordingly, courts and regulators have moved away from examining institutional structures or referencing doctrines and tenets, which had long been the accepted means for defining religion, and have instead begun exploring other methods of establishing the veracity and status of an organisation or individual's professed beliefs.

This new approach was one which also, finally, saw the repeal of the law relating to blasphemy. It is quite interesting that not until 6th May 2008 did a Lords amendment finally abolish the common law offences of blasphemy and blasphemous libel. The fact that in this jurisdiction a criminal offence derived from canon law and dating from at least the seventeenth century, specifically protecting Christianity and clearly constraining the human right to freedom of expression, should have lasted as long as it did provides a revealing indicator of the entrenched nature of the Church/State relationship.

8.6.2 Beliefs Not Dependent Upon Doctrines

Until 1995, except for two cases, neither the ECtHR nor its predecessor the European Commission on Human Rights had admitted applications from religions that could be called "new", "minority", or "nontraditional".

Subsequently, the Convention has been interpreted more broadly to allow a range of beliefs to qualify as 'religious'. This is signifies a recognition of and a response to the ever expanding list of religious-type organisations which, along with the more traditional religions, must now be accorded an equivalent legitimacy and weighting by courts and regulators: the emphasis is on the right of the individual to hold and manifest their sincerely held beliefs (subject to the rights of others) rather than on the institutional significance of a religion. However, such 'beliefs' as defined in European Convention case law, must amount to "more than just mere opinions or deeply held feelings", they must involve "a holding of spiritual or philosophical convictions which have an identifiable formal content".

In *Campbell and Cosans v. United Kingdom*,[40] for example, the ECtHR had served notice that non-theistic beliefs would be human rights compliant when it ruled in favour of complainants who alleged that the system of corporal punishment in Scottish state schools offended their philosophical convictions under Article 2 of Protocol 1 of the ECHR. This interpretation was endorsed by the Employment Equality (Religion or Belief) Regulations 2003 which made provision for a philosophical belief to have a similar weight and significance as a religious belief in the context of human rights jurisprudence. Following the initial introduction of definitional change in the 2006 Act, Weatherup J, in *Christian Institute*,[41] while suggesting that some boundaries were needed to determine whether a system of belief would warrant charitable status, stressed that a 'believer' is not necessarily a person whose beliefs are as set down in a doctrine to which he or she subscribes and which brings with it membership obligations to behave in a prescribed manner (see, also, Chap. 6). Thereafter, a number of cases further explored the range of beliefs that could qualify for charitable status alongside the traditional religious bodies. In *Grainger v. Nicholson*,[42] for example, the Employment Appeal Tribunal concluded that a strongly held philosophical belief about climate change, and the accompanying implication that carbon emissions must be urgently cut to avoid catastrophic climate change, were capable of constituting a 'religious or philosophical belief'.[43] Subsequently, in 2010 and 2011, the Charity Commission registered the Druid

---

[40] [1982] 4 EHRR 293.

[41] *Christian Institute and Others v. Office of First Minister and Deputy First Minister* Neutral Citation no. [2007] NIQB 66.

[42] [2009] UKEAT 0219 09 0311 (EAT).

[43] This wording resulted from an amendment inserted in April 2007 by the Equality Act 2006, s77(1). Prior to the amendment, the word "similar" appeared before the words "philosophical belief" but to be defined as 'similar' to religion was viewed by some as offensive to humanists and atheists.

Network[44] and the British Humanist Association,[45] respectively, as charities in acknowledgment that their beliefs similarly met the same criteria.

The implications of this broader approach for the Church and the wider Anglican Communion are that the status of Anglicanism, both as a religion and as a charity, need not be dependent upon its doctrines as applied through canon law: beliefs that are not referenced to canon law would still meet the necessary definitional requirements of Convention law and charity law.

8.6.3 Criteria Applied to Confirm Status of a Religion or Belief System

The focus of assessment has shifted from religion as an institution to the authenticity of an individual's subjective interpretation and experience of it.[46] This development is particularly significant in view of the established judicial principle that it is not for the court to inquire into any asserted belief and judge its validity by some objective standard: the right to freedom of religion protects the subjective belief of an individual. It is a development that may facilitate the realising of the Habermas proposal for dialogue between those of religious belief and secularists[47] and it could also possibly provide a margin of flexibility to encourage moves towards a rapproachment within the Church and the broader Anglican Communion.

8.6.4 Subjective Experience

The assertion by Nicholls LJ in *Williamson*[48] that "the freedom of religion protects the subjective belief of an individual"[49] was echoed by the comment of Baroness Hale for the Court of Appeal in *Ghai*[50] that "it matters not for present purposes whether it is a universal, orthodox or unusual belief," by the observation of Laws LJ in *McFarlane v. Relate Avon Ltd*[51] that "in the eye of everyone save the believer

---

[44] See, *The Druid Network* [2010] Ch Comm Decision (21 September 2010). The Druid Network explains that it exists for "Informing, Inspiring and Facilitating Druidry as a Religion".

[45] See, further, at: http://www.charity-commission.gov.uk/.

[46] See, Edge, P.W. 2012, January. Determining religion in English courts. *Oxford Journal of Law and Religion*, OUP.

[47] Habermas, J. 2006. Religion in the public sphere. *European Journal of Philosophy* 14(1): 9.

[48] [2005] UKHL 15, [2005] 2 AC 246 (HL) at para 75. An approach very much in keeping with the views expressed by Lord Greene MR in *Re Samuel* [1942] 1 Ch 1, CA at p. 17.

[49] *Ex parte Williamson*, op cit, at para 22; though expressed obiter.

[50] *Ghai, R (on the application of) v. Newcastle City Council & Ors* [2010] EWCA Civ 59.

[51] [2010] EWCA Civ B1 (29 April 2010).

religious faith is necessarily subjective" and by the EAT view in *Eweida*[52] that "it is not necessary for a belief to be shared by others in order for it to be a religious belief".[53] Such judicial and regulatory pronouncements would seem to firmly establish the subjective interpretation of a religion or philosophy as all-important.

In *Ex parte Williamson*,[54] for example, a case determined by the House of Lords, immediately preceding the introduction of the 2006 Act, the court was concerned with a number of schools collectively seeking to be exempted from the statutory ban on the use of corporal punishment on the grounds that the claimants represented a large body of the Christian community whose fundamental beliefs included the use of such punishment on behalf of parents.[55] The court proceeded on the basis that: where adherents profess a shared belief or beliefs of central importance to their sense of collective identity this calls for some examination; it is permissible and necessary for the court to enquire into the basis for that belief and determine whether it is held in good faith; without going as far as to assess its validity. What was of central importance, in the opinion of Nicholls LJ, in any case where the genuineness of a claimant's professed belief was at issue, was whether[56]:

> an assertion of religious belief is made in good faith: 'neither fictitious, nor capricious, and that it is not an artifice'[57]... But, emphatically, it is not for the court to embark on an enquiry into the asserted belief and judge its 'validity' by some objective standard such as the source material upon which the claimant founds his belief or the orthodox teaching of the religion in question or the extent to which the claimant's belief conforms to or differs from the views of others professing the same religion. Freedom of religion protects the subjective belief of an individual.

These and other judicial views in this landmark case have set standards for regulators and courts. Indeed in the following year, the House of Lords in *Begum*[58] considered the wish of a schoolgirl to wear the jilbab in keeping with the professed religious beliefs of herself and family despite the prohibition on doing so in the school dress code. The court heard evidence that the wearing of the jilbab was not considered necessary by a considerable proportion of those who shared the plaintiff's religious beliefs, but nonetheless upheld her right to consider it to be necessary for her. Lord Bingham of Cornhill added that "it was not the less a religious belief because her belief may have changed, as it probably did, or because it was a

---

[52] [2010] EWCA Civ80 (12 Feb 2010). OUP, 2012, at p. 14.

[53] *Eweida v. British Airways* [2008] UKEAT 0123, 08, 2011 (EAT) at para 29.

[54] [2005] UKHL 15, [2005] 2 AC 246 (HL) at para 75. An approach very much in keeping with the views expressed by Lord Greene MR in *Re Samuel* [1942] 1 Ch 1, CA at p. 17.

[55] See, *R (Williamson) v. Secretary of State for Education and Employment* [2005] 2 AC 246. See, also, *Campbell and Cosans v. United Kingdom* [1982] 4 EHRR 293, where the complainants were successful in their claim that the system of corporal punishment in Scottish state schools offended their philosophical convictions under Article 2 of Protocol 1 of the ECHR.

[56] *Ex parte Williamson*, op cit, at para 22; though expressed obiter.

[57] Citing Iacobucci J in *Syndicat Northcrest v. Amselem* (2004) 241 DLR (4th) 1, 27 at para 52.

[58] *R (On the application of Begum (by her litigation friend, Rahman) v. Headteacher and Governors of Denbigh High School* [2006] UKHL 15 (HL).

belief shared by a small minority of people".[59] So also in *Azmi*,[60] the court upheld the earlier Employment Tribunal finding that the claimant's beliefs concerning the veil were "genuine and held by a sizeable minority of Muslim women."[61] More recently, in *Ghai,*[62] the Court of Appeal considered a request from Ghai, a Hindu, that the Council make available some land outside the city precincts to allow the practice of open-air cremation as his religion required that cremation take place by traditional fire, in direct sunlight and away from man made structures. This had been rejected by the Council as in breach of the Cremation Act 1902 but it also argued that to fall within the protective ambit of Article 9 a belief must be of central importance to the religion concerned, and open air cremation was only peripheral to Hindu religious beliefs. The judicial view, however, was quite different and the court held that Mr Ghai's wishes as to how, after his death, his remains were to be cremated could be accommodated under the Act. Of particular significance is the fact that the Master of the Rolls, following the approach taken earlier by Baroness Hale in *Williamson*,[63] emphasised the importance of the individual's belief: "What we are concerned with in this case is, of course, what Mr Ghai's belief involves when it comes to cremation …".[64] These cases clearly illustrate that for the judiciary in this jurisdiction, it is no longer to an organisation's body of doctrines that the court must now look if it is to establish the nature and status of an adherent's professed religious beliefs (see, also, Chap. 6).

By way of contrast, the dangers of dogma were evident to Laws LJ in *McFarlane v. Relate Avon Ltd*[65] when he drew attention to the need for caution when faced with the implacable beliefs of a representative of institutional religion expressing perceived 'truths'[66]:

> … the conferment of any legal protection or preference upon a particular substantive moral position on the ground only that it is espoused by the adherents of a particular faith, however long its tradition, however rich its culture, is deeply unprincipled. It imposes compulsory law, not to advance the general good on objective grounds, but to give effect to the force of subjective opinion.

That there are limits to the latitude permitted a 'believer' in their interpretation of what constitutes a relevant manifestation of their organisation's beliefs was demonstrated in in *Playfoot (a minor), R (on the application of) v. Millais School,*[67] where the court found that an item of jewelry (a 'purity ring') was used as an ornament to reflect the wearer's personal preferences rather than her religious

[59] Ibid, at para 18.

[60] *Azmi v. Kirkless Metropolitan Borough Council* [2007] UKEAT/009/07.

[61] Ibid, at para 101.

[62] *Ghai, R (on the application of) v. Newcastle City Council & Ors* [2010] EWCA Civ 59.

[63] *R (Williamson) v. Secretary of State for Education and Employment* [2005] 2 AC 246.

[64] *Ghai, R (on the application of) v. Newcastle City Council & Ors* [2010] EWCA Civ 59, at para 19.

[65] [2010] EWCA Civ B1 (29 April 2010).

[66] Ibid at paras 23–24.

[67] *Playfoot (a minor), R (on the application of) v. Millais School,* [2007] EWHC 1698 Admin.

beliefs or, as it was put, "representative of a moral stance and not a necessary symbol of Christian faith".[68]

The significance of this subjective approach for the current dilemma facing the Church and the Communion is very straightforward: canon law need not be interpreted as an absolute prescriptive injunction uniformly binding upon all Anglicans; it should not preclude those adherents who sincerely believe, with justification, that their religion allows for an alternative but relevant interpretation, to pursue that interpretation as a legitimate manifestation of their religious beliefs; while remaining within the Anglican fold. Perhaps such thoughts were on the mind of Dr Rowan Williams, the former Archbishop of Canterbury, when he wrote recently to Anglican leaders worldwide "Our churches should not be places where we retreat into the relief and safety of being with people who are just like ourselves".[69]

8.6.5 Discrimination and the Law

Arguably, for all religious organisations, and particularly so for an established Church, there is little honour in claiming exemption from a moral code that otherwise applies to all citizens.[70] A position that relies on the moral authority of canon law and the Scriptures, but simultaneously requires exemption from that of human rights provisions, so that the Church may act in a discriminatory manner denied to everyone else, is difficult to defend. The freedom of religion is itself at risk if citizens see that the law leaves a choice to made between the moral authority of Church or State.

Walker LJ made a good point in the House of Lords' decision in *Carson*[71] when he drew attention to the fact that this area of difficulty is managed differently in the US:

> The proposition that not all possible grounds of discrimination are equally potent is not very clearly spelled out in the jurisprudence of the Strasbourg court. It appears much more clearly in the jurisprudence of the United States Supreme Court, which in applying the equal protection clause of the Fourteenth Amendment has developed a doctrine of "suspect" grounds of discrimination which the court will subject to particularly severe scrutiny. They are personal characteristics (including sex, race and sexual orientation) which an individual

---

[68] Ibid at para 8.

[69] Ecumenical Christmas Letter to the heads of other Churches and Christian world communions, Friday 21st December 2012. See, further, at: http://rowanwilliams.archbishopofcanterbury.org/articles.php/2762/archbishops-ecumenical-letter-to-churches.

[70] This argument could also be applied to the presumption, in charity law, that religious organisations (or purposes for the advancement of religion) are for the public benefit: it suggests a moral mandate not always sustainable given the evidence that some such organisations can and do breach the law and indeed have been held to bear corporate responsibility (requiring financial reparations to be paid) for the criminal conduct of their members.

[71] *Carson v. Secretary of State for Work and Pensions* [2005] UKHL 37, per Lord Walker of Gestingthorpe at p. 191F.

> cannot change …and which, if used as a ground for discrimination, are recognised as particularly demeaning for the victim.

Walker LJ may well have had in mind the combined effect of the 'neutrality test' and the 'permissive accommodations' doctrine employed by the Supreme Court when dealing with issues that raise a question as to whether a person or organisation is acting in a religiously discriminatory manner contrary to the Constitution's Fourteenth Amendment. While the 'neutrality test' requires the law to function in a manner that is neutral towards religion,[72] the 'permissive accommodations test' asks what religious accommodations are allowed – but not required.[73] The combined effect being to provide a degree of latitude in a small number of cases to counter-balance any particular disability suffered by a religion (or religious person or religious organization) as a consequence of the operation of a law. That latitude is such as to enable court or regulator to adjust the onus resting on the religious person or organization (or on any person or organization suffering discrimination by a religiously motivated act) in a graduated manner depending entirely upon the particular circumstances. Some such approach might offer a more defensible alternative to the present prescriptive morality that prevails on the Church/State interface in relation to matters of religious and sexual discrimination.

8.6.6 Cultural Context

In New Zealand and Australia there have recently been cases of interest in the present context both because the issues raised are very relevant to those currently faced by the Church but also because of the approach adopted by the judiciary: religious beliefs were interpreted against the prevailing contemporary cultural context, not simply brought forward from the time the relevant religion was established and 'read into' the presenting issue. It is interesting that such cases should emerge from countries both of which have a strong indigenous population, each with ancient and authentic cultural heritages, rooted in belief systems that have bound their communities for countless generations, and differing greatly from the developed western standardised urbanised culture that is otherwise the prevailing norm. These particular countries, with their Pacific Rim hinterland, have had greater and more direct exposure to the effects of cultural differences than others in the common law world and have had to work at differentiating rather than discriminating and at creating ways and means of balancing different cultural values in relation to issues affecting family, community and society more broadly.

The recent decision of the Supreme Court in *R (on the application of Hodkin and another) v. Registrar General of Births, Deaths and Marriages* [74] would seem to be very much in keeping with the approach of the antipodean judiciary (see, also, Chap. 6).

---

[72] See, for example, *Church of Lukumi Babalu Aye, Inc. v. City of Hialeah,* 508 U.S. (1993).

[73] See, *Corp. of Presiding Bishop v. Amos*, 483 U.S. 327, (1987).

[74] [2013] UKSC 77.

8.6.7 New Zealand

The case of *Quilter v. Attorney General*[75] was the first and by far the most significant of a succession of cases in which the judiciary wrestled with new definitions of 'family' and the transposing of familiar concepts into a reconfigured and more challenging social and legal landscape.[76] The Court of Appeal was then concerned essentially with the issue of whether being denied the right to marry under the Marriage Act 1955 constituted discrimination against the plaintiff lesbians, contrary to s.19 of the Bill of Rights Act which guarantees the right to freedom from discrimination based upon sexual orientation. The court noted that equality is one of the core principles underlying New Zealand's law on discrimination: the Human Rights Amendment Act 2001 required that government activities be subject to the anti-discrimination standards set out in s.19 of the Bill of Rights Act 1990 and s.21 of the Human Rights Act 1993; the prohibited grounds of discrimination included sexual orientation. While the court concluded that the Marriage Act 1955 specifically applied to marriage between a man and a woman only and that excluding same sex couples did not constitute discrimination, some of the judges were openly critical of the legislation: Tipping J stated, bluntly "I see the inability of homosexual and lesbian couples to marry as involving (indirect) discrimination against them on the grounds of sexual orientation"[77]; and Thomas J, agreeing, said that the effect of restricting marriage to heterosexual couples necessarily involved discrimination against those of gay and lesbian sexual orientation and warned of "the danger of looking to the past to determine whether discrimination exists today … in a real sense, gays and lesbians are effectively excluded from full membership of society".[78]

Following the court's decision, the government was, therefore, obliged to rectify the inequitable if not outright discriminatory provisions in marriage law. Acknowledging that making separate and different provision for same sex couples (by way of civil partnership) would not address issues of either discrimination or equality, it was felt necessary to amend the Marriage Act to make marriage as available to same sex couples as it is for heterosexual couples. Therefore, on April 17, 2013 the New Zealand Parliament passed the Marriage (Definition of Marriage) Amendment Act 2013 enabling gay, bisexual, lesbian, transsexual and intersex marriages to be legal. New Zealand's legalization of same-sex marriages makes it the first country in Asia-Pacific to make the change and the 13th country in the

[75] [1997] 14 FRNZ 430.

[76] See, for example: *VP v. PM* (1998) 16 FRNZ61 (lesbian mother retains custody of two children); *Re An Application by T* [1998] NZFLR 769 (second parent adoption by lesbian mother of partner's child by donor insemination refused); and *A v. R* [1999] NZFLR 249 (non-biological mother in *Re An Application by T*, ibid, held liable for child support payments as a step-parent).

[77] Ibid at pp. 575–6 (admittedly obiter).

[78] Ibid at p. 550 and p. 537.

world to do so. The logical sequence of steps that enabled New Zealand to make room in its traditional legal framework to accommodate contemporary social change was perhaps a more natural process in a jurisdiction accustomed to balancing cultural differences.

8.6.8 *Australia*

The protracted proceedings that constituted the *OV and OW*[79] case essentially concerned the right of the Wesley Mission to withhold services, by not accepting an application to place a child in the foster care of a same-sex couple who were living in a homosexual relationship, on the grounds that the Mission's religious beliefs would be breached if it treated the applicants the same as it did those whose status complied with the core Wesleyan doctrine of 'monogamous heterosexual partnership within marriage'. The central issue turned on the general exception for "religious bodies" provided by s.56 of the Anti-Discrimination Act 1977 (NSW) which gives protection for the actions of such a body where the actions conform to the doctrines of its religion. At the first hearing the Equal Opportunity Division of the Administrative Decisions Tribunal (NSWADT) considered that the issue gave rise to the question – what is a religion? It determined that the relevant religion was the Christian religion. The Wesley Mission sought to rely upon the "fundamental Biblical teaching that 'monogamous heterosexual partnership within marriage' is both the 'norm and ideal'". However, the Tribunal found, given the diversity of views across Christendom on this issue, that: "it does not follow, and nor is it asserted, that that belief can properly be described as a doctrine of the Christian religion". At the second hearing, the Appeals Panel found the Tribunal to be in error in the definition it reached, ordered that the matter be reconsidered, and directed the Tribunal to ascertain whether 'monogamous heterosexual partnership within marriage is both the norm and ideal' was a doctrine of 'Wesleyanism'. The Court of Appeal, however, found that both the Tribunal and Appeal Panel were in error. Basten JA and Handley AJA stated that "there is no basis in section 56 to infer that Parliament intended to exempt from the operation of the Anti-Discrimination Act only those acts or practices which formed part … of the religion common to all Christian churches, or all branches of a particular Christian church (in the sense of a denomination), to the exclusion of variants adopted by some elements within a particular Church".[80] The consequent search for 'a doctrine of "the Christian religion," and the need to establish conformity or otherwise with the act or practice of

[79] *OV v. QZ (No 2)* [2008] NSWADT 115; *Member of the Board of the Wesley Mission Council v. OV and OW (No 2)* [2009] NSWADTAP 57; *OV & OW v. Members of the Board of the Wesley Mission Council* [2010] NSWCA 155.

[80] *OV & OW v. Members of the Board of the Wesley Mission Council* [2010] NSWCA 155 (06 July 2010) at para 41.

the Mission, was misguided. No such doctrine had been found because the evidence was directed specifically to the beliefs and teachings of Methodism or Wesleyism'.[81] The Court of Appeal concluded that this reasoning led to the incorrect finding that, as the actions of Wesley Mission were not in accordance with its doctrines, it could not therefore enjoy the sanction of the exempting provision in the Act. Instead of adopting a broad focus on the Wesleyan understanding of Christianity the enquiry should have been confined to the terms of the specific complaint and it should have ascertained whether or not the grounds for complaint conformed to the doctrines of the religion of the Wesley Mission as those doctrines stood at the time of that complaint and not at the time of the founding of the Mission (bearing in mind that the doctrines adhered to by the Wesley Mission may have evolved over the years, or changed with the establishment of the Uniting Church in Australia). In reconsidering the matter in December 2010, the NSWADT took the view that 'doctrine' was broad enough to encompass, not just formal doctrinal pronouncements such as the Nicene Creed, but effectively whatever was commonly taught or advocated by a body, including moral as well as religious principles. Taking its lead from the Court of Appeal, the Tribunal accepted evidence: from the Superintendent and CEO of the Wesley Mission that in 2003 the Wesley Mission had a doctrine that 'monogamous heterosexual partnership within marriage is both the norm and ideal'; and from a minister that the provision of foster care services by a homosexual couple would be contrary to a fundamental commitment of the organisation to the Biblical values as reflected in its doctrines. Hence the defence under s.56 was established. It concluded that as the cause for complaint conformed with this doctrine which the Mission was, at the relevant time established to propagate, its decision was protected by the religious exemption found within s.56 of the Act.

Cobaw Community Health Services Limited v. Christian Youth Camps Limited & Anor[82] concerned the WayOut project a youth suicide prevention initiative operated by Cobaw Community Health Service that targets homosexual young people in rural Victoria. WayOut wished to have a 2-day forum at the Phillip Island Adventure Resort operated by Christian Youth Camps Limited which was established by the trustees of the Christian Brethren Trust for purposes connected with the Christian Brethren religion. The WayOut project co-ordinator, had sought to make a telephone booking at the resort which she considered had been refused on the basis of the sexual orientation of the proposed attendees and alleged that the resort had contravened the Equal Opportunity Act 1995 (Vic) by discriminating against them in the provision of services and accommodation on the basis of their sexual orientation. Following the *OV and OW* rationale, Hampel J determined that, as regards the respondents, the relevant 'religion' was the Christian Brethren denomination of Christianity. Having heard expert evidence from theologians on the meaning of 'doctrines of religion' and the interpretation that should be given to 'conforms with the doctrines of the religion', the judge found that plenary inspiration (the words of the Bible must be believed and acted upon) is a doctrine of the religion, but that not

[81] Ibid at para 40.

[82] [2010] VCAT 1613 (8 October 2010).

everything in Scripture amounts to 'doctrine', the prevailing cultural beliefs at the time must also be taken into account. As the evidence showed no references to marriage, sexual relationships or homosexuality, in the creeds or declarations of faith adhered to by members of the Christian Brethren, she held that their beliefs about these matters could not be construed as 'doctrines of the religion'.

The rulings in *OV and OW* and *Cobaw* are clearly jurisdiction specific, they have no precedence value for this jurisdiction. However, the rationale employed is relevant and has considerable persuasive value. Together they provide authority for the view that it is the contemporary application of a religious body's doctrines that is important: the doctrines are not required to be those that applied at the time of a religious body's establishment; over time these undergo change and must be contextualised so that their meaning relates to (or is drawn from) contemporary cultural norms; and religious bodies or individuals may avail of statutory protection from alleged discriminatory acts or practice when they can show that such conduct is required by or conforms to their religious doctrine, even where the doctrine is held by only some elements in a particular denomination. Their significance for the current dilemma facing the Church and the Communion is again uncomplicated: canon law cannot be viewed as a 'stand alone' injunction and not all Scripture is of doctrinal value, both require to be interpreted in conjunction with all other relevant and contemporary principles; a religion is capable of housing many different variants.

8.7 Conclusion

When, in March 2005, the Joint Standing Committee of the Primates and of the Anglican Consultative Council took the first step towards launching the Covenant initiative,[83] it may have been with some trepidation but, if the Church had any inkling of the consequences, it would not have considered venturing down that road. As it is the Covenant would seem to have flushed out many who would have prefered to keep their dissent private. While the predicted outcome might have been the isolation of the small minority of North American Anglicans, whose position was already well known, it was clearly not apparent that so many in the Church itself shared the same views. What might have been a strategy to convince a numerically very small minority that their position was untenable, with an accepted risk of losing that minority, turned into something much more morally compromising for the Church as many of its dioceses openly dissented from the Covenant and sided with their North American counterparts. This already decidely uncomfortable position became a good deal more so with the media interest in reports of Church child abuse[84] and with the debacle over the proposed appointment of women bishops. In

[83] See, further, at: http://www.anglicancommunion.org/commission/covenant/consultation/index.cfm.

[84] See, the Meetings Report 2009, the Butler-Sloss Report 2011, and the Addendum to the Butler-Sloss report in March 2012. See, further, at: www.diochi.org.uk.

the light of such events, it might be not unreasonable to query whether the leadership is really speaking for the Church, let alone the Anglican Communion, on the moral issues it now faces.

It is hard to avoid concluding that the 'inhouse' issues of gender and sexuality inequality are a residual legacy from the Church's past which cannot hope to subsist alongside modern human rights requirements. The current lockdown into the moral code of Scriptures and canon law could be somewhat blinkered in view of the relentless pace and direction of cultural change as reflected in the legislative reforms of charity law and equality law coupled with ECtHR case law developments. The approach demonstrated by some judiciary, in adjusting traditional religious beliefs to take into account the subjective interpretation of the 'believer' together with changes in cultural context, to thereby achieve a closer fit between beliefs and contemporary circumstances, has much to commend it.

Conclusion

The purpose of this book has been to gain a sense of how the Church of England's present equivocation in relation to certain aspects of human rights – such as gender and sexuality as criteria for the ordination of its clergy – fits with the broader, but not dissimilar, morally charged agenda of social dilemmas currently generating controversy in this and other jurisdictions. It would seem that the common nexus is a shared difficulty in achieving congruity between canon law inspired morality and the modern requirements of charity law and human rights. The issues that have arisen for the Church and more broadly for western society are no more – or less – than indicators of a fundamental conflict between these three areas of law.

In the early history of Protestantism in England can be seen a convergence of religion, charity law and the accompanying particular set of Christian values that first bound, and still continues to loosely underpin, our now more varied common law societies. Along with language, the institutions of democracy and many other characteristic traits, were bequeathed a shared understanding of: theology and the transcendental; theism, religious belief and altruism; the Nazarene model of the family unit with accompanying legally defined roles, relationships and reciprocal duties; the correlative acceptance that any sexual relationship outside that model is sinful and, more broadly; a shared grasp of what constitutes morality. It was a bequest entrusted to the established Church of England. It travelled first with the armed forces of the British Empire throughout the common law world and subsequently its reach was further extended by the Church to envelop all nations that now comprise the Anglican Communion. Under the protection of canon law, this legacy did much to instill and nurture an awareness of a shared moral code, bringing a semblance of unity to otherwise very disparate cultures. As a corollary of having something approaching a collective faith based morality, the countries concerned also became accustomed to a shared view that any conduct judged to be non-compliant with that moral base was reprehensible and intolerable: Church and State for centuries concurring that such conduct should be treated as both a sin and a crime.

However, much time has passed. The Judeo-Christian religious ethos, as refined by the sixteenth century experience of Protestantism in England – which engendered

K. O'Halloran, *The Church of England - Charity Law and Human Rights,* Ius Gentium: Comparative Perspectives on Law and Justice 36, DOI 10.1007/978-3-319-04319-7,

the shared common law concept of 'charity' and shaped the development of the charitable purpose 'the advancement of religion' – does not fit well with contemporary multi-culturalism. The western bias in the legal determination of what constitutes a 'religion' does not quite match the eastern interpretation: the distinctions between religious belief and religious life, between the religious and the secular, the public and the private experience of religion, are different. Arguably, 'religion', 'faith' and other forms of 'belief' now need to be given a legal definition that more accurately reflects their role in our modern multi-cultural societies: on a spectrum from public institution to private piety; with clear distinctions drawn between religious and secular activities; accompanied by reasonable constraints on proselytism and the public manifestation of private religious belief; and with equal recognition and protection given to the interests of secularists. Any such redefinition also needs to be matched appropriately with requirements regarding both the public benefit test (charity law) and exemption privileges (tax and equality laws) for all religious entities.

'Society' in the developed common law nations is, with gathering momentum, becoming not just culturally differentiated but culturally incoherent. Increasingly comprised of a patchwork of communities and scattered groups, with seemingly little in common with their neighbours other than geographic proximity, the varied cultural components are left to seek an affinity with parallel pockets within or outside the jurisdiction; which in turn introduces pan-national cultural stratification issues for 'civil society'. In conjunction with the cultural fracturing of modern developed societies, the gap between these and the developing nations of the Anglican Communion is widening. As the latter tend to have retained more intact cultures, their adherence to traditional faith based morality is stronger and their alienation from those that have digressed is all the greater. It matters, for both the Church and the Anglican Communion, that those holding to the traditional canon law protected morality vastly outnumber those that dissent. It also matters for the Judeo-Christian religions as a whole that Anglican dissent represents a rejection of doctrines long held to be deeply significant for Christianity, certainly for Catholicism and Judaism: the challenge presented by the grounds for dissent is not restricted to Anglicanism. Consequently, the prospect of furthering what until recently has been a process of incremental steps towards a new rapprochement between Protestantism and Catholicism is at best uncertain.

The gauntlet thrown down by the traditionalists – in the form of Lambeth Resolution 1.10 as endorsed in the Covenant – is, therefore, unsettling. In falling back on canon law prescriptive injunctions this approach resonates with the authoritarian Christianity of Church and State that once prevailed in a context of relative cultural hegemony. By making a stand on canon law precepts the Church of England risks lending its weight to the current wave of didactic moralism[1] and feeding the

[1] See, Grote, J. 2004. *A treatise on the moral ideals*. Whitefish, Montana, USA, (1876). Kessinger Publishing, who explains:

> "Didactic moralism proceeds always more or less on something of a previously formed ideal of what a man ought to be, and might be, and refers the particular actions to this rather than dissects them by themselves" at p. 476.

An approach that has fuelled a degree of moral judgmentalism among some religious groups, certainly in America and to a lesser extent in England, in recent decades.

growing mutual antagonism between those with and those without religious belief, within and between common law nations, on an agenda of complex faith based moral issues. Given the evidence of a creeping polarisation, on faith-based differences, most often on matters relating to the definition of 'family', Church leadership is now important. Internationally, the political significance of religion, apparent before 9/11, has since become steadily consolidated. Religious confrontation is drawing in more countries and ratcheting up the tension that divides some elements of Islam from some nations of the Judeo-Christian tradition. Domestically, there are now few societies in the western world that are not riven with disputes between those which share conservative religious beliefs and those which do not, on much the same agenda of moral issues – including artificial insemination, abortion, homosexuality, gay marriage[2] and adoption, and euthanasia – that constitute an ever extending list of 'moral imperatives' or red line issues for those of religious belief. On both fronts, as the standoff grows more strident, so pluralism becomes more elusive. Nationally and internationally the frontline separating religious and secular authorities is becoming longer, sown with minefields, and evermore confrontational. In such a context, Lambeth Resolution 1.10 is too doctrinaire to provide the high moral ground for the leadership that contemporary pluralist societies now sorely need.

Recent law reform outcomes would seem to have reinforced the position of the dissenters and undermined that of the traditionalists. Charity law reform has placed on the statute books: a broader definition of 'religion', one which no longer requires a God; questions as to whether an entity meeting that definition is necessarily a 'good thing', is serving the public benefit; and requires evidence regarding the subjective understanding of the individual, rather than from doctrines and tenets, to determine what constitutes religious belief. Human rights law has brought developments with regard to the definition of 'discrimination': restrictions on the exemptions available to religious organisations are matched by increased recognition given to the rights of secularists; employers have to be more vigilant to ensure service access and a non-discriminatory workplace; government must exercise caution in relation to contracting with religious organisations; when interpreting religious belief, reference should be made to the contemporary cultural context rather than exclusively to tradition; proselytism is not always permissible; and discrimination on the basis of gender or sexuality is becoming more rigorously policed.

However, reform has failed to harmonise the legislative intent governing charity law and human rights. The "islands of exclusivity" rationale would seem to have intruded to create or reinforce important points of difference between the two as they relate to religion: for example, in terms of exemption privileges and the role of the public benefit principle. The effect of reform in both those areas of law has nonetheless served to isolate, as comparatively anachronistic and dogmatic, the doctrines of canon law. Whereas the reform outcomes demonstrate the capacity of the respective bodies of law to respond to social change, be flexibly attuned to cultural differences and retain a functionality that is relevant to a broad range of believers and non-believers, canon law can only carry forward the articles of faith

[2] Note that by March 2013, 9 US states had legislated to permit same-sex marriages.

as formed and applied in a more despotic age. And yet there are interesting judicial rulings indicating how canon law doctrines can, and perhaps should, be contextur-alised so as to take into account the prevailing cultural norms of the society in which they are applied rather than reflect those of the society from which they emerged.

The struggle to achieve a triangulated alignment between religious beliefs, human rights and charity law is currently attracting considerable attention from governments, academics and others in all developed nations of the common law world. It is a struggle epitomised by the dilemmas now facing the Church of England. As the progenitor jurisdiction for both Anglicanism and charity law, and the initiator of a new statutory definition of 'religion' that does not necessarily include a god or gods, England is the jurisdiction that provides a focus for all concerned with such matters. Within that jurisdiction, the special position of the established Church with its institutional weight and its leadership of the worldwide Anglican Communion, illustrates how those of traditional Christian beliefs – together with those of other religions and those of none – are coping with the challenges presented by cultural change and contemporary lifestyle choices in an increasingly human rights oriented legal environment.

The results of this short study indicate that the Church is now in difficulty. The implications for its future, and the prospects for restoring equanimity in this and other jurisdictions in relation to a weighty and ever extending agenda of moral issues, are troubling.

Index

K. O'Halloran, *The Church of England - Charity Law and Human Rights*, Ius Gentium: Comparative Perspectives on Law and Justice 36, DOI 10.1007/978-3-319-04319-7,

CPSIA information can be obtained at www.ICGtesting.com
Printed in the USA
LVOW10*0821180214

374168LV00010B/171/P

9 783319 043180